KU-486-553

Arthur C Clarke's
MYSTERIOUS WORLD

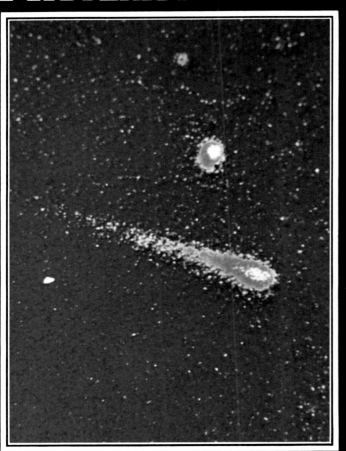

Endpaper: Yeti footprints (Don Whillans 1970)

Arthur C Clarke's
MYSTERIOUS WORLD

Simon Welfare & John Fairley

Collins
St James's Place, London

William Collins Sons and Co Ltd
London · Glasgow · Sydney · Auckland
Toronto · Johannesburg

First published in the United Kingdom in 1980 by
William Collins Sons & Company Limited
14 St James's Place, London SW1A 1PS

This book was designed and produced by
George Rainbird Limited
36 Park Street
London W1Y 4DE

Design: Martin Bristow
Picture Research: Frances Roxburgh

Text © 1980 Trident International Television Enterprises Limited
Introduction & comments © 1980 Arthur C Clarke

ISBN 0 00 216536 8

All rights reserved. No part of this publication may be
reproduced, stored in a retrieval system, or transmitted,
in any form or by any means, electronic, mechanical,
photocopying, recording, or otherwise, without the prior
permission of William Collins Sons & Company Limited.

Filmset by SX Composing, England

Printed and bound in Japan

Contents

	Foreword	6
	Introduction by Arthur C Clarke	8
1	The Missing Ape Man	12
2	A Cabinet of Curiosities	32
3	Ancient Fires	50
4	Monsters of the Deep	68
5	Circles and Standing Stones	84
6	Creatures of Lakes and Lochs	100
7	Figures in a Landscape	116
8	Of Beast and Snake	134
9	The Great Siberian Explosion	152
10	UFOs	168
11	Strange Skies	184
12	Giants in the Earth	200
	Acknowledgments	214
	Index	215

Foreword

The subjects covered in this book are the result of many months of discussion between Simon Welfare, John Fairley and myself. During more than half a century of omnivorous and indiscriminate reading (as a schoolboy, I ploughed through the Taunton Public Library at the rate of several volumes a day — a feat no longer possible in the TV age) I came across countless puzzles and mysteries that intrigued me. Many have now been solved; most have not, and it is from the remaining hard core that we selected the themes of our series. Once I had suggested them, Simon, John and their colleagues did the detailed research, and sent camera teams all over the world in search of relevant footage. It is our hope that all this effort may lead to solutions to *some* of these mysteries; but I think I speak for my friends when I say that I should hate to see them all well and truly settled. Not that there is much danger of this. . . .

The main text that follows is entirely due to Simon and John, who had to do all the hard work in putting book and series together. In matters as controversial as UFOs, Sea Serpents, unknown monsters and the other exhibits in our 'Cabinet of Curiosities', there must obviously be many opinions and viewpoints, but I have no disagreement with my colleagues on any major points and have left their text entirely unchanged. What I have done is to add postscripts to individual chapters, when I thought that I might have something new to add to the discussion. But in many cases I have preferred to accept Wittgenstein's wise advice 'Whereof one cannot speak, thereof one must be silent.'

Arthur C Clarke

Introduction
by Arthur C Clarke

Mysteries come in so many shapes and sizes that it is almost impossible to classify them. One useful way of doing so is to divide them into three categories, based on our current level of understanding. Borrowing shamelessly, let us call them Mysteries of the First, Second and Third Kind.

A Mystery of the First Kind is something that was once utterly baffling, but is now completely understood. Virtually all natural phenomena fall into this category; one of the most familiar, and beautiful, examples is the rainbow. To ancient man, this must have been an awe-inspiring, even terrifying sight. There was no way that he could explain it, except as the creation of some superior intelligence; witness the version in *Genesis*, when Jehovah tells Noah that he will set His sign in the heavens. . . .

The true explanation of the rainbow had to wait for Sir Isaac Newton's proof that 'white' light is really a blend of all possible colours, which may be separated by a prism— or by drops of water floating in the sky. After the publication of Newton's *Optics* in 1704, there was no further mystery about the rainbow—but all its magic and beauty remained. Some foolish people think that science takes the wonder out of the universe; the exact opposite is the truth. *Genuine* understanding is not only more useful than superstition or myth; it is almost always much more interesting.

There are countless other Mysteries of the First Kind. Still more awe-inspiring than the rainbow is the aurora, and only since the dawn of the space age have we learned how that is created by electrified particles blasted out of the sun, and trapped in the upper atmosphere by the earth's magnetic field. Even now, there are still many details to be worked out; but there is no doubt about the general principles of the aurora.

Of course, as any philosopher will be glad to tell you, no 'explanation' of *anything* is ever complete; beyond every mystery is a deeper one. The dispersion of light in the spectrum causes the rainbow—but what is light itself?—and so on, indefinitely. However, most of us are content to accept the common-sense or man-in-the-street attitude towards the universe, well summed up by the comedian Shelley Berman: 'If you give a philosophy student a glass of water he says: *Is* this a glass of water? And if so, *why* is it a glass of water? And pretty soon he dies of thirst.'

Mysteries of the Second Kind are what this book, and the television series on which it is based, are all about. They are mysteries which are *still* mysteries, though in some cases we may have a fairly good idea of the answers. Often the trouble is that there are too many answers; we would be quite satisfied with any one of them, but others appear equally valid. The most spectacular modern example is, of course the UFO phenomenon, where the range of explanations extends from psychic manifestations through atmospheric effects to visiting spaceships—and, to make matters even more complicated, the range of eager explainers runs from complete lunatics to hard-headed scientists. (There are some soft-headed scientists in this field as well.) All that I will say about the controversial subject of UFOlogy at this point is that, where there are so many answers, there is something wrong with the questions.

Another mystery, which does not arouse quite so many violent emotions, is the Great

Sea Serpent. Most zoologists would be quite willing to admit that large unidentified marine creatures may exist—perhaps, as in the case of the coelacanth, even survivors from primeval times. And *if* they are still around, one day we should be able to prove it. (Though not necessarily; at this very moment, the last surviving Sea Serpent may by dying from an overdose of industrial pollutants. . . .)

Barring such exceptional bad luck, most Mysteries of the Second Kind are eventually solved, and graduate to those of the First Kind. In witnessing this process, our generation is the most fortunate one that has ever lived. We have discovered answers to questions that have haunted all earlier ages—to questions, indeed, which once seemed beyond all possible solution. No more dramatic example could be mentioned than the Far Side of the Moon, once the very symbol of the unknowable. Now it has not only been completely mapped, but men have gazed upon its plains and craters with their own unaided eyes.

Yet there are some Mysteries that may remain forever of the Second Kind. This is particularly true where historical events are concerned, because once the evidence has been lost or destroyed, there is no way in which it can be recovered. One can conjecture endlessly about such famous enigmas as the true identities of Kaspar Hauser, or the Dark Lady of the Sonnets, or Homer. Unless someone invents a method of looking into the past—extremely unlikely, yet not quite impossible—we may never know. Scientists are more fortunate than historians, for Nature does not destroy evidence; all the questions they ask are ultimately answered—though in the process they invariably uncover new and more difficult ones.

Mysteries of the Third Kind are the rarest of all, and there is very little that can be said about them; some sceptics argue that they do not even exist. They are phenomena—or events—for which there appears to be *no* rational explanation; in the cases where there are theories to account for them, these are even more fantastic than the 'facts'.

Perhaps the quintessential M3K is something so horrible that—even if the material existed—one would prefer not to use it in a television programme. It is the extraordinary phenomenon known as Spontaneous Human Combustion.

There have been many recorded cases, supported by what seems to be indisputable medical evidence, of human bodies being consumed in a very short period of time by an extremely intense heat *which has often left the surroundings—even the victim's clothing!—virtually untouched.* The classic fictional case is in Dickens' *Bleak House*, but there are dozens of similar incidents in real life—and probably a far greater number that have never been reported.

The human body is not normally a fire hazard; indeed, it takes a considerable amount of fuel to arrange a cremation. There seems no way in which this particular mystery can ever be solved, without a great deal more evidence—and who would wish for *that*?

A less appalling, though sometimes very frightening, Mystery of the Third Kind is the Poltergeist (from the German—literally, 'noisy spirit'). Although a healthy scepticism is required when dealing with all paranormal phenomena, because extraordinary happenings require extraordinarily high standards of verification, there is impressive evidence that small objects can be thrown around, or even materialized, with no apparent physical cause. Usually there is a disturbed adolescent somewhere in the background, and although adolescents—disturbed or otherwise—are perfectly capable of raising hell by non-paranormal means, this persistent pattern over so many cultures, and such a long period of time, suggests that *something* strange is going on. If so, it is a complete mystery, and such labels as 'psychokinesis' are only fig-leaves to conceal our ignorance.

In this series, we have avoided M3Ks for several good and sufficient reasons. In the first case, there is no general agreement that they even exist, so discussions of their reality are inconclusive and unsatisfying. At best, the parties concerned agree to disagree; at worst, confrontations end up as slanging matches with charges of fraud or narrow-mindedness winging across the battle lines. This can be amusing for a while, but soon gets boring.

Secondly, such evidence as *does* exist is almost all in the form of eyewitness accounts —often fine for radio, but poor fare for television, unless one cheats and 'reconstructs' reported events. Needless to say, none of *my* colleagues would ever be guilty of so heinous a crime. . . .

Finally, even if the existence of a particular M3K is established, where does one go from there? Nothing could be more important than the *conclusive* demonstration of some anomalous event outside the frontiers of accepted science; it is by such discoveries that knowledge advances. However, until there is some plausible theory or working hypothesis to explain the phenomenon, there is little that one can say intelligently about it. Few things are more frustrating than isolated enigmas that seem to admit of *no* rational explanation. With the Mysteries of the Second Kind, we have at least something to get our teeth into.

If they are real, M3Ks quickly graduate to M2Ks, and eventually to M1Ks. A perfect example is the discovery of radioactivity at the end of the nineteenth century. The late Victorian scientists were amazed to find that certain uranium compounds continually emitted energy; the discovery was not only totally unexpected, but defied all that was then known about physics. However, the facts were swiftly established beyond controversy and led in a very short time to the first real understanding of atomic structure.

The fact that this process has *not* happened in the case of paranormal phenomena is one of the strongest arguments against their real existence. After more than a hundred years of effort, the advocates of the paranormal have still been unable to con-

vince the majority of their scientific peers that 'there is anything in it'. Indeed, the tide now appears to be turning against them with recent revelations of fraud and incredibly sloppy techniques in what once seemed to be well-established results.

But the verdict is not yet handed down, nor will it be in our time. Those who think that Science has accounted for everything are just as stupid—and that is not too strong a word—as those who accept the most fantastic stories on the flimsiest of evidence.

Which leads me to my final point. I said at the beginning that there were three kinds of Mystery; now let me add a fourth—Mysteries of the Zeroeth Kind. . . .

The only mystery about *these* is that anyone ever thought they were mysterious. The classic example is the Bermuda Triangle, though this has not prevented countless writers, some of whom may even believe the rubbish they are regurgitating, repeating the same nonsense over and over again. The stories of vanishing aircraft and ships in this region, when the *original* sources are examined, usually turn out to be perfectly explicable and commonplace tragedies. Indeed, it is a considerable tribute to the Florida Coast Guard that there are *so few* disappearances in this busy area, among the legions of amateur sailors and weekend pilots who venture out across it, often with totally inadequate preparation.

A glance at any display of paperbacks will, alas, disclose a ripe collection of Mysteries of the Zeroeth Kind—the mental junk food of our generation. It is a pity that there is no way of labelling books that rot the mind: WARNING! READING THIS BOOK MAY BE DANGEROUS TO YOUR MENTAL HEALTH! but the practical difficulties are obvious. What a pity it is not possible for some public-spirited benefactor to purchase copies of the latest flying saucer guide book, revelation from Atlantis, or pyramidal insanity, and then sue the author for incompetence. Even if he was awarded no more than the price of the book, it would be a lot of fun!

Sometimes it doesn't really matter, and

there may even be occasions when the most rubbishy of books may open up a mind to the wonders of the universe (as bad science fiction can also do). But there are times when real harm can be done to serious and important studies, or to the elucidation of genuine mysteries, by the activities of frauds, cranks and hoaxers. Thus the idea that earth may have had visitors from space is a perfectly reasonable one; indeed, I would go so far as to say that it is surprising if it has *not* done so during the past billions of years of its existence. Unfortunately, books full of faked 'evidence' and imbecile archaeology have scared serious researchers away from the field. So it is with the study of UFOs— which, despite all the nonsense that has been written about them, may yet turn out to be important and interesting.

It is my hope that this book, and the series on which it is based, will help all those interested in the truth to distinguish between real mysteries and fraudulent ones. True wisdom lies in preserving the delicate balance between scepticism and credulity. The Universe is such a strange and wonderful place that reality will always outrun the wildest imagination; there will always be things unknown, and perhaps unknowable.

Which is very lucky for us; because it means that, whatever other perils humanity may face in the future that lies ahead, boredom is not among them.

Arthur C Clarke
Colombo, January 1980

11

The Missing Ape Man

The footprints meandering across these pages have travelled from the high peaks of the Himalayas, the mountains of Soviet Georgia and of northwest America and Canada, into the imaginations of thousands of scientists, zoologists, mountaineers and showmen whose dream is to find the 'Missing Link', the half ape half man of countless fabulous tales. In the process these prints have trampled on many reputations, launched huge expeditions and parted fortunes from otherwise shrewd businessmen.

The names of the mysterious creature are the stuff of the most ludicrous tall stories: the 'Abominable Snowman', 'Bigfoot', the Russian 'Man of the Mountains' and its description belongs to the world of nursery rhyme: seven, eight, nine feet tall, vile and ugly of face, covered in long hair, strong enough to wring the necks of full-grown cattle, fast enough to outrun man or dog, or, in Russia, even a horse, attacking young virgins and battering men to death with a club.

On the other hand, Lord Hunt, leader of the expedition that first conquered Mount Everest, believes that such a creature may exist. As recently as 1978, he and his wife found and photographed convincing tracks in the Himalayas. In America, Dr Grover Krantz of Washington State University is also convinced of the reality of Bigfoot, or the sasquatch as it is called by the North American Indians. In 1978, the University of British Columbia organized an academic conference in which thirty-five separate papers of analysis and speculation were on offer, from universities all over the world. In Russia there is a whole department at Tbilisi in Georgia, under Professor N I Burchak Abramovich, devoted to the search for the Neanderthal 'Man of the Mountains'. Every now and then the New China News Agency reports that Chinese soldiers in Tibet have shot and eaten a snowman. In the wild country either side of the Cascade Mountains, which run down the Pacific Coast of America from Canada through Washington and Oregon, reports of sightings of Bigfoot or the sasquatch now run into hundreds.

As recently as 1979, a British expedition which conquered a 14,840 ft (4,520 m) peak

Left: Yeti footprints on Annapurna, photographed by Don Whillans
Right: Lord Hunt's photograph of yeti footprints in the Himalayas taken in 1978

in the Himalayas for the first time found distinct footprints in the Hinken Valley and heard 'scream-like calls'.

The lead climber, Squadron Leader John Edwards, said '. . . there is firm evidence of a strange creature in the Himalayas. One footprint we found was a really clear example and I think our pictures will prove to be the best taken yet. What is more, we heard this high-pitched scream and our Sherpas said it was a yeti.'

Although most zoologists scoff at the idea that there can exist, undiscovered, a manlike creature, a missing link in the evolutionary chain, it was that great zoologist, Charles Darwin, who provided the theoretical basis upon which many yeti hunters have built. Particularly in the USSR, Darwin's theory of evolution has been taken to imply a 'missing link' and the huge, uncharted mountains of Soviet Central Asia provide perfect cover for an animal shy of humanity.

Fly from northern India to Nepal, Sikkim, Bhutan or over India's old North East Frontier and range after range of inhospitable hill and mountain lies beneath, for the most part hardly inhabited.

Even in the Pacific northwest of North America dense forests blanket the country along the Columbia river. Fifty miles can

Area of yeti and alma sightings

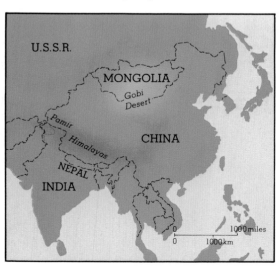

separate one small road from the next and since the Second World War more than seventy aircraft have disappeared in the area without trace. Indeed, there is a macabre joke among people who know the area that, apart from the sasquatch or Bigfoot, another monster, which enjoys eating aircraft, lurks in the hills. But of all the 'missing ape men' it is the yeti, the Abominable Snowman, who is the most celebrated.

The Abominable Snowman

The Abominable Snowman, the yeti as the Sherpas call him, is the most venerable of all the mysterious ape men of the high country. He is tangled in a web of fantasy, religion, legend, chicanery and commercialism. He has been seen by supposedly reliable witnesses, his droppings have been analysed, his footprints recorded and examined in apparently unimpeachable circumstances. He was dismissed as a legend by expeditions in the late 1950s and 1960s but now the evidence for his existence seems to become stronger every year.

A traveller to Katmandu is embroiled, even before he arrives, in the yeti business. The Royal Nepalese Airlines' flight skims over the lower mountain ranges, the villages perched absurdly right on the peaks, seemingly in hourly danger of toppling into the ravines. Then, suddenly, the line of the great summits of the Himalayas comes into view, white and jagged, the rest of the earth blocked out by cloud. Shangri-La, the Lost Horizon, secret valleys, unknown tribes, the yeti— all seem plausible. But in the aircraft seat pocket is the menu for the airline's Yeti Service, and the new hotel for which you are bound, built by the World Bank, is called the Yak and Yeti. The yeti is a highly commercial legend, perhaps even Nepal's principal foreign currency earner.

The stories of the yeti, the great monster of the Himalayas, are legion among the Nepalese themselves and especially the Sherpas who live in the high mountains. At Thyangboche monastery in the shadow of Everest, the abbot talks quite matter-of-

Thyangboche monastery in the shadow of Everest often visited by the yeti

Though prints had been reported by Westerners as far back as 1887, and then again by a British Army officer 21,000 ft (6,400 m) up Everest in 1921, it is the photographs of them that present the main challenge. F S Smythe's were the first, taken at 16,500 ft (5,000 m) in 1937. Eric Shipton's photographs —with an ice-axe carefully laid against the prints for scale—started serious enquiry. McNeely and Cronin from the 1972 American expedition found footprints clear and sharp enough for plaster casts to be taken. The following year Lord Hunt found prints and his 1978 pictures show huge footprints, 14 in (355 mm) long and 7 in (177 mm) wide.

Speaking at the Royal Geographical Society in London, Lord Hunt said:

'We were in a side valley below Everest. It was late in the evening and getting dark when my wife and myself came across the traces. They were very fresh indeed, and I will even say that they were certainly made that day. There was deep snow on a

Eric Shipton's photograph of a yeti footprint on a glacier of the Menlung Basin in Nepal in 1951

factly of the yetis that visit the monastery garden. Each year vivid descriptions of attacks by yetis are reported in Katmandu. One Sherpa girl, Lakhpa Domani, described an incident to a Peace Corps volunteer, William Weber, who was working in the area of Machherma village in the Everest region. The girl said she was sitting near a stream tending her yaks when she heard a noise and turned round to confront a huge apelike creature with large eyes and prominent cheek bones. It was covered in black and red-brown hair. It seized her and carried her to the water, but her screams seem to have disconcerted the creature and it dropped her. Then it attacked two of her yaks, killing one with blows, the other by seizing its horns and breaking its neck. The incident was reported to the local police and footprints were found. Weber says: 'What motive could there possibly have been for a hoax? My conclusion was that the girl was telling the truth.'

The actual evidence for the yeti falls into three main categories: footprints, eyewitnesses and physical evidence such as skulls and skins.

The footprints are certainly intriguing.

rather steep little slope and the creature was a heavy one, because he had broken through hard crust on which we could walk without making an impression through the snow at all. The prints were oval, elongated. I put down an ice axe to measure. They were 14 in long and just about half as wide.'

Lord Hunt, who has seen tracks several times over some thirty years, and heard what he calls 'high-pitched yelping cries', 'can find no other explanation but that there is an unidentified creature still to be discovered.'

British mountaineer and surgeon, Michael Ward, was with Eric Shipton when the 1951 prints were photographed. 'We were about 30 or 40 miles west of Everest,' he relates, 'and we crossed a large mountain range at about nineteen to twenty thousand feet and went into what is called a "blank" on the map. The map was absolutely white and there was no topographical detail at all.' On a glacier they came across some mountain goats and saw their tracks. Then suddenly there was another track.

'These were really well defined and quite different. We could see the toes of all the feet. The prints led off right down the glacier for several miles as far as I could see. My own feeling was the tracks had probably been made at night or earlier

Eric Shipton

that day, because there was absolutely no blurring round the edges. In fact in some of the places you could see where this animal had crossed a small crevasse and you could actually see nail marks where he'd jumped from one side to the other. As you can see in the pictures, the tracks were much deeper than we were making. We'd have probably spent a great deal longer photographing them and describing them, but we were short of food and our main concern was to make our way out of this completely unexplored country where not even the Sherpas and Tibetans had ever been, and certainly no European.'

Their concern was well founded, for Shipton and Ward had strayed into Tibet and were subsequently captured by armed Tibetan guards, only to be ransomed after protracted bargaining by their Sherpas for the princely sum of £1.

The sceptical view is that the footprints are those of other species distorted by the sun or snow conditions—perhaps the Tibetan blue bear, itself rare enough to be almost legendary, or a langur monkey, which is known to live at considerable heights. The snow leopard has also been named as the guilty party and one letter to the British magazine *Country Life* even suggested that it might

The tracks of the snow leopard – not, perhaps, very like a yeti's

be a bird—the Alpine chough—which had been observed to leave snowmanlike traces as it hopped across the snow.

However, the zoologist, W Tschernezky, of Queen Mary College, London, did a most exhaustive analysis of the Shipton footprints, using a reconstructed model and comparing it with gorilla, fossil man and human footprints. Noting the unusually large second toe and very short metatarsal bone, he concludes they are very unlike a bear or a langur monkey. 'All the evidence suggests,' he says, 'that the so-called snowman is a very huge, heavily built bipedal primate, most probably of a similar type to the fossil *Gigantopithecus*.' Such an assertion takes the yeti as near to being a living version of the 'missing link' as any reputable scientist would dare.

Of the people who have actually seen the tracks, the most convincing are probably those whose backgrounds do not lead them easily to espouse the yeti legend. Captain Emil Wick, Swiss pilot with Royal Nepalese Airlines, has an elegant house on the outskirts of Katmandu. Sitting in his garden at dusk over a bottle of beer he was forthright:

'My God, I tell you I had no interest at all in these damned yetis when I came to Nepal. I came here to fly close to the mountains with the tourists because I am a damned good flyer in these little planes, and to enjoy myself when I am not flying, just like I did in Bangkok and Indonesia and wherever. Then, one morning last year, I was flying some Japanese to Kangchenjunga when I saw these tracks at a terrific height. There were three of them, three separate tracks and it was obvious that they were made by a two-legged creature. They came up either side of a steep ridge, then they came together and went down to a lake which I had never seen before, perhaps for a drink. I know it was fresh snow and it wasn't later than half-past seven in the morning so the sun cannot have played tricks. I went round for two or three looks and you'll never be-

lieve me—there was a Japanese woman beside me with a camera and I begged her to take pictures. "I will even give you the flight free", I said. But she just said "Stop flying around for your own amusement. We pay you to go to Kangchenjunga. That's where we want to take our pictures".'

A Frenchman, the Abbé Bordet, of the Paris Geological Institute, followed three separate lots of tracks on a 1955 expedition. In his account for the *Bulletin* of the Musée National d'Histoire Naturelle, Paris, he says he followed one track for more than half a mile. At times, the impression was so clear he could make out the snow marking the separation of the toes. At one point, the creature had jumped off a little rock wall 4 or 5 ft (1–1.5 m) high and its footprints had sunk 6 in (150 mm) or so into the snow. Father Bordet had his photographs examined by the two most senior mammalogists in France and they declared the tracks to be those of an unknown species.

Squadron Leader Lester Davies of the Ullswater Outward Bound School, in England, was also struck by the depth of the prints he filmed in 1955 on the RAF Himalaya Expedition.

'They'd sunk in about 5 or 6 in. With cine cameras and rucksack, I was weighing about

Lester Davies' 1955 yeti footprint. This shows the toe mark which is not always to be seen, perhaps because the toe is sometimes clenched or raised

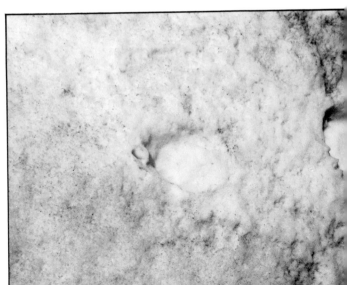

$12\frac{1}{2}$ stone, and only went in about 1 or $1\frac{1}{2}$ in. I thought, this thing is huge!'

Men of unquestioned probity say they have actually seen the creature. Don Whillans is the dour and down-to-earth proprietor of a Welsh guest house and indomitable hero of climbs on Everest and Kangchenjunga. He was on Annapurna in June 1970.

'We were in the Annapurna sanctuary as it is called, which is a ring of very high mountains. I was anxious to find a decent place to camp for the night and as we slowly came round a spur of the mountain, I heard what sounded like bird cries from behind me. I looked at the Sherpa and he said "Yeti coming, Sahib". So I whipped round and looked up the mountain and I saw two black crows flying away and a black shape drop behind the ridge. My first thoughts were, "What do I do now, grab the ice-axe

Don Whillans

or what?" Anyway, it didn't reappear so I said, "Come on let's get the camp up." The following day, we continued up the valley to complete this reconnaissance of the south face and I saw the tracks obviously left by the creature, the night before. These tracks were nearly 18 in [457 mm] deep, the snow was very soft and they seemed to be roughly about the same size as my own foot, which sort of corresponded with what the Sherpas had said, that they were baby yeti. I suppose yetis, if such a thing exists, come in different sizes, the same as people.

'Later on that evening, it was a very, very moonlit night and, for some reason, there had been a strong feeling as far as I was concerned that this creature was actually still around. So I stuck my head out of the tent. It was so moonlit that you could actually read. I watched for about a quarter of an hour and I was just beginning to think, "Oh well, maybe whatever it is has gone", when I saw something move. When you do a lot of climbing, you get used to looking at mountains and looking for very small figures and very small alterations. And this creature, which looked to me in its movements ape-like, sort of bounded along in a funny gait towards what obviously in a few weeks' time, when the snow had gone, would be a clump of trees. It appeared to be pulling some of the branches. Anyway I watched for about twenty minutes. I got the binoculars out and all I could make out was a black apelike shape. Then, quite suddenly, it was almost as if it realized it was being watched, it shot across the whole slope of the mountain. It must have travelled half a mile before it disappeared into the shadow by some rocks. What was really strange to me was the behaviour of the Sherpas. If it had been a bear—they're very familiar with bears—they would have said "Oh, it's a barlu" as I believe they call it and that would have been the end of it. But they were very subdued for a couple of days and if I ever tried to

Sir Edmund Hillary holding the legendary yeti scalp during his worldwide tour in 1960; with him is Khunjo Chumbi, a village elder from Khumjung, Nepal, the scalp's custodian

mention the subject or was looking at the tracks through the binoculars during the day I would hear them passing comments to one another.

'Now whether it was a langur monkey, as has been said, I don't know. It might have been an extremely thin bear, just come out from the winter. But it didn't seem like that to me. And the actual tracks that I saw had very peculiar indentations between the actual footprint, which didn't strike me until about twelve months later when I was looking at a picture of a gorilla in a normal animal book. That could very well be the knuckle marks of this creature, between the actual footprints.'

In 1975, a Polish trekker, Janusz Tomaszczuk, claimed to have had a terrifying encounter. He had been hiking in the Everest area and had sprained his knee. As he limped back to a nearby settlement, he saw a figure approaching him. When Tomaszczuk shouted for help, the figure came nearer. It was then that he saw that the 'man' he had asked for help was an apelike creature over 6 ft (1.8 m) tall with arms down to its knees. His screams drove it away.

Such stories are accepted as normal by the Sherpas. In 1978 there were more reported attacks by yetis, particularly in Sikkim, where the Forestry Department sent out a series of fruitless expeditions in pursuit. The most serious attempt to resolve the enigma of the yeti was sponsored by the American *World Book Encyclopedia*. An expedition set out in 1960, led by Desmond Doig and Sir Edmund Hillary, the first man

19

(along with Sherpa Tenzing) to stand on the summit of Mount Everest. They stayed ten months, through a fierce winter, in the region where most of the yeti sightings had been reported. The expedition was lavishly equipped with trip-wire cameras, and time-lapse and infra-red photography. There was worldwide excitement when Hillary persuaded the villagers of Khumjung to lend their legendary yeti scalp for six weeks for scientific examination. This scalp, along with two others and a couple of skins (which were later identified as blue bear) were alleged to be the only remnants of the yeti in existence.

Hillary and Doig set off in the autumn with the guardian of the scalp, Khunjo Chumbi, on a worldwide tour that took them to Honolulu, Chicago, Paris and even Buckingham Palace. At every stop Chumbi imitated for the television crews the high-pitched howl that the yeti is supposed to make. Meanwhile, posses of experts examined the scalp.

Like latter-day Phineas Foggs, Hillary and Doig had to return to Khumjung within forty-two days otherwise, by agreement, the land and property of their Sherpas would have been forfeit. They arrived on the last day, dropping out of the sky in a helicopter with the scalp safe in its box, but sadly convinced that the scalp was almost certainly made from the hide of a serow goat. The expedition had no better luck with its cameras and hideouts and Hillary turned to the problems of a difficult climb of Mount Makalu.

In their accounts of the expedition, Hillary and Doig dismissed the yeti as the stuff of myth and legend. After all, they had exposed one of the scalps as false and devoted nearly a year, in the heart of the supposed yeti habitat, to as thorough a search as experience and technical virtuosity could devise.

Today, reclining less energetically on the carpets of his fine house opposite the American Embassy in Katmandu, Desmond Doig is wryly sceptical of the 1960 expedition and has reversed his opinion, now believing that the yeti exists. 'After all, we may not have seen a yeti,' he says, 'but we didn't see a snow leopard either and we *know* they exist. In fact, we hardly saw any creatures at all. The expedition was too big and clumsy. Also, years afterwards, I think I solved the scalp mystery.' He tossed what appeared to be a perfect facsimile of the Khumjung scalp across the room. 'I was travelling near the Sikkim border when I met a tribesman wearing that thing and not much else. It turns out that they are made quite regularly around there to be worn as hats.' So the scalp may have been a genuine mistake—but even if it was a deliberate fake it does not mean that yetis do not exist.

It was Doig, too, who subsequently obtained from a monastery in Bhutan a magnificent blue-bear skin which was sold at Christie's in London in 1978 for £1200. The catalogue note said: 'It has been suggested that this very rare skin is that of the Yeti or Abominable Snowman.'

Doig, who has spent thirty years in the Himalayas and speaks many of the area's languages, points out that the Sherpas talk of three different kinds of yeti. There is the dzu teh, which is large, shaggy and attacks and eats cattle. This, he feels, is almost certainly the Tibetan blue bear, which has never been seen by a Westerner even though the first skin found its way to the Asiatic Society in London in 1853. To this day there are only half a dozen known blue-bear skins, a skull and some bones. 'I once met a Tibetan lady who told me there had been one in the Panchen Lama's zoo in Shigatse in Tibet,' Doig went on. 'She said it walked on two legs, was as big as a tall man and had a face like an ape or a bear. Unfortunately, it and the whole zoo were swept away in a flood.'

The second type of yeti is called the thelma by the Sherpas; 'a "little man" that runs along hooting and collecting sticks.' Doig says 'I don't think there's much problem about that. It's almost certainly a gibbon, even though conventional zoology says that they are not found north of the Brahmaputra River in India.'

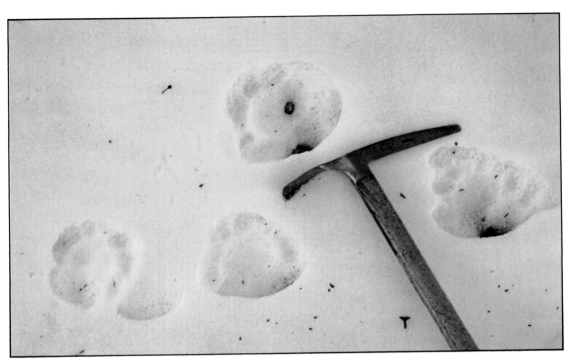

A 1979 photograph of two yetis' footprints

The third, the true snowman of the legend according to Doig, is the mih teh. It is savage, looks like an ape, is man-eating, covered with black or red hair, has the classic 'reversed toes' and prowls about at anything up to 20,000 ft (6,100 m) or even higher.

'In 1961 we dismissed the mih teh as pure myth. I now think we were wrong. I've often shown Sherpas who claim to have seen the mih teh a sort of identity parade of different bears, humans, drawings of Neanderthal Man and *Gigantopithecus*, gorillas, chimps, gibbons, and the orangutan. Invariably, though they have no knowledge whatsoever of the great apes, it is an ape they point to, usually an orangutan. We know from fossils that the orangutan once lived in northern India. Who knows? There are still immense jungles which could conceal whole tribes of yetis. Perhaps their rare excursions to the high slopes are, as Abbé Bordet suggested, in search of water. It can be very dry on the upper margins of the forest.'

The yeti case rests on tales from the Sherpas, some Western eyewitnesses, but above all on the footprints of which there are now more than twenty reliable records including the pictures brought back at Christmas 1979 by the Royal Air Force expedition. Doubters question where such a creature could find food at such altitudes. Believers quote the lynx, the woolly wolf, the ibex and the yak, which have all been seen at more than 18,000 ft (5,490 m). But no one has come up with a convincing explanation for photographs like Shipton's and Lord Hunt's, which seem to show with such clarity the tracks of a creature much heavier than man, which walks for long distances on two legs, and leaves a footprint unlike any other known animal.

Bigfoot
Compared to the Himalayan yeti, the North American Bigfoot or sasquatch is almost insolent in the frequency of his reported appearances. A regular journal, *Bigfoot News*, for years was large with Bigfoot sightings, often by ordinary people who

had no interest in publicity and no previous knowledge of the Bigfoot story. And, obligingly, Bigfoot occasionally leaves his tracks behind to lend some substance to the stories of witnesses.

A typical encounter took place in the Mount Hood National Forest in northern Oregon. Three loggers, Fermin Osborne, J C Rourke and Jack Cochran, were working in a clearing. On a July morning, Cochran was working the crane when he saw a man-like figure watching him. He got out of his cab to look. The figure was massively built, covered in dark hair and was walking upright. Fermin Osborne said:

'I didn't see it that time and apparently it just walked quickly away into the forest. But the next day I was with Rourke and we decided to take a break from work. We walked into the edge of the forest. All of a sudden, this great creature got up out of the undergrowth, right in front of us, not more than ten yards away. It was covered with dark hair, even over the head and face, and really heavily built. Rourke chased after it but he couldn't catch up with it. He just chucked a couple of stones at it. I've seen plenty of bears and it certainly wasn't a grizzly. More like a gorilla really.'

Bigfoot country

Bigfoot put in an appearance for the law in the person of Sergeant Larry Gamache of the Yakima Sheriff's Department in Washington State. Sergeant Gamache was driving back from a fishing trip with his brother and sister-in-law, Kathy.

'My brother was asleep in the back of the pick-up. Suddenly I saw what I thought was a man coming out of the timber on the shoulder of the road. Then I realized this was no man. It was naked and covered in long hair. I drove slowly past and then Kathy screamed. The creature had come over and peered in at her through the passenger window. She was terrified. And my brother slept through it all.'

Over more than half a century, the sasquatch has made innumerable other personal appearances. In Canada in 1928, an Indian named Muchalat Harry told Father Anthony Terhaar that he had been kidnapped by a male Bigfoot and carried off to a 'camp' where there were twenty assorted Bigfeet, including wives and several curious young ones. They did him no harm and after a while, when their interest in him slackened, he escaped in his canoe. Father Terhaar met him when he arrived at Nootka on Vancouver Island clad only in his torn underwear. The experience had turned his hair pure white. In 1922 a miner called Fred Beck and some companions were working a claim on Mount St Helens, Washington, when they saw and shot at what seemed to be giant apes. One was hit and, for several nights after, the miners' cabin was bombarded with stones and lumps of rock until finally, unnerved, they packed up and left. In 1966 two young men out hunting coyotes, in Jackson Hole, Wyoming, shot a 'gorilla-like' figure which, when they ran up to it, turned out to be massive and hairy, with a bare face and huge hands and feet. The men thought they might have shot a man, a local freak, so they leaped in their car and fled back home to Iowa.

The incredulity and mirth that these tales arouse starts to fade away under the sheer

Glenn Thomas on a pile of rocks thrown up near Estacada, Oregon by a group of Bigfoot he saw hunting for food in 1967

they found thirty or more holes with rocks, obviously moved during the digging, that weighed 250 lb (114 kg) or more, and there was an abundance of chucks and marmots. Marmots do hibernate in nests under rocks, and it was October when Glenn Thomas claimed to have seen his Bigfoot family.

A Californian wildlife writer and his wife were driving on the road from Paradise to Stirling City one night when they saw a manlike figure in their headlights: 6 ft or more tall, covered with black hair but with a white, hairless face. The head was small and came to a peak at the top. It did not run but shuffled away, seemingly with a limp. 'My husband specializes in writing for such publications as *Field and Stream* and *Sports Afield*,' wrote Mrs Robert L Behme. 'I mention this in the hope that you will believe we are reasonable, not given to hallucinations brought on by the novelty of a backwoods road at midnight.'

Six people, family and friends, were with Robert Bellamy when he saw a Bigfoot in the Tygh Valley, Oregon, and they all watched it for several minutes. The two Welch brothers, Canadian mining prospectors, saw a Bigfoot, then followed tracks on to a lake to find a substantial hole knocked in the ice and the snow swept back. A creature was seen by boatmen, wandering along the shore in British Columbia, apparently feeding off the oysters in the shallow water.

The most fascinating of all the sightings is the famous, brief and jumpy film of Bigfoot rollicking about in the forest, taken in 1967 by Roger Patterson at Bluff Creek, northern California. As the clearer of the frames show, the creature is most assuredly female with breasts and very prominent buttocks. In the film she lopes along with a jolly gait which usually produces fits of laughter in people who see the footage for the first time.

However, the film has many intriguing features. The exact site, beside a small road near Onion Mountain, was not only known but other investigators were able to reach it soon afterwards and, like Patterson and his companion Bob Gimlin, take casts of the

frequency and detail of the North American sightings, often reported by sensible people at the risk of considerable local derision. Glenn Thomas, a logger from Estacada, Oregon, was walking down a path at Tarzan Springs near the Round Mountain when he says he heard a noise.

'I was screened by the trees, but through them I could see these three huge figures digging in a rock pile. They looked just like Bigfoot is supposed to: hairy, huge hands and very powerfully built. There was a big one with a female and a young one. They were lifting rocks out, the big male one, and digging down all of 6 or 7 ft. Then the male reached down and took out a nest of rodents and ate them.'

This story may answer one of the many questions surrounding Bigfoot: what does he eat? When investigators went to the area

A 'still' from Roger Patterson's celebrated film of Bigfoot, which was taken in 1967

creature's footprints and measure its stride. Furthermore, as the positioning of trees and fallen logs shown in the film was unchanged, it is possible to make some reasonably accurate estimate of the creature's height.

The most careful analyses of the film have been made by Dr D W Grieve, Reader in Biomechanics at the Royal Free Hospital in London, and by a group of Russian scientists. By comparing film of humans at the same spot, Dr Grieve calculates that the creature is about 6 ft 5 in (1.95 m) high—tall indeed if it is a human in a suit, but possible. The shoulder and hip widths, however, are well beyond the human range and, assuming that they are not padded with polystyrene, suggest a weight of 280 lb (127 kg). The length of stride seems to be about 42 in (1.07 m), which is very long for a man. Dr Grieve remarks that it would be very difficult to imitate the free striding and arm swinging seen in the film if it was in fact a man in a furry suit encumbered with shoulderpads

and a corset of cotton wool. 'If it is a fake, it is a very clever one,' he says.

Three senior Russian scientists, Doctors Bayanov, Burtsev, and Donskoy, spent a long time examining the film in Moscow, and came to broadly similar conclusions to those of Dr Grieve. Donskoy said: 'We can evaluate the gait of the creature as a natural movement without any of the signs of artfulness that one would see in an imitation.' Bayanov and Burtsev noted that the creature has an apelike head and almost no neck and that the tracks show, here as elsewhere, that the creature walks with less weight on its heels than a normal man, has no foot arch and seems to walk with slightly bent legs. They suggested that the nearest analogy is with Java Man or *Pithecanthropus erectus*, the apelike creature which, unlike even early *Homo sapiens*, is classified as an animal not a man, but which is thought to stem from the same evolutionary root.

The doubts about the film centre on the fact that it is not known at what speed—24 or 16 frames per second—it was shot. The two speeds produce very different impressions when it is screened. Also the footprints found on the ground at Bluff Creek do not chime with the film. They are 14 or 15 in (38–41 cm) long and suggest a much taller creature than 6 ft 5 in (1.95 m) and one that should have a much longer stride.

Like the yeti, the most dispassionate evidence probably comes from the footprints. Trails with more than three thousand footprints have been followed over distances of several miles, hard work for any faker. Tracks have been found in the most remote spots where it would ordinarily be pointless to indulge in a hoax. The footprints have been subjected to minute examination at Washington State University, in the Soviet Union and in many institutions in Canada and the United States. A typical print is 16 to 18 in (41 to 46 cm) long and 7 in (18 cm) or more wide. There is no sign of a foot arch as in man, except in prints that seem to come from young ones. There is a distinct double ball, unlike the single ball on a man's foot, which indicates an adaptation of the foot to take great weight. The depth of the footprint impressions and projections from the creature's reported height suggest a bulk of at least 300 lb (136 kg), and some estimates put it at 500 to 1,000 lb (227 to 454 kg).

Grover Krantz of Washington State University and Robert Morgan, President of the American Anthropological Research Foundation, examine a cast of a Bigfoot print. This is one of 161 tracks found near Merwin Dam, Washington in 1974

Roger Patterson with a cast of a Bigfoot track found at Bluff Creek, California in 1967

Elaborate curves, ratios, formulae and projections, pages of calculations, graphs, diagrams, articles in learned journals like *Northwest Anthropological Research Notes*, have all been devoted to Bigfoot's feet. A glance at the pictures of the footprints confirms that they are not those of a bear, which is the usual explanation of the sceptic, as there is no sign of claws. Grover S Krantz, who has contributed a lot to the slide-rule assessment of the sasquatch prints, says: 'Even if none of the hundreds of sightings had ever occurred, we would still be forced to conclude that a giant bipedal primate does indeed inhabit the forests of the Pacific North West.'

It is Krantz who advises anyone who sees a sasquatch to shoot it, as the only final way of providing scientific proof. And he matches action to word by driving round in Bigfoot country with a high-powered rifle constantly at his side and special swivelling fog lamps on the side of his car for penetrating the gloom of the roadside forests.

Convincing though the stories are, however, this is also the country of the hoaxer and the huckster. There are certainly at least two entirely fake films, and fake footprints have been made with anything from re-moulded wellington boots to specially carved wooden feet. From San Francisco to Vancouver people go out either seeking Bigfoot or faking him.

There are stories of people reporting the colour of his eyes at 300 yd and the shape of his toenails from even further. However, a real hoax might be a dangerous business. Drive up any road into the Cascades and you will find almost every sign and half the road-side trees riddled with bullet holes where gun-toting locals have indulged in target practice as they have careered home on a Saturday night. Any joker capering around in a funny suit risks his life, especially as there is rumoured to be a million dollar reward for the finder of the first carcass of a Bigfoot. Unlike the Himalayas, where the hunt for the yeti is the concern of the select few who venture to 20,000 ft (6,100 m) or more and know the hazards of the world's greatest mountains, the hunt for the sasquatch is a popular passion that brings out coach parties from Portland and Seattle and tempts every cowboy for 500 miles around to spend a weekend on the trail with a rifle across his shoulder.

The wave of publicity has produced a relentless increase in Bigfoot reports—now certainly more than 2,000 accounts of finding prints or making sightings—and more alarmingly, he seems to be wandering far afield. In 1978 and 1979 alone, there were reports from Florida, Tennessee, Michigan, Alabama, North Carolina, Iowa and Arizona as well as from his home country of the North West.

Then there is the story of the Minnesota Ice Man exhibited at a Chicago fair and throughout the northern states, which a Belgian zoologist, Dr Bernard Heuvelmans and others saw and photographed. They were convinced it was Neanderthal Man or something like him, yet the Smithsonian Institution in Washington claims to know not

only that it was a rubber fake, but where and how it was fabricated: Hollywood. The ice-man saga languishes now in limbo. Heuvelmans is certain that what he examined for three days in 1968 frozen in a block of ice was an authentic body. He even smelled the

The Minnesota Ice Man

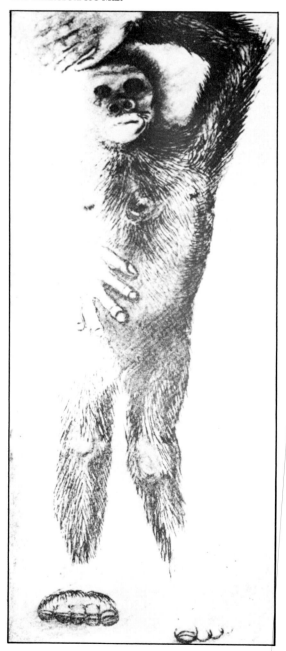

Dr Igor Burtsev holding a cast of an alma's footprint found in the Gissar Range of the Pamir Mountains, Tadzhikistan, 21 August 1979

putrefaction when some of the flesh had been exposed by melting ice. The derision with which Heuvelmans' account of what many regarded as a showman's fake was greeted, almost broke his spirit. Though the exhibit in its ice sarcophagus was around for three years, no one else contrived to examine it properly before its proprietor Frank Hansen, an ex-Air Force pilot, quietly disposed of it to avoid the hue and cry. Heuvelmans, armed with many good photographs of the ice man, is convinced it was a troglodyte or Neanderthal type, probably shot in Vietnam during the war and smuggled into the United States by the notorious dope route using the grim corpse bags marked, to hide the mutilation of the casualties, 'Not To Be Opened'.

But then some of the sasquatch's pursuers in North America do seem more unlikely than the beast itself. KFYR Television News from Bismarck reported, with film to prove it, that a posse had been put together by Lieutenant Verdell Veo of the Bureau of Indian Affairs in South Dakota, to hunt down Bigfoot after his foul-smelling presence was detected at Little Eagle, South Dakota. Their bait: a chicken-wire bag of 'used feminine articles' in deference to the notion that Bigfoot is particularly attracted to menstruating women.

The alma

No such exotic devices are known to be in use in the Soviet Union, but the search for the alma, the Russian version of the yeti and the sasquatch, is undoubtedly on a more continuous and scientific basis than for either of its rival hominids.

Many stories have filtered out of Siberia, the Russian steppes and the Caucasian mountains of sightings of manlike creatures.

An alma as described by Slavomir Rawicz and drawn under his guidance in 1977 by the zoologist, Dr W Tschernezky of Queen Mary College, London

During the Second World War prisoners and refugees fleeing either the Germans or the Russians or both claimed to have seen the alma. Slavomir Rawicz, in his controversial book *The Long Walk* about a 4,000-mile escape from a Siberian labour camp into India, claimed to have met a male and female alma which blocked his route for two hours and forced a disastrous detour; and in the prosaic surroundings of the seaside resort of Blackpool in Lancashire, England, a Pole, Mr Wiktor Juszczyk, regales his family with the story of his meeting with the alma in the area of Sinkiang and Soviet Turkestan. He was escaping from a Soviet prison camp when he was captured by Chinese soldiers who told him they regularly put food out for an alma—a piece of fish and a large loaf of black bread. On the second night, according to Mr Juszczyk, it appeared.

'It loped through 2 ft of snow right up to the table. Then it sat on its haunches, grabbed the loaf and ate. He must have been 7 ft high. He had a broad nose and slanting eyes, small and staring. I have never seen such a powerful-looking creature: long body, short legs, his chest, shoulders and arms covered in red-brown hair, but his hands were just like human hands. He spent a couple of minutes eating the bread and part of the fish, gave a few animal grunts and then ambled off.'

Mr Juszczyk subsequently escaped to England, married an Englishwoman and now has three children. 'It sounds fantastic, I know,' he says, 'but I saw it.'

The alma seems to be quite distinct from the yeti, inhabiting areas of inaccessible mountains right across from the Caucasus in the west of the Soviet Union to the Altai and the Gobi Desert in Mongolia in the east. Furthermore all reports indicate a manlike creature, as opposed to the more apelike form of the yeti.

The Russians are nervous about revealing too much about their alma researches, apparently for fear of being ridiculed in the West. Inquiries on the spot in Moscow and at the Darwin Museum there are met with classic evasions. Individuals are 'not available' or 'cannot be contacted' or have moved their office. As Moscow does not boast a telephone directory of private numbers, such tactics are effective. But there is a band of dedicated scientists, centred on the Darwin Museum and inspired originally by Professor Porchnev, who have gathered probably the most exciting and overwhelming case of all. They have shown that sightings of the alma go back at least to Przhevalski, the great nineteenth-century explorer and zoologist, who discovered the wild Mongolian horse which is named after him, and the wild camel too. On his expedition of 1879 one of his party, the Cossack Egorov, saw several wild men 'covered with hair and uttering inarticulate cries'.

Professor Rintchen of Ulan Bator University collected innumerable reports from among his fellow Mongols of alma sightings.

And unlike the yeti or the sasquatch there are many accounts of almas being shot and killed, but the exigencies of war or expeditionary logistics have invariably prevented the corpses being brought back for scientific examination. In 1944 a hairy man was shot and killed in Tashkurghan near where the borders of India, China, Pakistan, Afghanistan and the Soviet Union all meet. Professor B A Fedorovich cross-questioned many of the witnesses subsequently and was convinced the story was true. A Moscow factory chief, G N Kolpachnikov, relates that he was leading a reconnaissance unit in Mongolia during the Japanese invasion of 1937. One night two sentries saw a pair of silhouettes descending the side of a hill. Challenged, they made no response, so the sentries shot them. Kolpachnikov describes his astonishment when he saw the bodies in the morning. 'They were not enemies, but strange hairy creatures more like an anthropoid ape. But I knew that there were no anthropoid apes in the Democratic Republic of Mongolia.' He questioned an old man who told him that wild men were sometimes encountered in the high mountains. Kolpachnikov recalls that the bodies were about the height of a man covered irregularly with reddish hair, sometimes thick but often with the skin showing through. The face was like a very coarse human face with prominent eyebrows.

With a war going on there was no opportunity to do anything more than bury the bodies.

There are dozens of exemplary reports of sightings. In 1948, the geologist, M A Stronin, was prospecting near the Tien Shan and made camp with his two Khirgiz guides in a valley. In the first light of dawn he was woken by his guides shouting that their horses were being stolen. Stronin grabbed his rifle. In his own words: 'I saw this figure beside the horses. It was standing upright but the arms seemed longer than a man's. I shouted "Hey, why are you trying to rob us?" The figure turned at the sound of my voice and calmly walked away from the horses.'

Again Stronin describes the reddish hair

and upright stance. He chased after it. 'It wasn't quite human, nor quite animal, but even though it was in my sights, I couldn't decide to shoot what might have been some kind of man.'

From stories like this, the Russians have built up a very detailed picture of the alma. It corresponds largely with Mr Juszczyk's tale, and Professor Boris Porchnev of the Moscow Academy of Sciences has published an account in the fullest terms:

'There is no underlayer of hair so that the skin can sometimes be seen . . . infants are born without hair . . . the head rises to a cone-shaped peak . . . teeth are like a man's but larger, with the canines more widely separated . . . they often grasp objects without using the thumb, just the fingers and palm . . . they can run as fast as horses, climb trees, and swim in swift currents . . . breeding pairs remain together, often sheltering in holes in the ground . . . they have a distasteful smell, can throw stones but not make tools and like to warm themselves near the embers of an abandoned fire . . . they eat small animals and vegetable foods and are active mainly at twilight or at night.'

So convincing were the reports, including accounts of albino types, that in 1958 the Soviet Academy of Sciences mounted a full scale expedition to the Pamirs led by K V Staniukovich and including Porchnev to look for the 'snowman'. Although the expedition came up with some startling eyewitness stories, including an account of almas stoning a village and making off with food during particularly severe weather, they came up with no hard evidence. Porchnev, the chief protagonist of the alma, found himself under attack at a bitter meeting in 1959 and the subject has never since had the open support of the academy.

Certain workers, including Dr Bayanov and a remarkable French-born Moscow doctor Marie Jeanne Koffman, have been allowed to continue their investigations and even correspond with the West. They have put together an enormous dossier, with casts of outsize but humanlike footprints, samples of hair and dung and a continuous record of sightings. As recently as 1979 an amateur expedition led by Igor Tatsl brought back photos and plaster casts of prints in the Gissar Mountains in Soviet Central Asia.

All this evidence has now been brought into sharp focus by Dr Myra Shackley of Leicester University in England, an archaeologist who is one of the world's leading authorities on Neanderthal Man. She believes that the almas may well be the last surviving examples of Neanderthal Man, who is supposed to have been wiped out 40,000 years ago by the rise of modern man, *Homo sapiens sapiens*. She explains:

'It has never made sense to me that a vigorous and actually rather inventive tool-making culture which had been around for very many thousands of years should just succumb during the last ice age. The pattern of Neanderthal sites which have been excavated across Soviet Asia accord very closely with the sightings of the alma. If Neanderthal man should survive he would need a remote area, but with sufficient food and certainly the right sort of geological formations to provide the rocks for his tool making.'

The Altai mountains (Myra Shackley, 1979)

In the summer and autumn of 1979 Dr Shackley managed to get to Mongolia and make an expedition into the remotest parts of the Altai mountains where they thrust dramatically down into the Gobi desert.

'I think I was probably the first European for years, perhaps the first European ever, to penetrate some of those mountains,' she said. 'Nor do the Mongolians go there. They have no reason to, and in any case they are afraid of the creatures that live there.'

Though it was only a reconnaissance, Dr Shackley had an early success. In a high river valley she came across what appear to be Neanderthal tools, though not of recent vintage.

'It turns out the whole area is rich in Mousterian Neanderthal artifacts,' she says. 'If Neanderthal were to have survived it would most likely be in exactly those areas where the alma has been most persistently reported. It may seem bizarre, but could it be that Neanderthal Man is alive and well and living in Outer Mongolia?'

The search for the yeti, the sasquatch and the alma, has stretched around the world. But they remain elusive. Like Sir Edmund Hillary, most people dismiss them as legends, part of the endless panoply of ghosts, monsters and giants that have always peopled the human imagination. Naturalists are, in the main, confident that the earth has few

great secrets to surrender. But the mountain gorilla was dismissed as fantasy until it was finally captured at the turn of the century; the panda was first shown to people in the West only when it was delivered to Chicago Zoo in the 1930s; the orang-utan, closest of all to the mythical version of man's ancestors, had to be captured to be believed in the West.

On the other hand, if the yeti, Bigfoot and alma exist, why have no bones, skin or bodies been found? If they are not now on the verge of extinction, as Desmond Doig fears, they have not only been careful but very lucky indeed to escape the clutches of man.

The sceptics have written off many of the eyewitnesses. But can they all be hoaxers, fools, visionaries? If they are not seeing an unknown creature, what are they seeing? In North America, and even in the Himalayas, it might be a bear, but so many reports of sightings come from people who are experienced forest and mountain men who would be expected to recognize a bear or any other such familiar animal. And why do the descriptions tally so well, even those from people who have never heard of the alma or the Bigfoot? Why do the Sherpas of Nepal insistently identify an apelike creature?

Through all the uncertainties, comes the evidence of the footprints. None of the theories seems to explain them, either in the Himalayas or in America, or in the Soviet Union where according to Professor Khalkov they are very similar to those of Neanderthal Man. Hoaxers may operate in the Pacific North West but would they go 20,000 ft up the slopes of Everest and Kangchenjunga or venture into the wildest part of the Pamirs? Yeti, alma, Bigfoot—whatever its name, something seems to be there.

Arthur C Clarke comments:

Personally, I would take reports of contemporary apemen more seriously if there were not so many of them, and in such heavily populated places. But if 'Bigfoot' *does* exist, I would like to propose an open season for shooting those people who want to shoot

The mountain gorilla, until 1901 dismissed as fantasy

him—even in the name of science. . . .

Although there is nothing impossible in the idea that some of our remote ancestors might have survived down to quite recent times, the sad fate of the Tasmanian and other aborigines suggests that it is rather unlikely. The Tasmanians were members of our own species; and where are they now?

Yet we may have missed the Neanderthals by only a few centuries, not by millennia. For many years I have been intrigued by a Ceylonese legend that could be interpreted in this manner. The island's shy, forest-dwelling Veddas, who until recently* lived a virtually Stone Age existence, tell stories of conflict with even more primitive, apelike creatures who were able to talk but did not possess fire. The last of these man-apes, so the Veddas claim, were driven into a cave and then suffocated by fires built outside it.

This is supposed to have happened only a few lifetimes ago. So, just possibly, somewhere in the remote jungles of Sri Lanka, there may be a cave holding bones that would revolutionize the science of anthropology. . . .

*A few are still around. They grab their bows and arrows and hide their transistor radios when they hear the tourist buses approaching.

2

A Cabinet of Curiosities

No book of mysteries should fail to acknowledge the work of Charles Fort, an American who devoted his life to collecting reports of bizarre happenings. Fort was born in the Bronx district of New York in August 1874 and for many years worked as a journalist with a notable lack of success. However, a small inheritance which came his way at the age of forty-two gave him the freedom to devote himself full-time to the work for which he is now remembered.

For almost a quarter of a century, Fort sat in the New York Public Library or, when he was living in London, in the Reading Room of the British Museum, scouring scientific journals and newspapers for reports of anything that could not easily be explained or did not fit into accepted categories of knowledge. From this eye-straining labour and the almost indecipherable notes he made, came four exotic books published between 1919 and 1932: *The Book of the Damned, New Lands, Lo!* and *Wild Talents.*

Near the beginning of *The Book of the Damned*, he proclaims his method: 'I have gone into the outer darkness of scientific and philosophical transactions and proceedings, ultra-respectable, but covered with the dust of disregard. I have descended into journalism. I have come back with the quasi-souls of lost data.'

Fort is true to his word; his books are bizarre catalogues of unexplained events which have become known in memory of their recorder as *Forteana*. Within the pages of *The Book of the Damned*, for example, he records falls from the sky of red dust, frogs, 'manna', jelly-like substances, grain, vegetable matter, carbonate of soda, nitric acid, limestone, salt, coke, cinders, snakes, ants, worms and cannon balls.

Today, more than sixty thousand of Fort's notes are preserved in the New York Public Library. They contain accounts of UFOs collected decades before the terms 'flying saucer' or 'UFO' were coined, like the 'splendidly illuminated aeroplane' which passed over the English village of Warmley in 1912, or the triangular shapes reported in the sky over Bermuda in 1885, a strange foretaste of this century's alleged discovery of a Bermuda triangle said to be fatal to ships and aircraft. There are phantom soldiers, luminous owls, mirages, 'new' stars and planets, extraordinary coincidences, and strange booming sounds.

Left: 'Raining cats and dogs and Pitchforks!' from a nineteenth-century print
Right: Charles Fort at his checkerboard

Fort died in 1932, but his work is continued by dedicated followers throughout the world. Many of them publish magazines crammed with Forteana, gathered, according to Fort's method, from newspapers and scientific journals. Indeed, there are so many mysteries to record that one Fortean, a Canadian, even stores data on a computer. Typical of the bizarre tales that have been reported in recent years are the stories of two eminently trustworthy Englishmen, Roland Moody and Wilson Osborne.

Raining seed

Roland Moody and his wife live in a suburb of Southampton. Their neighbours on one side are Mr and Mrs Gale, on the other Mrs Stockley and her son, Patrick. Theirs is a quiet, friendly street, and nothing extraordinary seemed to have happened there, until 12 February 1979.

Roland Moody in his conservatory

Appropriately, as it turned out, Mr Moody is a keen gardener and at about 9.30 on that particular morning, as snow fell and a strong wind blew, he and his wife were pricking out seedlings in the warmth of the conservatory at the back of their house. Mr Moody remembers every detail of what happened next:

'I heard this whooshing sound, which was on the glass above me. I didn't take a lot of notice of it, but about three-quarters of an hour afterwards, it did it again, and I looked up and found the whole of the glass above me covered in what we found out afterwards was mustard and cress seed. But the most peculiar thing about it was that the cress seed was covered in jelly. In fact, if you were to put your finger down on the seed to pick it up it stuck to your fingers and you couldn't get rid of it. And afterwards this occurred five or six times during the course of the day. Each time, more and more of this mustard and cress seed came down, and it covered the whole of the garden, and it was most peculiar because we then started treading it indoors on our feet, and there you could smell the mustard and the cress without a shadow of doubt.'

Perplexed, Roland Moody went round to see his neighbours to ask if they had had a similar experience. Mrs Stockley had suffered a lesser bombardment of mustard and cress, but she also had a confession to make: she had not told anyone that the year before, mustard and cress seed had fallen all over her front garden, and she had spent a year clearing the plants from the flower borders.

As the week went on, things got worse. 'The following day, on the Tuesday,' says Mr Moody, 'we were still pricking out the seeds—I grow quite a lot of seeds; about thirty boxes every year—and down came a shower of peas and maize and haricot beans.' By now, Mrs Moody had had enough and took refuge inside the house. Meanwhile, Mr and Mrs Gale next door had ventured out into their garden which had already been 'rained' on by bean and pea seeds. 'Presently,' remembers Mrs Gale, 'a load of broad bean seeds came over and we both ducked down.' Mrs Stockley did not escape either: 'I got masses of broad beans every time I opened my front door. We were literally showered with them. They travelled right up the hall, right into the kitchen, which is some ten yards, I suppose, and they came in with such velocity.' On one occasion, Mrs Stockley was hit by dozens of broad beans when her son opened the front door while she was making a call from the telephone in the hall. Every time the front door was opened, broad beans came in, and several visitors were showered by them as they waited to be let in to the house. Mrs Stockley even called in the police but they could find nothing that could have caused the seed fall. Eventually, the puzzled neighbours began to collect the seeds, amassing some 10 lb (4.5 kg) from at least twenty-five falls, and, being thrifty gardeners, they planted them. 'I cleared up to eight full buckets of mustard and cress from the garden', says Mr Moody. 'The beans grew, the peas grew, everything grew.' Mr and Mrs Gale had a 'beautiful crop of beans', and Mrs Stockley still has some of the heavenly harvest in her freezer to prove it all happened.

But where did the seeds come from? To this day, none of the neighbours know. There was no real pattern to the falls: Mr Moody's seeds came mainly from the south-east, Mrs Gale's fell into the back garden, while Mrs Stockley's beans shot through the front door. The nearest house Mr Moody's seeds could have come from was 700 yd (640 m) away. If they had been thrown, a cannon would have been needed to send them through Mrs Stockley's door with such violence: and there was no sign of anyone or anything unusual in the street when the falls happened. Strangely, too, the seeds only fell on three houses in the road, and there were not even any on the path outside.

These days, as he tends his garden, Mr Moody still ponders not only the cause of the falls, but also the origin of the jelly that he

Wilson Osborne and his wife standing where they were showered with nuts

found sticking to the first batch of mustard and cress seeds. But expert gardener though he is, he can find no answer: 'It is just as big a mystery today as it was back in February 1979,' he says.

Nuts in March

Almost two years earlier, on 13 March 1977, Mr Alfred Wilson Osborne (a chess correspondent for a newspaper) and his wife were on their way back from church near their home in Bristol when they experienced what Mr Osborne describes as 'a most amazing thing'. They were passing a large car saleroom when, according to Osborne, 'there was a click as if I'd lost a button, and I realized that it was not a button which I had lost, but something had fallen from the sky.' That 'something' was a hazelnut, and at once the Osbornes found themselves caught in a whole shower of them: they estimate that there were between 350 and 400. 'They were just pinging on the cars as they went down,' says Mrs Osborne. To be caught in a shower of hazelnuts on a Sunday morning in Bristol at any time would be strange enough, but not only were there no nut trees in the road, but hazelnuts are not in season until September or October—and this was March. 'Yet', says Mr Osborne, 'they were quite fresh and sweet and nice.' Moreover, the Osbornes are certain the nuts were not thrown in some way from the flat roof of the nearby car saleroom: they were coming from the sky, which was 'practically clear and blue with one cloud drifting over'.

In the hope of solving the mystery, Mr Osborne kept a few of the nuts and told his friends about the shower; but, he says, 'the first reaction I got was that I was nuts like the hazels.' One of the Osbornes' friends, however, also walked through the falling nuts, when he passed the car saleroom about three minutes later, but neither he, nor the readers of the local newspaper to whom Mr Osborne turned for help, could provide an explanation. 'It's impossible to account for it, actually', says Mr Osborne. 'How they came and where they came from, I have no idea, but I have thought that it might be a vortex sucked them up, but I don't know where you suck up hazelnuts in March.'

Charles Fort would certainly have enjoyed and noted the stories of Mr Moody's seeds and Mr Osborne's hazelnuts, although he seems to have failed to record a shower of *fossilized* hazelnuts in Dublin in 1867, which, according to *Symons Monthly Meteorological Magazine*, fell with such force 'that even the police, protected by unusually strong head covering, were obliged to seek shelter from the aerial fusillade!'

He does, however, tell of several seed falls, including 'wheat' enclosed in hailstones in the English county of Wiltshire in 1686, and 'little round seeds' at Marienwerder in Germany.

Fish and frogs

Strange falls from a clear sky are the main-stays of Forteana, and several people, including scientists, have kept lists of the bizarre deluges that have been reported. Here, for example, are some falls culled from records old and new by David Ludlum, the editor of *Weatherwise*, an authoritative American meteorological magazine: a herring, 13 in (33 cm), fell on Main Street, Buffalo, New York in 1819; a 'heavy shower' of herring fell on the Odd Fellows Cemetery in Sacramento in 1879; a shower of fishes, including a 10-in (25-cm) squid, landed on Boston in 1841; a gopher turtle encased in ice fell on Bovina, Mississippi in 1894; iced ducks crashed at Worcester, Massachussetts in 1933; thousands of fish covered Magnolia Terminal in Thomasville, Alabama in June 1957 (fish had also fallen at Wichita, Kansas in 1899); water lizards dropped on Utah in 1870; 'catfish, perch and a few that looked like trout' showered Kershaw County, in 1901; and eight years before, at Wentworth and Anson Street in Charleston, an alligator had dropped from the sky.

Anyone who has experienced such a fall demands an explanation. Not surprisingly, explanations are almost impossible to find. There is nothing, for example, more likely to make a scientist squirm than a frog fall, such as the one witnessed by a British woman on 12 June 1954.

That afternoon, Mrs Sylvia Mowday took her small son and daughter to a display given by the Royal Navy in a park in Sutton Coldfield, Birmingham. She says:

'After seeing the exhibition, we went to the fair which was on the other side of the park. As we were making our way there, we had this sudden heavy storm. We tried to reach a belt of trees and my four-year-old daughter put her little red umbrella up and we heard these things thudding against it. And, when we looked, to our amazement it was a shower of frogs. They were coming from the skies, hundreds of them. The umbrella was covered, all our shoulders were covered, and as we looked up we could see the frogs coming down like snowflakes. When we looked down, we found the ground was absolutely covered with them, over an area of about fifty square yards. We were afraid to tread on them, they were so tiny.

They were half to three-quarters of an inch big, a khaki colour with little touches of yellow on them, just like they are when they emerge from frogspawn.'

As it turned out, Mrs Mowday was not the only citizen of Sutton Coldfield who had witnessed a fall of frogs: so had Mr John W Pittman, and his sighting had been ten years earlier in August 1944, also in the English Midlands. Mr Pittman, his wife and two children had gone by bus to a small village between Tamworth and Lichfield. It was a hot day, but, as they walked down the road, they were caught in a shower of rain. Suddenly, the road was covered with tiny frogs, which could only have come down with the rain. Fort, who enjoyed any sort of coincidence, would have loved the name of the village: it was called Hopwas.

A more widely publicized frog fall is the one reported by the well-known newspaper columnist, Veronica Papworth. In 1969, she was living in a house high on a ridge in Penn in Buckinghamshire. Here is how she told the story in the London *Sunday Express*:

'I well remember when we were going to a dinner party and we had a sudden storm and the doors and windows were open and it rained *frogs*. Little ones. Hundreds and thousands of them leaping in and all over the floor and you can't clobber frogs with a newspaper.

'As fast as we chucked them out they leapt back in again. So we were ages late for the party and fortunately when we *did* arrive, I found a couple up my baggy pants to prove it.'

Charles Fort collected reports of many frog falls. Among the most dramatic is this strange story of frogs and horses: 'Mr Stoker was driving along the Newark Valley, one of the most extensive of the desert regions of

Veronica Papworth in 1969

Nevada. Thunderstorm: down came frogs. Up on their hind legs went the horses.' There are many accounts, however, that are even older, such as this one from the *Histories* of Heraclides Lembus:

'In Paeonia and Dardania, it rained frogs, and so great was their number that they filled the houses and streets. Well, during the first days the people killed them and shut up their houses and made the best of it. But soon they could do nothing to stop it; their vessels were filled with frogs, which were found boiled or baked with their food. Besides, they could not use the water, nor could they set foot on the ground amidst the heaps of frogs piled up, and being overcome also with disgust at the smell of the dead creatures, they fled the country.'

Fort also reported a frog fall in Southgate, north London, in 1921. Mrs Joan Battell, who saw it, remembered it vividly and told us how, after a sudden rain shower, the road was 'literally swimming' with frogs.

Every so often, further reports crop up in small paragraphs in newspapers, almost always unleashing the pent-up wit of the sub-editors. 'Raining cats and frogs', announced *The Guardian*, describing a fall in Perpignan, France; the London *Daily Mirror*, noting a fall at the village of Darganata in Soviet Central Asia in July 1979, resorted pithily to 'Village Hop'. In December 1977, the London *Sunday Times* reported another frog fall in the desert—the Moroccan Sahara.

Many unimpeachable eyewitnesses have also reported falls of fish. Indeed, they are apparently so common in India and Australia that the newspapers have almost given up mentioning them. One Australian naturalist, Gilbert Whitley, was able to publish a list of no fewer than fifty rains of fish in *Australian Natural History* of March 1972. They include a fall of thousands of 'creek minnows' at Cressey, near Lake Corangamite, Victoria, in 1879; shrimps near Singleton, New South Wales in 1918, and pigmy perch in Heyfield, Victoria in 1933; and small freshwater fish which rained on the suburbs of Brisbane. From India, a scientist reported in the *Journal and Proceedings of the Asiatic Society of Bengal* that a tennis court near Muzaffarpur in northern India was 'literally white with small fish' that had fallen from the sky. In one case it is said that fallen fish were put to good use and turned into curry. Among many such stories from the East is that of Ron Spencer who told a BBC radio programme in 1975 about a fall at Comilla near the Burmese border in the Second World War. As fresh water was scarce, he used to stand in the monsoon rains with nothing but a bar of soap.

The cover of *Lo!* by Charles Fort (1931)

'On one occasion [he wrote] I was in quite a lather when things started to hit me, and, looking around, I could see myriads of small wriggling shapes on the ground, and thousands being swept off the roofs . . . These were small, sardine-sized fish. Needless to say, very shortly after the heavy storm, none were left. The scavengers had gobbled them up.'

From Britain come further reports. One of the earliest is a letter to a Fellow of the Royal Society describing a remarkable rain:

'On Wednesday before Easter, Anno 1666, a Pasture Field at Cranstead near Wrotham in Kent, about Two Acres, which is far from any part of the Sea or Branch of it, and a Place where there are no Fish Ponds but a Scarcity of Water, was all overspread with little fishes, conceived to be rained down, there having been at that time a great Tempest of Thunder and Rain; the Fishes were about the Length of a Man's Little Finger, and judged by all that saw them to be young Whitings, many of them were taken up and shewed to several Persons! . .'

In August 1918, there was a famous fall of sand eels, 3 in (76 mm) long, in the Hendon area of Sunderland, while in 1948, Mr Ian Patey, of Hayling Island in Hampshire, was caught in a shower of herring. Mr Patey remembers that they fell on him and his three companions as they walked along a fairway on the Barton-on-Sea golf course near Bournemouth during a game of foursomes.

Crabs and periwinkles have also fallen on the peaceful English countryside. At the end of May 1881, there was a thunderstorm near the city of Worcester. In the St John's area, many houses were damaged, but the attention of the local people, and of the readers of Berrow's *Worcester Journal*, was captured by one amazing aspect of the storm:

'A man named John Greenall, taking shelter in a shed in his master's garden at Comer-lane, states that he observed large masses of periwinkles fall, some of them being buried a considerable depth in the ground and others rebounding from the surface. The fall was confined to the market garden belonging to Mr Leeds and the Comer-lane. An army of Worcester street arabs soon took possession and gathered the periwinkles . . . In one large shell, which a boy picked up in the lane and gave to Mr Joseph Phillips of St John's, was a living hermit crab.'

And Lord Eastnor had something similar to report in a letter written in 1836:

'Soon after a most violent storm of rain and wind, in the summer of 1829, three small crabs, weighing from $1\frac{1}{4}$ to $1\frac{3}{4}$ oz., were found in the area of the workhouse at Reigate; and a fourth was afterwards found at a little distance, I think the following morning. . . . They were found by a boy, who told the governor that he had found a comical sort of a frog.'

The conventional explanation for these, and, indeed, many other strange 'rains', is that the creatures have been lifted from the ponds or rivers where they normally live by a freak whirlwind. But, if that is the case, the whirlwind must have been very selective, as William R Corliss points out in his *Handbook of Unusual Natural Phenomena*:

'First, the transporting mechanism (whatever it may be) prefers to select only a single species of fish or frog or whatever animal is on the menu for that day. Second size selection is also carefully controlled in many instances. Third, no debris, such as sand or plant material is dropped along with the animals. Fourth, even though saltwater species are dropped, there are no records of the accompanying rainfall being salty. All in all, the mechanism involved is rather fastidious in what it transports. The waterspout or whirlwind theory is easiest to swallow when the fish that fall commonly shoal on the surface in large numbers in nearby waters. It is much harder to fit the facts when the fish are from deep waters, when the fish are dead and dry (sometimes headless), and when the animals fall in immense numbers.'

Falling ice

Potentially far more dangerous are falls of large blocks of ice, a phenomenon reported frequently in modern times as well as in the past. Indeed, according to a list of such events published in *INFO Journal*, Spring 1968, a carpenter working on a roof at Kempten, West Germany, was struck and killed by an icicle 6 ft (1.8 m) long and 6 in (15 cm) round that fell from the sky. There are many cases of near misses, such as the time a lump of ice over a foot long and shaped like a rugby ball crashed through the roof of a house belonging to Doris Coult in the Humberside steel town of Scunthorpe, or the cube—described as about 'eighteen inches square'—that hit a car belonging to a Mrs Wildsmith, in the London suburb of Pinner in March 1974.

In America, the strange case of the block of ice that smashed through the roof of a house in the small town of Timberville, Virginia, still defies explanation. It happened on 7 March 1976 as Wilbert Cullers, his son and his son's girlfriend were watching *The Six Million Dollar Man* on television. The local *Daily News-Record* reported what happened next on that peaceful Sunday evening:

> '"We heard a roar just like dynamite, and pieces of the ceiling came through," Mr Cullers said. The pieces of ceiling and several large pieces of murky ice splatted onto the floor near the middle of the room, about a yard from the television. Several of the pieces bounced into the two rooms adjoining the living room. When they looked up through the large hole in the living room ceiling, they could see all the way into the clear, star-speckled sky outside.'

The *Daily News-Record* turned up a valuable witness to the ice fall in Johnny Branner, Mr Cullers' next-door neighbour. He had been standing out in his driveway just before the ice hit the Cullers house. 'It sounded like a muffled shotgun' he was reported as saying. A few seconds later, as the bewildered Mr Branner looked around, another chunk of ice hit the road. Within minutes, deputies from the Rockingham County Sheriff's Office, led by Sergeant Carl 'Butch' Hottinger, were on the scene. While Wilbert Cullers cleared up the pieces of ice from the floor and wondered how to repair the two-foot-square hole in the tin roof of his house, the deputies collected samples in a bucket and took them off to be analysed. Sergeant Hottinger's 'Offense Report' states that 'the total amount of ice looked to be the size of a basketball,' and adds, 'upon examining the ice I found it to be a milky white, cold, and compressible in the hand.'

Some of the ice was taken to the nearby Eastern Mennonite College in Harrisonburg, where it was tested by Robert Lehman, the Physics Department Chairman, and two chemistry students. As the tests began, the local police laboratory, which had also received samples from the Sheriff's office, reported, to the relief of the local inhabitants, that the ice had not been radioactive. This was confirmed by Dr Lehman and his students, who concluded that the ice was very like ordinary tapwater.

Where, then, had the ice come from? A question the Harrisonburg *Daily News-Record* lost no time in putting to all available authorities. An astronomer from the University of Virginia and officials of the National Weather Service were found to be in agreement: the ice probably came from an aircraft. Dr Lehman and his colleagues surmised that ice had formed at a broken water vent on a plane and had fallen off when it reached a weight of 10 or 15 lb (4.5–7 kg). Others, however, seemed to be less sure. Not only did local meteorologists say there was nothing in the atmosphere that night that could have caused a large block of ice to form on aircraft, but none of the people who were outside in the area of Wilbert Cullers' house saw or heard an aircraft, although the night was clear. And then there was the problem of some pieces of

Wilbert Cullers (left) and Carl Hottinger

gravel, which had been found *inside* one of the ice fragments. How would gravel have got on to an aircraft?

Some ice falls are certainly attributable to liquid falling from aircraft passing overhead. Take, for example, the 'Green Glob', weighing about 25 lb (11 kg), which fell at Ripley, Tennessee one Sunday afternoon in 1978. It caused a sensation among the people of the small township about 60 miles north of Memphis. 'This is more excitement than we've had in this little town for a long time,' Debbie Crowell, who worked in the sheriff's office, told a reporter. 'It had a nice little odour to it,' she added, and in that lies a clue to the origin of the 'Green Glob'. Local officials of the Federal Aviation Authority were able to confirm after an analysis that it was the result of a leak in an aircraft's plumbing system. The blob will have formed as the green-blue chemicals used to flush the lavatories seeped from a tank. The low temperatures at the kind of high altitude at which most planes fly would have caused the fluid to freeze. Vibrations, a current of warm air, or sheer weight must have caused the frozen mass to fall away from the aircraft. This phenomenon also accounts for the Shenandoah 'Blue Blob', a lump of dark-blue ice

weighing about 10 lb (4.5 kg) that crashed into a house in Shenandoah, Pennsylvania, in 1970, and, according to the local paper, prompted at least one resident to think that 'the end of the world had come'.

Not all the ice falls, however, can be explained away as easily as that, because there are many instances of blocks that fell to earth before the invention of aircraft. The largest scientifically verified hailstone is known as the Coffeyville Hailstone, after the town upon which it fell in 1970. It measured $17\frac{1}{2}$ in (44 cm) in circumference and weighed 1.67 lb (7.6 kg). And what are we therefore to make of the ice encountered by a Captain Blakiston on one of his voyages? He later wrote:

'On 14 January 1860, when two days out from the Cape of Good Hope, about three hundred miles SSE of it, in lat 38° 53′ S, long 20° 45′ E, we encountered a heavy squall with rain at ten am lasting one hour, the wind suddenly shifting from east to north (true). During the squall there were three vivid flashes of lightning, one of which was very close to the ship; and, at the same time, a *shower of ice* fell which lasted about three minutes. It was not hail, but irregular-shaped pieces of solid ice, of different dimensions, up to the size of half a brick. . .'

41

Even more remarkable is the ice block that fell from the sky on to an estate in Ord in Scotland in 1847:

'Immediately after one of the loudest peals of thunder heard there, a large and irregular shaped mass of ice, reckoned to be nearly 20 ft in circumference, and of a proportionate thickness, fell near the farmhouse. It had a beautiful crystalline appearance, being nearly all quite transparent, if we except a small portion of it which consisted of hailstones of uncommon size fixed together. It was principally composed of small squares, diamond-shaped, of from one to three inches in size, all firmly congealed together. The weight of this large piece of ice could not be ascertained; but it is a most fortunate circumstance, that it did not fall on Mr Moffat's house, or it would have crushed it, and undoubtedly have caused the death of some of the inmates. No appearance of either hail or snow was discernible in the surrounding district.'

Such falls have left scientists at a loss with some of them doubting the accuracy of the original reports and others suggesting that they have an extraterrestrial origin and come from comets. Even since the invention of aircraft, the origin of some blocks of ice remains obscure. The best-documented of such recent falls is undoubtedly one that occurred in a quiet, tree-lined street on the outskirts of Manchester, England, on 2 April 1973. On that evening, Dr Richard Griffiths, who was then a postgraduate student at Manchester University, was walking along Burton Road on his way to buy a bottle of whisky, when he noticed a single sudden flash of lightning. Since he was a registered lightning observer for a research association, Griffiths made a careful note of the time of his sighting of the lightning stroke, 7.54 pm. He then bought his bottle of whisky at a nearby shop, and, at 8.03 pm, as he set off back to his lodgings, a large object hit the road just outside the shop. It was a huge block of ice, which Griffiths later estimated

may have weighed up to $4\frac{1}{2}$ lb (2 kg), in itself extraordinary, since the Coffeyville hailstone weighed only just over $1\frac{1}{2}$ lb (0.7 kg).

Because he was a scientist and a part-time weather observer, Richard Griffiths immediately picked up the largest chunk of ice, wrapped it, and raced home to his kitchen. There he placed it in the freezing compartment of his refrigerator. The next morning, he took the precious sample, in a pressure cooker wrapped in a blanket, to his laboratory at the Manchester Institute of Science and Technology and began to analyse the ice in the hope of determining its origin.

There are standard tests that can be made to determine the history of a hailstone. One of them is to slice the ice into thin sections and examine it not only in ordinary reflected light but also through sheets of crossed polaroid. This reveals its crystal structure. By applying these techniques, Griffiths found that the piece of ice he had saved was made up of fifty-one layers of ice separated by some thinner layers of trapped air bubbles. However, it did not seem to resemble any known hailstone, either in the size of its crystals which were much larger than are normally found, or in its layers, which were far too regular to conform with those he had ever previously come across.

Another test showed that the ice had been formed from cloud water, but how had it grown and where? Perhaps it had grown in some sort of container: so Griffiths tried to produce similar ice by filling balloons with water and hanging them in a refrigerator. The ice made in this way, however, bore no resemblance whatsoever to the ice-block from the sky and this ruled out the possibility of a hoax. Perhaps, then, Griffiths wondered, the ice had, after all, fallen from an aircraft. But, he says:

'I made enquiries at the engineers' department at the airport. There were two aircraft following a flightpath in the area at the time. One of them landed just before this piece of ice came down, and the other one landed somewhat after. But I made

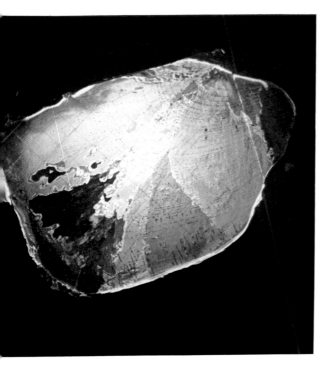

Richard Griffiths' ice

specific enquiries as to whether or not either of these aircraft reported any icing on their fabric and the engineers advised me quite categorically that there was no icing on these aircraft. So, unless other evidence comes to light, I would say it couldn't have come from either of those two.'

So Dr Griffiths is still baffled. All he can now say is 'It's all negatives. Lots of things that it isn't, and not a word about what it is. I can't give you an answer.'

The Chinese seals

While Fort gleefully collected tales of objects that fell from the sky, he was also intrigued by things that have turned up in unexpected places on the ground. Strangest of all these is undoubtedly the collection of ancient Chinese porcelain seals found all over Ireland in the late eighteenth and nineteenth centuries. They were, as Fort puts it, 'not the things with big, wistful eyes that lie on ice, and that are taught to balance objects on their noses, but inscribed stamps, with which to make impressions.'

The seals are tiny, consisting of a cube measuring about 1⅛ in (28 mm) surmounted by the figure of an animal, and are made of a type of hard porcelain known as *blanc de chine*. It is now known that such seals were made for Chinese scholars. Each seal bore an auspicious message, and the scholar, who would have owned twenty or thirty, would have sealed his letter with the one he deemed to be the most appropriate. They were common in the East, but what were they doing in Ireland? Especially as they were found at a time when there were no known direct trading links between China and Ireland. Moreover, such seals have never turned up in a similar manner elsewhere in the British Isles.

It was a Mr Joseph Huband Smith of Dublin who first brought the seals to the attention of his countrymen in a paper he read to the Royal Irish Academy in 1839.

He had an extraordinary story to tell. For several years, Chinese seals had come to light in obscure places in the towns and countryside of Ireland. The first seems to have been found in about 1780, when a turf cutter found one buried in a bog at Mountrath near Portlaoise in what was then called Queen's County. Another was discovered in about 1805 in a cave near Cork harbour; yet another by some men who were digging up the roots of an old pear tree in an orchard in County Down. Then there was the seal found at Clonliffe Parade near the Dublin Circular Road in 1816. A sixth seal was turned up by a plough in a field in County Tipperary, and two more, in the bed of the River Boyne in County Meath, and in Killead, County Down, respectively.

In the years that followed Huband Smith's revelations, the mystery of the Chinese seals stirred fierce passions among Irish antiquarians. None of them could agree where the seals came from, what the animal on top of them was, whether the inscription on the underside actually meant something in Chinese, or how it was that such exotic objects had seemingly been scattered years before in such unlikely places. Smith lost little time in informing the Academy of his own theory: 'It is therefore, at least, possible that they may have arrived hither from the East, along with the weapons, ornaments, and other articles of commerce, which were brought to these islands by the ships of the great merchant-princes of antiquity, the Phoenicians, to whom our ports and harbours were well known.'

In the 1840s, a man named Edmund Getty from Belfast decided to try to answer some of the questions about the seals. He consulted a naturalist who confirmed suspicions that the apelike animal on the top of them had been modelled to look like a Chinese monkey. He then decided to take impressions of all the seals that had so far turned up—there were now about twenty-six of them—to determine whether they bore an inscription in Chinese. This was quite an undertaking, but fortunately one of his friends was appointed to a job in Hong Kong, and he was able to ask two groups of Chinese scholars to attempt to translate them.

Such was the pace of communications between Ireland and the East in Victorian times, that two years went by before Getty received the answer to his question. It was that the seals were undoubtedly Chinese and that the type of script on them was in use in about 500 BC, the time of Confucius. The scholars agreed on the meaning of many of the inscriptions; one seal, for example, bore the legend: 'A pure Heart', and another 'The Heart though small, most generous'. Sometimes, however, the Chinese scholars disagreed with each other as to meaning. According to a group of scholars in Nanking, one seal's inscription read 'Some Friend', while Shanghai academics maintained that it meant 'Plum trees and Bamboos'.

Still, some progress had been made, and by 1853, at least fifty seals had been found. By 1868, the Royal Irish Academy learned from a Dr Frazer that there were now sixty-one seals but he believed that they were relatively modern, probably dating from the

Chinese seals and where they were found

fourteenth or fifteenth centuries, or even later.

But the mystery of how the seals got to Ireland still remains. A few of the seals are to be found on the top shelf of a glass case in the National Museum of Ireland in Dublin. With them are four seals which the museum's catalogue says were 'bought at Canton, 1864', and were ordered by Dr Frazer for comparison.

At our request, they were examined for the first time in many years by Jan Chapman, an orientalist from Dublin's Chester Beatty Library. To begin with, she noted that the fact that the seals were made of porcelain was very unusual, since they are usually carved from minerals. Their size, too, surprised her, for most Chinese seals, including some on other shelves in the museum are much larger. She was, however, able to identify the porcelain itself as the product of a factory situated near one of China's main trading ports, Amoy. Although the factory started making porcelain in the twelfth century, Miss Chapman believes the seals found in Ireland date from the early eighteenth century, which is when the factory exported porcelain of that type. But, beyond that, she can shed no light on the mystery. All the seals were, it is true, found east of a line drawn from Lough Foyle to Cape Clear, and it may be that they entered Ireland at Cork. But this is too vague a pattern to be of any real use, and the Chinese seals of Ireland remain as puzzling as they were in Fort's day.

The 'Devil's footprints'
Whereas the Chinese-Irish seals were found over a period of many years the 'Devil's footprints' appeared in the beautiful English county of Devon literally overnight. The year was 1855, and the winter that January and February was exceptionally hard. At one moment the Exe estuary was frozen over and, while some people enjoyed the skating which this made possible, others were suffering badly: there were bread riots in Torquay, because the normal supplies had failed to get through, and many people died

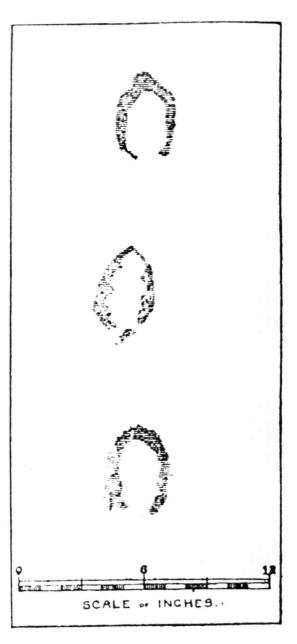

An eyewitness sketch of the 'Devil's hoofprints'

of the cold. On Friday 9 February, the people who lived in the villages and towns around the Exe estuary awoke to find the countryside covered with strange footprints. To many, it seemed that to add to all the troubles the winter had caused them, they had had a visit from the Devil.

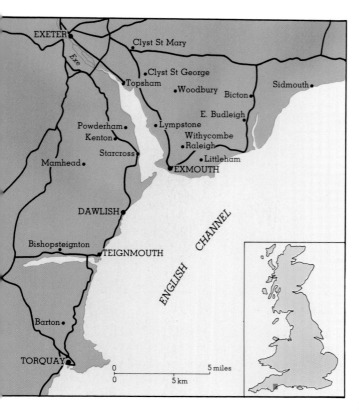

The part of Devon visited by the 'Devil' in 1855

At the town of Dawlish, this account of the footprints was recorded many years later by the daughter of the Vicar, Miss Henrietta Fursdon, in *Devon and Cornwall Notes and Queries*:

'The footprints occurred in the night, and owing to my father being the Vicar he was immediately visited by curates, church-wardens and parishioners to ask him his opinion of the footprints, which were all over Dawlish. They were in a straight line, in the shape of a small hoof, but con-tained in the hoof were the marks of claws. One track especially attracted attention, which went direct from the Vicarage to the Vestry door; other tracks were found leading straight up to dead walls, and again found on the other side, many were found on the roofs of houses; and in all parts of Dawlish. . . . I myself remember distinctly seeing the footprints,

and my terror as a child of the unknown wild beast that might be lurking about, and the servants would not go out after dark to shut outer doors.'

Other people clearly had similar feelings, because the *Torquay Directory* reported that 'a party of tradesmen and others armed themselves with guns and bludgeons and spent the greater part of the day in tracing the footsteps.' Upriver at Mamhead, General Edward Mortlake Studd was called from his lunch to inspect tracks in the garden of his home, Oxton House. At Pytte, a trail led up to a closed garden door at the house of a Mr Doveton, and then appeared on the other side of the 8 ft wall and ran all round the garden. At Lympstone, Woolmer's *Exeter and Plymouth Gazette* reported 'hardly a garden . . . where footprints were not observ-able . . .' A local clergyman, the Reverend H T Ellacombe observed: 'At a house at Marley near Exmouth, marks were seen on the sill of a window two stories high,' while near Withycombe Raleigh, a gentleman had followed the tracks under gooseberry bushes and found that they entered and passed through a 6 in drain. Not all the tracks appeared on the same day: the Reverend Ella-combe, Rector of Clyst St George, wrote that he first saw them three days after they had been found elsewhere: 'There is scarcely a field or an orchard or a garden where they were not—all in a single line—under hedges and in one field near me we met with excre-ment.' 'Four oblong globes of a whitish colour —the size and shape of a large grape.'

An anonymous correspondent writing in

Oxton House, Devonshire, from a contemporary print

46

the *Illustrated London News* of 24 February 1855 gave what remains the most famous account of the Great Devon Mystery:

'The marks which appeared on the snow (which lay very thinly on the ground at the time) and which were seen on the Friday morning, to all appearances were the perfect impressions of a donkey's hoof—the length of four inches by two and a quarter inches; but instead of progressing as that animal would have done (or indeed as any other would have done), feet right and left, it appeared that foot had followed foot, in a *single line*; the distance from each tread being eight inches or rather more—the footprints in every parish being exactly the same size and the steps the same length! This mysterious visitor generally only passed *once* down or across each garden or courtyard, and did so in nearly all the houses in many parts of the several towns . . . , as also in the farms scattered about: this regular track passing in some instances over the roofs over houses and hayricks, and very high walls (one fourteen feet), without displacing the snow on either side or altering the distance between the feet, and passing on as if the wall had not been any impediment. The gardens with high fences or walls, and gates locked, were equally visited as those open and unprotected. Now, when we consider the distance that must have been gone over to have left these marks—I may say in almost every garden, on doorsteps, through the extensive woods of Luscombe, upon commons, in enclosures and farms—the actual progress must have exceeded a hundred miles. It is very easy for people to laugh at these appearances, and account for them in an idle way. At present no satisfactory solution has been given. No known animal could have traversed this extent of country in one night, besides having to cross an estuary of the sea two miles broad. . . .'

From contemporary press reports and old

The Rev. H T Ellacombe (1790–1885)

letters found in parish archives, Miss Theo Brown, a lecturer at Exeter University, has helped to reconstruct the astonishing scene that the people who lived around the Exe estuary found on that snowy morning in February. There were separate tracks at Teignmouth, Dawlish, Starcross, Kenton, Mamhead and Powderham on the west side of the Exe and at Topsham, Clyst St Mary, Clyst St George, Woodbury, Lympstone, Exmouth, Littleham-cum-Exmouth, Withycombe Raleigh, East Budleigh and Bicton. At Barton, south of Teignmouth, the prints crossed the Barton Hall estate; while at Teignmouth itself, the aptly named Mr Hook, a fisherman, told Theo Brown that his father remembered that the tracks had come up over the beach, across the town, up a lane called The Lea behind the present gasworks, and away across country in the direction of Bishopsteignton.

There was great excitement and not a little fear in the small Devon villages. Everyone seemed to have a theory about the origin of the strange footprints. The Reverend George Musgrave of Withycombe Raleigh announced from the pulpit that the prints must have been made by a kangaroo that had recently escaped from Mr Fish's zoo in

Sidmouth. A correspondent called 'Ornither' suggested that a large bird, the great bustard, was responsible; a farmer said they must have been cats' paw prints that had thawed and then refrozen. The famous zoologist Professor Richard Owen gave his considered opinion that they were badgers' tracks. Toads, otters and crippled hares were also suspected. To most people, the footprints looked as if they had been made by a donkey, but how could a donkey, they wondered, have crossed the estuary so many times in one night, let alone negotiated walls 8 ft high, as well as 6 in drainpipes and windowsills? It is hardly surprising that the superstitious settled for a visit from his satanic majesty himself.

Today, we are little the wiser about the true origin of the Devil's footprints. Theo Brown thinks they may have been caused by a combination of different creatures: donkeys, ponies with broken shoes, which would have given the impression of the cloven hoofs that so scared the local people, birds with iced-up feet. It is also possible that some of the tracks—particularly those which appeared after the first 'outbreak'—were made by practical jokers with a heated shoe iron. Miss Brown thinks that meteorological phenomena may also have been responsible, and there is support for this from a Scottish explorer James Alan Rennie who, in 1952, near the Scottish village of Cromdale near Inverness, came across 'tracks every bit as mysterious as those seen in Devon'. These tracks leaped over a sunken roadway, stopped at a pine tree, and finally after several gaps, ended up opposite the village churchyard. Rennie rushed home to get his camera, photographed them, and showed them to his mystified friends. Rennie, however, had an explanation: he had actually seen tracks like these being made when he was exploring in Canada in 1924. He had been snow-shoeing over a frozen lake, when he had come across tracks which had terrified his companion, a French-Canadian dog skinner. The dog skinner crossed himself and said his prayers. The next morning, he

had disappeared but Rennie, undaunted, set off again across the frozen lake. As he walked, the tracks appeared right in front of him. They were being made by 'some freakish current of warm air, coming in contact with the low temperature' which 'had set up condensation which was projected earthwards in the form of water-blobs.'

None of these explanations is entirely satisfactory: if the atmospheric conditions in Devon in February 1855 had been similar to those described by Rennie, then it is likely that someone would have noticed them, particularly since the discovery of the first footprints excited such attention. If the tracks had been made by a combination of creatures, what were they, which ones had gone under the gooseberry bushes or onto windowsills or up 6 in drain-pipes? As Theo Brown remarks, 'You wouldn't get a donkey walking over house roofs.' And what would have caused all these creatures to emerge and leave such tracks over so wide an area but not in villages away from the district on the night of 8 February, when few such tracks have ever been seen since?

Forteana

The problem with Fortean phenomena is that it is not always easy to treat them seriously. Yet the request, advanced by the *Illustrated London News* correspondent on the 'Devil's footprints' that people should not 'laugh at these appearances and account for them in an idle way' is apt. Falls of fish, frogs and ice from a clear sky often sound comic, but, when hoaxes and misreporting are eliminated, there are real meteorological mysteries to explain and questions that demand sensible answers. If whirlwinds are the cause of frog falls, what are the circumstances in which they occur? How is it that blocks of ice which do not share the characteristics of hailstones can form in the sky before crashing down to earth? What weather conditions, if any, could be the cause of the 'Devil's footprints,' or if, as some argue, they were made by a whole series of animals, what were the animals, and what brought them out on that particular snowy night? Outlandish though these occurrences may be, they demand serious investigation, although their very unpredictability increases the difficulty of studying them scientifically.

It is no use turning to Fort for explanations of frog falls, ice blocks from the sky, rains of fish, or even the Chinese Seals or the Devil's Footprints. His aim is to establish that strange things happen that scientists cannot easily explain. He himself does not even try to offer any explanation, except of the most light-hearted sort. He suggests, for example, that the objects that rain down on the earth come from a kind of 'Super-Sargasso Sea' in the sky, or from a place he calls 'Genesistrine': 'Whether it's the planet Genesistrine, or the moon, or a vast amorphous region superjacent to this earth, or an island in the Super-Sargasso Sea, should perhaps be left to the researches of other super- or extrageographers.'

It is a truism to say that we live in a strange and unpredictable universe, but Fort believed so with a passion tempered by a sense of humour and of wonder. He was not against science, he was against scientific dogmatism, and opposed to scientists who are quick to reject accounts of strange phenomena out of hand. Things have changed little since the days early in this century when Fort sat poring over ancient journals in reading rooms. His books and the events in them are a warning against the belief that modern science has begun to comprehend the total complexity of the universe. In his books and notes, Fort celebrates the natural world's unpredictability and any rationalist tempted to dismiss reports of extraordinary happenings should pause and think again, lest he should hear the wise laughter of Charles Fort as that great archivist of the world's mysteries rests from his labours among the falling frogs and leaping fishes on the ice-strewn shores of his Super-Sargasso Sea.

Arthur C Clarke comments:
Organic matter falling from the skies! How

perfectly ridiculous. . . .

Well, just a moment; by a strange coincidence, if there is such a thing as a strange coincidence, only a few days ago I attended a lecture by the distinguished Sri Lankan astronomer, Professor N C Wickramasinghe, who, with his colleague Sir Fred Hoyle, has put forward the truly revolutionary theory that life did not originate in the oceans of this earth—but in outer space. More than that, Professor Wickramasinghe has made the astonishing suggestion that many of the great clouds of obscuring gas—a kind of cosmic smog—that lie between the stars consist of *bacteria*! Perhaps not living, but freeze-dried. . . .

Even now, he believes, some epidemics may be caused by extraterrestrial organisms drifting down from the stars (shades of *The Andromeda Strain*!). It is not such a long step from this to globs of jelly . . . but frogs, fish—and hazelnuts? These must surely have a terrestrial origin, and often it could be a very simple one. (Baby frogs can suddenly appear in such surprising numbers, when they have completed their metamorphosis from tadpoles, that they seem to have fallen from the skies.) But there are far too many cases which cannot be explained as easily as this. Charles Fort was on to something. But *what*, for Heaven's sake?

Falling ice, even without benefit of aircraft, does not seem to present such a problem. We are now fairly sure that frozen water (and ammonia, as well as more complex chemicals) is common in space; the rings of Saturn contain large quantities, and may indeed be described as orbiting icebergs. That term may also be applied to many comets and some meteorites; if an ice meteorite hit the earth's atmosphere, the outer layers could act exactly like the heat shield of a returning spacecraft, and the inner core might reach the surface intact.

And so Charles Fort's suggestion that such falls originate in 'vast fields of aerial ice from which pieces occasionally break away' may be the almost literal truth. . . .

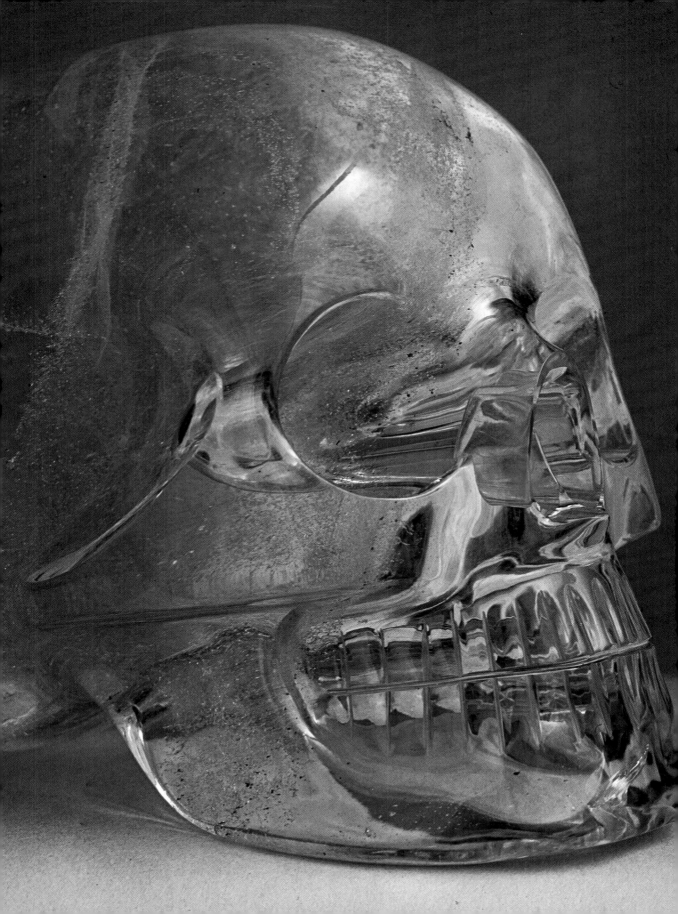

3

Ancient Fires

For the past twenty years, the weirdest gem in the world has belonged to a lady who keeps it on a velvet cloth on a sideboard in her house. It is a fearsome skull, weighing 11 lb 7 oz (5.19 kg), carved of pure quartz crystal, and its owner believes it comes from a lost civilization. Its eyes are prisms and, it is said, the future appears in them. It has been called the 'Skull of Doom'.

Since the skull came to light in the ruins of an ancient South American city, many researchers have tried to establish its origin: they have taken affidavits about the circumstances in which it was found, they have measured its enigmatic features with calipers, and have examined its shiny surface millimetre by millimetre, they have even shone coloured light through its clear crystal, but so far they have laboured in vain.

The crystal skull is one of a handful of strange man-made objects that have challenged the ingenuity of the world's scientists during the past half century. Some of them, like the crystal skull, or the perfect stone spheres known as the Giant Balls of Costa Rica, present daunting puzzles to the experts, since their origin and purpose are quite unknown. Others seem to challenge accepted modern ideas of man's scientific progress like the 'electrical battery' found in Baghdad and thought to have been made a good 1,500 years before Volta's invention in 1798, or the bronze 'computer' recovered from a ship wrecked in the Aegean and dating from 80 BC. They suggest that some ancient peoples possessed a technology far more sophisticated than modern civilization has believed possible. All these artifacts defy easy explanation.

Left: The crystal skull from the Museum of Mankind

The crystal skulls

There are, in fact, two mysterious life-size crystal skulls. One of them sits in a glass case at the top of the stairs in the Museum of Mankind (part of the British Museum) near London's Piccadilly Circus. There, it presents a special problem to the museum administrators, because the cleaners, worried by the skull's unrelenting gaze in the dim light of the exhibition room, have insisted that it should be covered with a black cloth before they will work near it at night. Surprisingly for a museum in which the details of each exhibit are authoritatively displayed to the public, the label on the crystal skull's case is vague. As to the date, it says merely that the skull is 'possibly of Aztec origin—the colonial period at the earliest'. The truth is that even this attribution is guesswork by the museum's experts, because there are almost no facts known about the skull's history. The museum bought it from Tiffany's, the New York jewellers, for the sum of £120 in 1898. No one at the Museum of Mankind knows where Tiffany's got it from, although it is said that it may have been part of the booty amassed in Mexico by a mysterious soldier of fortune during the nineteenth century.

The other skull belongs to a woman, Anna Mitchell-Hedges, and the story of how she came by it is exotic and confused. Anna's father was F A ('Mike') Mitchell-Hedges, a British adventurer who roamed the Americas during the early years of the twentieth century, gambling with millionaires, riding the range as a cowboy, and fighting with Pancho Villa during the Mexican Revolution. On one of his trips, Mitchell-Hedges met up with a group of men in a hotel in Port Colborne, Ontario. With them was a small

51

'Mike' Mitchell-Hedges leaving for Central America in 1926

orphan named Anna le Guillon whom he adopted and who later took his name.

It was Anna who discovered the crystal skull. In 1927, Mitchell-Hedges was excavating the great Mayan city of Lubaantum in British Honduras. Mitchell-Hedges had discovered the city a few years earlier, during a search for the lost civilization of Atlantis which he believed to be in the area. On her seventeenth birthday, Anna noticed something beneath an ancient altar: it was the top half of the crystal skull. Three months later, just a few feet away, she found its detachable lower jaw, which had become separated from the rest of the head.

According to Miss Mitchell-Hedges, her father gave the skull to the Mayans who lived in the area. 'They prayed to it', she says, 'and told father it was their god used for healing or to will death.'

When the Mitchell-Hedges' expedition left the ancient city later in 1927, 'the Mayan people gave my father the skull as a parting gift because he had been so good to them, bringing them medicines and clothing.'

Almost from the moment of its discovery, however, the crystal skull has been a cause of controversy. Not only are its origins obscure, but the exact circumstances of its finding have never been fully revealed. For this reason; although there was no doubt that Anna Mitchell-Hedges had found it under the altar at Lubaantum, questions were raised about the events surrounding the find. How was it, asked some commentators, that one of the largest gemstones in the world had turned up so suddenly in the midst of excavations, and how was it that Anna failed to find the skull's lower jaw until several months had gone by? Furthermore, why would neither Mitchell-Hedges himself, nor other excavators at Lubaantum, give further details of the discovery? Inevitably, the vagueness of the story led some people to speculate that the skull might not have come from the Mayan city at all, and that it had been 'planted' by the altar so that Anna would be sure to find it. Since the day of the find was her seventeenth birthday, and she had apparently been depressed after a bout of malaria, perhaps, the argument ran, her father had planned the 'discovery' to cheer her up. He could have acquired it on his travels in Mexico.

Certainly, the great explorer's own public attitude to the skull appears uncharacteristic at first sight. In his autobiography, *Danger My Ally*, published in 1954, five years before his death, he devotes only a few lines to it, and they are far from explicit. Writing of a trip to Africa in 1948, he says:

'We took with us also the sinister Skull of Doom of which much has been written. How it came into my possession I have reason for not revealing.

'The Skull of Doom is made of pure rock crystal and according to scientists must have taken 150 years, generation after generation working all the days of their lives, patiently rubbing down with sand an immense block of rock crystal until the perfect skull emerged . . . It is at least 3,600 years old and according to legend was used by the high priest of the Maya when performing esoteric rites. It is said that when he willed death with the help of the skull, death invariably followed. It has been described as the embodiment of all evil.'

To many readers of his vigorous prose, it seemed strange that a man who obviously enjoyed a good story should have devoted only thirteen lines of his autobiography to his most exotic possession, and stranger still that this cryptic passage should not have appeared at all in some later editions of Mitchell-Hedges' book.

Anna Mitchell-Hedges, however, is quick to discount such questions. She says any idea that the skull was 'planted' under the altar is 'nonsense' and that her father would not have spent many thousands of pounds on an expedition so that he could bury a crystal skull. As for Mitchell-Hedges' reluctance to discuss the skull and the story of its discovery: she explains this by pointing out that her father allocated the account of the various finds and incidents at Lubaantum to

different members of his team and was scrupulous in observing their right to give the facts first. He had decided that his daughter should tell the story of the crystal skull, and although more than half a century has now passed, she is still not ready to give her full version of the events that began amid the ruins of Lubaantum on her seventeenth birthday.

Anna Mitchell-Hedges has, however, shed some light on one much-discussed episode in the history of the skull she now owns. On 15 September 1943, it came up for auction in the famous salerooms of Sotheby's in London. It was listed as lot 54, and had been sent for sale, not by Mitchell-Hedges, but by a London art dealer, Sydney Burney. It had apparently come into Burney's possession as security for a loan made to Mitchell-Hedges. The files of the British Museum reveal that the museum tried to buy the skull at the sale, no doubt wishing to be able to display the world's only two life-size crystal skulls side by side. A terse pencilled note by H J Braunholtz, a member of the British Museum staff, records what happened when they bid for it through an art dealer. 'Bid at Sotheby's sale, lot 54, 15 × 43 up to £340 (Fairfax). Bought in by Burney. Sold subsequently by Mr Burney to Mr Mitchell-Hedges for £400.' This episode adds confusion to an already perplexing tale: the skull had obviously failed to meet Burney's asking price and had been withdrawn, but what does Braunholtz mean when he says 'Sold subsequently by Mr Burney to Mr Mitchell-Hedges for £400'? Miss Mitchell-Hedges says the skull was placed with Mr Burney as collateral for a a loan and redeemed by her father as soon as he saw it was for sale.

From that time onwards, the story becomes a little clearer. The skull remained in Mitchell-Hedges' possession until he died in 1959. Since then Anna Mitchell-Hedges, who has lived in both Britain and Canada, has kept the skull at home, occasionally lending it to exhibitions or researchers.

And, although she says that she will, in time, reveal the full circumstances of the skull's discovery, Anna Mitchell-Hedges is unable to shed any light on the central question of when the skull was made and scientific analysis of both crystal skulls has also failed to provide an answer. The most notable examination of the skulls took place in 1936, when Sydney Burney, who had the Mitchell-Hedges skull in his possession at the time, agreed to lend it to scientists at the British Museum.

The two skulls were compared in detail by the distinguished anthropologist Dr G M Morant, and his report was published in *Man*, the journal of the Royal Anthropological Institute of Great Britain and Ireland. Morant's report began by noting that while the skulls were similar in many anatomical details, the most significant difference between them was that the British Museum skull was in one piece, while the other skull's lower jaw was detached. Furthermore, the

The crystal skull from the Musée de l'Homme

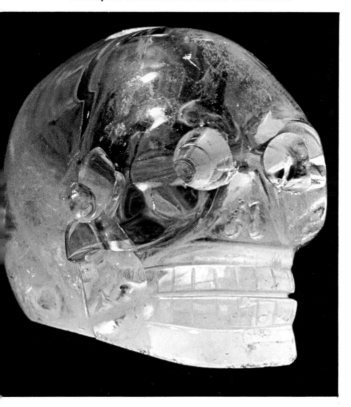

Mitchell-Hedges skull (or Burney skull, as Morant calls it) was far more lifelike and finely detailed than its counterpart. Morant, however, was most struck by the similarities he found between the two skulls. For a start, he decided that their general shape indicated that they had been modelled on a woman's skull. By superimposing tracings taken from photographs, he noted that the outlines of the lower jaws, teethlines and nasal openings matched almost exactly, and, although there were a few differences, he opined that it was 'impossible to avoid the conclusion that the crystal skulls are not of independent origin'. He added: 'In the writer's opinion it is safe to conclude that they are representations of the same human skull, though one may have been copied from the other.' Surprisingly, Dr Morant went on to claim that the more finely wrought Mitchell-Hedges skull may have been the earlier version, because it would have been unusual if a craftsman, copying from the cruder British Museum skull, would have been inclined or able to add anatomical details.

Morant's comparison, in fact, settled nothing. Other authorities immediately challenged his claim that one skull was a copy of the other, and none of them really tackled the crucial question of their date and origin, beyond mentioning that the museum skull, with its round eye sockets and 'merely indicated' teeth, was characteristic of ancient Mexican art. The Mitchell-Hedges version, on the other hand, had 'the character almost of an anatomical study in a scientific age'.

There can be little prospect of a definitive answer to the question of whether the crystal skulls are ancient or modern, because there is no scientific technique for dating crystal. Even deciding which country the skulls originate from is fraught with problems, not least because smaller ones are known to have been made in fifteenth-century Italy as well as in South America. French experts have, however, agreed on the date of a smaller crystal skull in the Musée de l'Homme, Paris. They believe it was made by the Aztecs in the fourteenth or fifteenth century, and that it may have been an ornament on a sceptre carried by an Aztec priest. The French argue that the Aztecs were obsessed with death and that it played an important part in their spiritual life. One typical fifteenth-century Aztec poem says:

'Where would we not go to find death?
For that desire, our heart bleeds.'

Moreover, to the Aztecs, crystal was a favourite material because of its transparency and its 'ability' to ward off poisonous snakes and to help people foretell the future. To clinch the argument, the French also say that they have found traces of copper tools like those used by the Aztecs on the skull's surface.

When the British Museum Laboratory examined the Museum of Mankind skull a few years ago, however, they found no helpful clues as to its workmanship, although on one tooth there was the vaguest indication that a powered cutter may have been used. While the British experts, therefore, remained puzzled by the origins of the Museum of Mankind skull, Anna Mitchell-Hedges is in no doubt at all that the one she found is Mayan, like the city in which she found it.

And there, for want of any further evidence, the story of the crystal skulls must rest, except to say that it would be sad if their mysterious past were to obscure an appreciation of their beauty. The Mitchell-Hedges skull, particularly, has an awesome power. Its prismatic eyes and movable jaw make it easy for anyone to imagine it as an object designed to strike terror into the hearts of primitive people. Perhaps it was lit from below, and, shining in the darkness of a temple, uttered prophecies through its crystal mouth. Even if it is relatively modern, as a work of art it is as unforgettable as it is terrible in its beauty.

The 'Giant Balls' of Costa Rica

Las Bolas Grandes—the Giant Balls of Costa Rica—present a rather different problem. Their place of origin is not in doubt, as it is certain that they come from the Diquís

The 'Giant Balls' in Costa Rica: a photograph taken in the 1940s by Dr Samuel Lothrop

Delta in Costa Rica—but they are, nonetheless, some of the strangest objects ever discovered by archaeologists.

They came to light, literally, in the 1930s when the United Fruit Company began to clear the thick jungle of the Diquís Delta for banana plantations. As workmen hacked and burned their way through the forests, they came across dozens of stone balls, many of them perfect spheres. They ranged in size from a few inches to 8 ft (2.4 m) in diameter: the smallest are the size of tennis balls, weighing only a few pounds, the largest weigh 16 tons or more.

When American archaeologists began to study them in the 1940s, they were astonished. One of them was Dr Samuel Lothrop of the Peabody Museum, Harvard University. Lothrop had run into one of the perennial problems of archaeology in Latin America: bandits threatened the safety of his team in an area in which he had planned to excavate, and he had to find something else to do. He decided to go to Palmar Sur, a farming community on the Diquís Delta, and it was on his way to a guest house there that he saw giant stone balls decorating a park and the lawns of private houses. It was, he wrote later, 'a fantastic sight'.

Like any archaeologist when faced with

Dr and Mrs Lothrop

previously unknown artifacts, Dr Lothrop hoped to be able to answer the questions: who made them, how, why and when? He soon found that there were no easy answers. It was impossible even to find out how many of them there were in the jungle, because a number of them had already been removed to people's gardens or had been broken into by the local inhabitants who believed they contained treasure. Others had been damaged by fire in the clearing of the jungle. There were certainly hundreds, probably thousands, and Lothrop learned of groups of them numbering up to forty-five. They were clearly man-made, because the granite from which most of them were fashioned did not occur naturally in the area where they were found. The strangest thing of all was that many of them were almost perfectly spherical. The larger ones, in particular, were so smooth and round that it was almost impossible to believe that they had been fashioned without some kind of mechanical aid, and Lothrop concluded that whoever carved the Giant Balls must first have made templates.

The giant stone spheres must have been of great importance to their sculptors, as their manufacture clearly demanded prodigious labour. There were no quarries in the Palmar area and Lothrop surmised that the stone must have been brought from the mountains many miles away. A few of the balls he came across were made of stone possibly from the

The Lothrops excavating in Costa Rica

mouth of the Diquís River—a journey of at least 30 miles (48 km) by river to the place where they were found. To carve a sphere 8 ft (2.4 m) in diameter, the ancient masons would have had to start with at least a 9 ft (2.75 m) cube of rock, and whole teams of people would have had to turn it as it was rubbed smooth with other stones. Then they, or others, would have had to drag the completed balls to the mountain ledges or the far banks of rivers where they were found.

Finding clues to their meaning is almost impossible, as they suggest no clear patterns of human behaviour. Some small ones were found in graves, larger ones in long lines, straight or curved, and sometimes arranged in triangles. The usual device of looking for pottery beneath the artifacts did not help either, because although many of the broken pieces found were sixteenth-century, there were shards dating from other centuries.

Today, the Giant Balls of Costa Rica are still a mystery, although many of them now adorn the gardens and business quarter of the country's capital San José. Local archaeologists are still recovering them from the mud of the Diquís Delta, and, as they do so, they marvel at the ingenuity of the people who fashioned and transported them, for they are difficult to move even with modern machinery. The archaeologists are satisfied they know how they were cut: probably, people first found a block of stone that looked as if it could easily be turned into a sphere;

then they ground it down with an abrasive of sand and water, pressing the sand onto the surface of the stone with another rock. But they can only guess why they were made. They are not mentioned in the early histories of Costa Rica written by the first Spanish settlers. Dr Luis Diego Gomez, Director of the Museo Nacional, Costa Rica, favours the idea that they represent the sun, moon, or the whole solar system; others theorize that they may be grave markers, that they were aligned on heavenly bodies, or that their makers saw them as the physical embodiment of perfection. One local archaeologist sums up the problem: 'If anyone knows about it, we do—and we know nothing.'

The controversies surrounding the Giant Balls have not always been academic. In the late 1970s, two of the largest ever found turned up near Palmar and were sold to two men from San José who tried to move them to the capital. But Dr Gomez and the Museo

Nacional decided they must be preserved, and sued on the grounds that their sale amounted to the desecration of the national heritage. The trucks carrying the Giant Balls were turned back on their way to the city and the precious national treasures were dumped by the airstrip at Palmar to await the court's decision. As the long legal wrangle went on, Gomez formulated a plan to display them if he won. Although his plan entailed knocking down the elaborate Spanish portico of the museum to roll them into the building, it was readily agreed to, because, whatever their significance when they were made, the Giant Balls of Costa Rica still have the power to intrigue and fascinate.

The vitrified forts of Scotland

High on a hill in the Scottish Highlands is a riddle which, like the crystal skulls, leaves experts struggling to find an explanation to fit the curious facts they have amassed.

Even from many miles away, the summit of the 1,850 ft (560 m) Tap O'Noth near the

The high oval rampart of melted rocks which form the vitrified fort on Tap O'Noth

village of Rhynie in northeastern Scotland looks oddly flattened; but its truly extraordinary nature is revealed only after an arduous climb to the top. Here, there is a high oval rampart of stones which once formed the defences of an ancient fort, built during the British Iron Age. It is a spectacular place, commanding views over a vast area of Aberdeenshire, but the strange thing about it is that the walls are made, not of dry stones, but of melted rocks. There are still vast blocks of them in position: what were once individual stones are now black and cindery, fused together by heat that must have been so intense that molten rivers of rock once ran down them. Now, cold once more, the walls are made of a material so hard and glassy that archaeologists call it 'vitrified'.

To find one vitrified fort would be strange enough, but there are at least sixty of them in central and northeastern Scotland: one of them, Dunnideer, is only a few miles from Tap O'Noth and clearly visible from its walls. Some of the forts are vast, like Tap O'Noth, built on thousands of square yards of headland or hilltop, others are tiny enclosures. All of them, to a greater or lesser degree, still have walls of melted rock. Nor is it a purely Scottish phenomenon: vitrified forts have been found in England, France and Germany.

It is understating the case to say that archaeologists have not known what to make of vitrified forts since they began to study them about two hundred years ago. The harder they have looked, theorized and argued, the more intractable the problem has seemed to become: no one can explain to everyone's satisfaction how or why the forts' walls have been melted.

As usual, there are many theories. One, favoured in the eighteenth century, is that the hills on which vitrified forts are found were originally volcanoes, and that the people who settled there used stones thrown up by eruptions to build their settlements; another advanced in recent years maintains that the rocks were melted by the ray

Vitrified rock, part of the vitrified fort at Craig Phadrig near Inverness

guns of that group so dedicated to the hoodwinking of modern archaeologists, the ancient astronauts. One rather more mundane notion is that melted rock was used as a kind of glue to bind loose stones together, but even this has been dismissed as impracticable by people who have taken the idea seriously enough to consider it: enormous crucibles would have been needed to prepare the 'cement', and no trace of them, or of the blast furnaces that would have been necessary to heat them, have ever been found.

The theories favoured by archaeologists depend on the assumption that the walls of the fort were made of stones laced with timber, and that there was a hollow in the middle filled with rubble—the wood acting as a stabilizing factor like the 'through-stones' used by drystone-wallers to hold the two faces of their walls together. Excavation has certainly revealed that this type of construction existed at forts at Abernethy near Perth and Dun Lagaidh in Ross and

Cromarty. Moreover, no less an authority on forts than Julius Caesar described a wood and stone defensive wall called a *murus Gallicus* in his account of his Gallic Wars.

But with vitrified forts nothing is easy, and the people who have studied them are not even able to agree on the details of their construction. For example, no one can decide how much wood was used: some archaeologists claim there were beams running along the wall; others that joists only ran across it; yet others that there was a combination of the two. There may also have been vertical posts on the outside of the walls. No one has even been able to say for certain whether hard- or softwood was used. The remains of vitrified forts are distorted and have usually collapsed, so it is hardly surprising that the archaeologists have no clear answer even to this basic question as they pick their way through the ruins.

Whatever the details, they do, however, agree that vitrification results from the burning of timber-laced stone walls, and the real controversy is over why the vitrification was produced; was it part of the building process—perhaps to make the walls stronger or to insulate them—or did it come about by chance, in the destruction of the forts by fire?

The idea that the fort builders deliberately melted the rock walls of their settlements was advanced by some of the first Scottish antiquarians when they came across the phenomenon two hundred years ago. Their theory was that fires had been lit, and inflammable material added, to produce walls strong enough to resist the dampness of the local climate or the invading armies of the enemy. It is a curious notion, and there are many objections to it, not least that there is no evidence that such a technique, if it was used, did strengthen the walls; rather the opposite, in fact, because in many cases firing seems to have caused the walls to collapse. Moreover, it could hardly have proved to have been an effective building method,

Bute-Dunagoil vitrified fort on the Sound of Bute, Arran

as the walls of many of the forts are only partially vitrified. A Scottish archaeologist, Helen Nisbet, who has excavated vitrified forts, has also provided another telling argument against the idea that vitrification was deliberately engineered. In a thorough analysis of rock types used, she reveals that most of the forts were built of stone easily available at the chosen site, and that, even when stones were brought from a distance, they do not seem to have been chosen for their property of vitrification.

Yet scientists who have studied the problem are reluctant to allow the archaeologists to abandon the idea that the walls were somehow designed to produce vitrification. One team of chemists from the Natural History Museum in London stated their view quite bluntly after studying material from several vitrified forts: 'Considering the high temperatures which have to be produced, and the fact that possibly sixty or so vitrified forts are to be seen in a limited geographical area of Scotland, we do not believe that this type of structure is the result of accidental fires. Careful planning and construction were needed.' Another team of chemists did not go as far as that but, after subjecting rock samples from eleven forts to a rigorous chemical analysis, stated that the temperatures needed to produce the vitrification were so intense—up to $1,100°C$—that they could not have been produced by setting fire to a simple *murus Gallicus*. 'Rather,' these researchers added, 'there must have been a careful design of the wall and a contained burning process.'

The argument that the forts became vitrified because they were accidentally destroyed by fire is just as imperfect and contradictory. Significantly, perhaps, there is more than one theory on how they came to be burned. One is that the walls were ignited by sparks from domestic fires, signalling beacons or foundries. This idea, however, has been generally discounted, not least because there are so many vitrified forts that chance destruction of this kind seems improbable, unless their inhabitants

were habitually and astonishingly negligent in their fire precautions.

The other main theory is that vitrification came about almost incidentally when the forts were destroyed by invaders, and the fact that there are clear signs that many of the forts were occupied for some time before being set on fire supports this. In two famous experiments in the 1930s, the great archaeologist Gordon Childe and his colleague Wallace Thorneycroft showed that forts could have been set on fire by invaders piling brushwood against the walls, and, more importantly, that the fires started in this manner could generate enough heat for the stones to vitrify.

In March 1934, a model *murus Gallicus*, 12 ft (3.66 m) long, 6 ft (1.8 m) wide and 6 ft (1.8 m) high, was built for them at Plean Colliery in Stirlingshire. They used old fireclay bricks for the faces, pit props as timber, and filled the cavity between the walls with small cubes of basalt rubble. Finally, they covered the top with turf. Then, they piled about four tons of scrap timber and brushwood against the walls and set fire to them. Despite a snowstorm the wood caught fire, and, three hours later, the wall began to collapse. This exposed the inner core which, fanned by a strong wind, grew hotter and hotter.

When Childe and Thorneycroft went through the remains of the wall the next day, they found that they had successfully reproduced the kind of vitrification they had seen in ancient forts. And they did it again in June 1937, when they fired another wall actually on the site of a vitrified fort at Rahoy in Argyllshire, using the rocks found there.

But the experiments do not by any means resolve the questions posed by the vitrified forts not least because Childe seems to have used a larger proportion of wood to stone than many experts believe made up the original structures. It is hard, for example, to understand why people should have built defences that invaders could destroy with fire, when great ramparts of solid stone

Gordon Childe (just visible) and his assistant about to fire a wall at Rahoy in 1937 to prove his vitrification theory

would have survived unscathed. It is also difficult to see why people should have persisted with the design for a thousand years or more, and in so many places in a relatively small area, if they were so susceptible to the firebrand. There is not even a clear answer to the question of who set the walls on fire: if it was the work of invaders, could the defenders of the forts not easily have put the flames out, for as Childe's experiments showed it took some time for the brushwood to ignite the main structure? And there is always the lingering doubt, raised by the chemists, that the walls must have been specially designed to allow the inner cores to

reach great heat and vitrify, suggesting that the fort builders of ancient Scotland may have known something about building which we today do not.

The Baghdad battery

In Baghdad, Iraqi archaeologists are glad to discuss what they believe to be proof that their ancestors could make electricity a full 1,800 years before Galvani produced enough current to make the famous frogs' legs twitch.

The story begins in 1936 when a consignment of finds from a settlement which had once been occupied by the Parthians was sent to the Iraq Museum laboratory. At the time, Wilhelm König, a German, was in charge. He wrote later:

'Something rather peculiar was found, and, after it had passed through several hands, it was brought to me. A vase-like vessel of light yellow clay, whose neck had been removed, contained a copper cylinder which was held firmly by asphalt. The vase was about 15 cm high; the sheet-copper cylindrical tube with bottom had a diameter of 26 mm and was 9 cm long. In it, held by a kind of stopper of asphalt, was a completely oxidized iron rod, the top of which projected about 1 cm above the stopper and was covered by a yellowish-grey, fully oxidized thin coating of a metal which looked like lead. The bottom end of the iron rod did not extend right to the bottom of the cylinder, on which was a layer of asphalt about 3 mm deep. The question as to what this might be, received the most surprising answer. After all the parts had been brought together and then examined in their separate parts, it became evident that it could only have been an electrical element. It was only necessary to add an acid or an alkaline liquid to complete the element.'

It seemed to be a battery. Yet it had been found in the ruins of a Parthian village, and the Parthians had lived in the area between 248 BC and AD 226. König was claiming that they had electricity, and that Volta and Galvani, who up to that time had been credited with the invention of the first batteries, had merely introduced them to the West.

Despite suggestions that König misinterpreted the find and that it is the remains of a scroll that was stored in a pottery container, or of a relatively modern battery dropped perhaps by telegraph engineers in the late nineteenth or early twentieth centuries, another German has provided dramatic support for König's theory. He is Dr Arne Eggebrecht, an Egyptologist from Hildesheim in West Germany, and he first came across the battery when a touring exhibition of treasures from ancient Iraq went on show

Components of the Baghdad battery on show in the Iraq Museum

at the museum where he works. Of all the exhibits—the lofty marble statue of an ancient king the hexagonal cuneiform tablets, and the finely worked vases—it was the apparently humble group of the copper cylinder, iron rod and pot that most intrigued him. Like König he says: 'If you take all these things together, they can only mean an electric cell or battery to a scientist.'

Since the first realization, Eggebrecht has tested the theory many times with a battery made with exact replicas of the pieces. For the alkaline liquid called for by König, he uses juice freshly pressed from grapes bought at a local fruit shop. As soon as the liquid is poured into the copper cylinder, a voltmetre connected to the battery registers half a volt of electricity. Eggebrecht's is no idle curiosity: he believes the existence of such a battery may help solve a mystery that

Dr Arne Eggebrecht with his replica of the Baghdad battery which he has used in successful experiments

Using the replica battery to gild a small statue

archaeologists have so far been unable to explain. The museums of the world are full of gilded objects, and, in many cases, the method used to gild them is obvious: sometimes gold leaf was pressed round them or even glued on. But such techniques do not seem to have been used in every case. For example, Eggebrecht has a small statue of the Egyptian god Osiris made in about 400 BC. It is made of solid silver topped with a layer of gold which he believes is far too thin and smooth to have been applied by the crude techniques of beating or gluing. Could batteries, he wonders, have been used to electroplate it? It was a question which, with the replica battery to hand, could be easily answered. By immersing a silver statuette in a gold-cyanide solution, and running an electric current through it from the Baghdad Battery, he was able to produce a finely gilded object in little more than a couple of hours. Having done this several times, a dis-

concerting thought struck him: perhaps many of the treasures that the museums of the world display in their collections as being made of gold are, in fact, made of silver with a thin veneer of gold, and he hopes that, in the light of his finding, many museums will begin the unwelcome task of re-examining their treasures to make sure that all that glisters in the display cases really is gold. In the case of the Baghdad Battery, therefore, the suggestion that an ancient civilization may have possessed electricity may prove to be a mixed blessing.

The Antikythera Mechanism

There is at least one artifact that proves beyond all doubt that one civilization in the ancient world possessed technical know-how which no modern scientist had previously suspected. Since it was found in the sea off Antikythera, a small island northwest of Crete, it is known as the Antikythera Mechanism.

It was recovered from a shipwreck discovered in 1900 by a team of divers who had decided to try to find sponges on a rocky ledge off Antikythera. They came across the hull of a ship laden with statues. Later that year, they returned to the scene, and, after many months of arduous and dangerous diving, brought up a haul of bronze and marble statues which were taken to the National Archaeological Museum in Athens for cleaning and restoration. The museum staff were overwhelmed by the beauty and sheer quantity of the finds and it is not, therefore, surprising that it was several months before anyone looked closely at a few pieces of corroded bronze which had been recovered with them. When, on 17 May 1902, a leading archaeologist, Spyridon Stais, finally examined them, he noticed the outlines of cog-

wheels in the ragged bronze lumps. Immediately there was controversy: some experts said they were the gear wheels of an astrolabe which astronomers had used for measuring the elevation of heavenly bodies; others disputed the claim. What was certain was that writing on the case indicated that the mechanism had been made in about 80 BC. It was not, however, until 1958 that the Antikythera Mechanism was first examined by the man who was to reveal the true extent of its maker's technical achievement to the world.

Derek de Solla Price, an Englishman who is now the Avalon Professor of the History of Science at Yale University in America, came across the mechanism while studying the history of scientific instruments. When he visited the Athens museum, he was astonished by what he saw: 'Nothing like this instrument is preserved elsewhere,' he wrote. 'Nothing comparable to it is known from any ancient scientific text or literary

The divers who discovered the Antikythera Mechanism in 1900

A fragment of the Antikythera Mechanism

allusion. On the contrary, from all that we know of science and technology in the Hellenistic Age we should have felt that such a device could not exist.'

Preliminary work on the bronze fragments had revealed its basic features: on the outside, it had consisted of dials set into a wooden box, and inside there were at least twenty gear wheels. The box was covered with inscriptions which included an astronomical calendar. But the most significant feature of all was that the mechanism included a system of differential gears. It was this that astonished Price, because, up to then, science historians had thought such complex gearing had first appeared in a clock made in 1575.

For more than a decade, Price struggled to reconstruct the mechanism from the corroded fragments, but it was not until 1971 that X-ray photographs taken for Price by the Greek Atomic Energy Commission finally revealed the Antikythera Mechanism's full array of meshing gears. Since clocks dating from the thirteenth century AD were known to have had simpler gearing, Price's reaction is understandable: 'I must confess that many times in the course of these investigations I have awakened in the night and wondered whether there was some way round the evidence of the texts, the epi-

graphy, the style of the astronomical content, all of which point very firmly to the first century BC.'

No one can be sure how the Antikythera Mechanism was used or what it was doing in a ship laden with statues, but Price himself thinks that it may have been a representation of the universe, more a work of art than a scientific instrument. He also believes that it may have been part of a tradition of gearing technology bequeathed by the Ancient Greeks to their Islamic successors, coming finally to fruition in the great European astronomical clocks of the Middle Ages. Certainly, the Antikythera Mechanism must rank, as Price claims, 'as one of the greatest basic mechanical inventions of all time.'

Its very existence is a warning against the arrogant modern notion that sophisticated

The X-ray photograph taken in 1971. Derek de Solla Price has drawn over it to illustrate how he believes the mechanism would have worked

science was beyond the capabilities and the imagination of the people of the ancient world.

Arthur C Clarke comments:

The saga of the 'Antikythera Mechanism' is one in which I feel personally involved, for a variety of reasons. In the late 1950s, I put Dr Price in touch with Dennis Flanagan, editor of *Scientific American*, who persuaded him to write the article which first presented this astonishing device to the general public. ('An Ancient Greek Computer': *Scientific American*, June 1959.) Over the years, I continually pestered Dr Price to complete his research, which was finally published in 1974 ('Gears From the Greeks', in the *Transactions of the American Philosophical Society*.) And in 1965, I took time off from the affairs of the International Astronautical Federation Congress to visit the Athens National Archaeological Museum, and to gaze with my own eyes at the corroded fragments lying at the bottom of an empty cigar box. Later I was to write*:

'Looking at this extraordinary relic is a most disturbing experience. Few activities are more futile than the "What if ..." type of speculation, yet the Antikythera mechanism positively compels such thinking. Though it is over two thousand years old, it represents a level which our technology did not reach until the eighteenth century. Unfortunately, this complex device described merely the planets' apparent movements; it did not help to *explain* them. With the far simpler tools of inclined planes, swinging pendulums, and falling weights, Galileo pointed the way to that understanding, and to the modern world. If the insight of the Greeks had matched their ingenuity, the industrial revolution might have begun a thousand years before Columbus. By this time we would not merely be pottering around on the moon; we would have reached the nearer stars.'

And I have often wondered what other

A twelfth-century astronomical clock

treasures of advanced technology may lie hidden in the sea. We can be absolutely certain that the Antikythera computer is the product of *human* skill; but if there is anywhere one might expect to find crashed spaceships or other alien artifacts, it would be in the oceans that cover three-quarters of our world.

* 'Technology and the Limits of Knowledge' in *The View from Serendip*.

4

Monsters of the Deep

Our planet, no doubt, should be called not Earth but Sea. And nothing is more certain than that the two-thirds of its surface that is covered with water still holds many surprises for Man.

Arthur C Clarke's bungalow at Unawatuna on the southernmost tip of Sri Lanka affords one of the most evocative ocean views in all the world. The watcher on the shore stands on the most perfect curve of golden beach, palm trees hustling, despite the tides, foolhardily close to the shore, the sea clear for sometimes hundreds of feet. Even when the southwest monsoon rolls in its formidable breakers, the water remains translucent. The skindiver loitering among the coral, seemingly unremarked upon by the legions of weird and exotic fish, can soon feel that he can make the underwater world his own. But it is this same idyllic Indian Ocean prospect that looks out too towards many of the great enigmas of the oceans. Beyond the horizon here is only more horizon, no land for 6,000 miles down to the Antarctic, and trenches in the sea bed as deep as the Himalayas are high. Few ships venture here save the noisy motor vessels ploughing the regular and predictable routes from the Cape to Australia or across to Singapore and the Indies. There are vastnesses enough where the great sea monsters can lurk.

To be sure, there are fearsome enough creatures already known and catalogued by science. The giant manta ray, often 20 ft (6 m) across, winged like some enormous marine vampire, occasionally surfaces in some terrified fisherman's net. Stories about it are common in the Maldives and the Andamans. In late 1979, the Sri Lankan papers carried a laconic paragraph about a boy, Mada Mahendra, killed by a 'devil fish' or manta ray while diving for coral. 'His two companions escaped,' the paper said by way of compensation. Here too are the sea snakes, the deadliest family in the world. The most sinister, 5 ft (1.5 m) long with a small head that allows it to pursue even burrowing prey, abounds in parts of the South Seas. Yet it was only 'discovered' in 1946 by Sir Edward Belcher. In 1974, a Japanese professor established that the venom from Belcher's sea snake is one hundred times more powerful than that of any other reptile, including the king cobra and even the black Australian tiger snake. The fishermen, whose leaf huts crowd down to the water's edge in Sri Lanka, talk too of the mightiest fish in the sea, the whale shark, 60 ft (18 m) long or more. The tales are of boats rammed, and overturned, men lost. Yet the whale shark, bigger than any previously known fish, has rarely fallen into the hands of men, dead or alive.

Left: The Indian Ocean: strange sea creatures periodically turn up in the nets of Sri Lankan fishermen
Right: The giant octopus, image of terror: an epic struggle inspired by the fiction of Jules Verne

The megamouth shark

The megamouth shark

The limits of the marine biologist's knowledge are **very** narrow. The hundreds of thousands of sperm whales still surviving in the southern oceans get more than three-quarters of their food from a sizeable squid called a cranichiid. Yet for all the research done in the whaling areas only one specimen of the cranichiid has ever been caught. But surprises from the deep come on a grander scale than that. In 1976, the US Navy ship *AFB14* hauled up its sea anchors one afternoon with rather more than usual difficulty, to find a massive and fierce-looking creature, 15 ft (4.5 m) long and weighing three-quarters of a ton, entangled in the underwater parachute. It had seven rows of needle-like teeth. The great fish turned out to belong to a completely unknown family which scientists have now dubbed the megamouth shark.

The US Navy has indeed good reason to respect the unknown monsters of the ocean, for, not long before, they had had a very bizarre experience. The USS *Stein*, a frigate, had pulled out of San Diego in California on a cruise across the equator to South American waters, her mission to track submarines. Soon after crossing the meridian, her vital sonar gear became unserviceable, with heavy 'noise' drowning out all useful signals. All tinkering with the equipment proved futile. So, defeated, the captain turned round for the long trip back to California and the dry dock at Long Beach Naval Dockyard. As the last few feet of water seeped out of the dry dock, the watching crew of the *Stein* saw their tough sonar dome emerge battered and rent, with dozens of huge gouges out of the rubber no-foul covering that protects the sonar dome from weeds and barnacles. As soon as the dock was dry, the officers descended the steps to examine the havoc. They found hundreds of pointed teeth embedded in the covering, sharp, hollow, some an inch or more long, which had broken off some creature as it grappled with the dome in senseless combat.

The Naval Oceans Systems Center was just down the road, so scientists were able to examine the damage and the teeth, or possibly claws, before the ship was repaired. After months of pondering, their only ver-

The whale shark

The legendary kraken – a giant squid which was held responsible for many a ship's unexplained loss at sea

dict: that the damage was caused by a creature that 'must have been extremely large and of a species still unknown to science.'

The kraken

But men have seen such creatures, and indeed been devoured by them. The exigencies of the Second World War took ships to waters round the globe which are otherwise seldom frequented. Lieutenants Rolandson, Davidson RN and Lieutenant R E Grimani Cox of the Indian Army, were caught by a German raider flying the Japanese flag in a remote part of the South Atlantic. After firing on the ship till she caught fire, the raider gave all aboard five minutes to take to the boats. The three officers found themselves left with a small raft and nine companions, taking turns to cling to the raft or sit upon it.

They were faced with all the traditional nightmares of the shipwrecked: a burning sun, a terrible thirst, attacks from Portuguese men-of-war, which Lieutenant Cox said 'stung like a million bees', and then, on the third day, the sharks appeared to pick off the wounded and those who had gone mad with thirst. After three more days, the sharks suddenly disappeared—not a relief but a prelude to the most appalling moment of all. Slowly, beside the raft, a gigantic shape appeared with huge tentacles. For some time it seemed to stand off and contemplate its strategy. Then, deliberately, it reached out onto the raft and grabbed one of the Indian survivors 'hugging him like a bear'. Cox and the others made a futile attempt to tear the tentacles away, Cox himself suffering several sucker wounds, but the creature slowly took the Indian away. Apparently one man sufficed, for Cox and the two navy officers, picked up by a Spanish ship, lived to tell the tale.

Today it is possible to speculate that the voracious monster was a giant squid, perhaps the most fiendishly equipped of all the great marine creatures that lie hidden beneath the oceans.

We know the squids are there, for several times in the last century, at intervals of thirty years, 20 or 30 ft (6 or 9 m) specimens, probably relative midgets, have floundered ashore in Newfoundland. They seem to be deceived by periodic changes in the cold Labrador current and decoyed into the shallows and away from the North Atlantic deeps. Their aggressive armoury is awe-inspiring: first the tentacles, which grab the prey; then the arms with sucker discs acting like vacuum pads on the victim's flesh; inside them, rows of claws dig in for a firmer hold. Then, as the prey is drawn in, it is cut by a beak, powerful enough to sever heavy wire. This beak, like a nightmare

The 21 ft squid that drifted ashore in Trinity Bay in 1965 being examined by Frederick Aldrich of Memorial University, Newfoundland

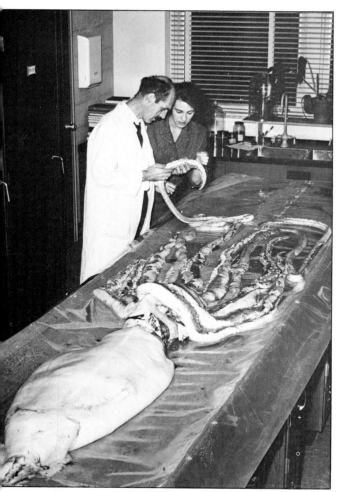

version of a parrot's but with the top closing over the bottom, tears chunks from the victim, before tiny teeth, further down in the mouth, finally shred the meat. It is thought that the squid prey even on the big sperm whales and the whales on them.

What is known is that squids have a strong attraction for the colour red. Off the shores of Newfoundland the squid fishermen often eschew bait and merely hang red-painted metal or spark plugs near the hooks. These suffice to catch the squid. There are ghoulish stories of what happened to torpedoed men in the area during the war as they floated in their bright-red lifejackets.

A hundred years ago, the British writer F T Bullen, aboard the whaleship *Cachelot*, described a titanic encounter between a whale and the kraken (the Norse name by which the whalers knew the squid) bursting out of the water. The whale was in the toils of the kraken, but with part of the squid's body already in the whale's mouth. They then disappeared again below.

In its death agony a harpooned sperm whale vomits up the contents of the stomach, often thousands of squids large and small. Bullen describes pieces of tentacles as thick as a man's body floating past his harpoon boat. Huge sucker marks found on the bodies of sperm whales seem to bear witness to these struggles in the deep suggesting vast creatures far bigger than the 21 ft (6.5 m) squid that drifted ashore in Trinity Bay, Newfoundland in 1965.

It was just a year after this that the US Navy had yet another of its encounters with the mysteries of the deep. The research vessel *San Pablo* was 120 miles (200 km) off Cape Bonavista, Newfoundland, on a normal oceanographic trawl in clear daylight. Suddenly a sperm whale hurled itself out of the water ahead of the ship, entangled in the tentacles of a giant squid. The scene was repeated, and the officers and men had time to go to their cameras as well as to their

Right: A gigantic squid encountered and almost captured by the French war steamer, *Alecton*, 120 miles (200 km) northeast of Teneriffe in 1861

binoculars. The *San Pablo* was hamstrung with paid-out cable and could not move closer, so the photographs are not too enlightening; however, the men of the *San Pablo* were oceanographic experts and they all agreed that the whale was at least 60 ft (18 m) long, yet the squid seemed to match it.

Vivid descriptions survive, again from the war, of truly enormous squids. One from J D Starkey, who says he was aboard an Admiralty trawler off the Maldives in the Indian Ocean. It was his habit on the midnight-to-four 'graveyard' watch, to lower a cluster of electric bulbs into the water . Shoals of fish of all descriptions were attracted to the light, and easy to catch. One night, Starkey, wrote, all the fish vanished.

'As I gazed, a circle of green light glowed in my illumination. This green unwinking orb, I suddenly realized, was an eye. Gradually I realized I was gazing at almost point-blank range at a colossal squid—the body alone filled my view as far as my sight could penetrate. I am not squeamish, but that cold, malevolent, unblinking eye seemed to be looking directly at me. I don't think I've ever seen anything so coldly hypnotic and intelligent before or since.

'I took my quartermaster's torch and shining it into the water I walked forward. I climbed the ladder to the fo'c's'le and shone the torch downwards. There in the pool of light were its tentacles.'

Starkey said the tentacles were 2 ft (0.6 m) thick, with the suction discs clearly visible.

'Then I walked aft again, keeping the squid in view. This was not difficult as it was lying alongside the ship, quite still, except for a pulsing movement. As I approached the stern again where my bulb cluster was hanging, there was the body still. Every detail was visible—the valve through which the creature appeared to breathe, and the parrot-like beak.

'Gradually the truth dawned: I had walked the length of the ship, 175 ft plus.'

Starkey, who had experience of most of the large sea creatures, says he had had fifteen minutes or more to study his giant. 'Then,' he said, 'it seemed to swell as its valve opened fully, and without any visible effort it zoomed into the night.'

Small wonder that there are reports of squid attacking, and even capsizing, ships. In the 1930s a 15,000-ton tanker, the *Brunswick*, was in the South Seas off Samoa doing twelve knots, when a great squid overtook her, then turned and attacked the ship amidships. It could not get a grip on the hull and was finally cut to pieces by the propeller. Her captain, Arne Grønningsæter, reports that the ship was attacked twice again in almost the same way. Undoubtedly, there was something specially provocative about the *Brunswick*'s shape or colour or speed: reminiscent, perhaps, of a whale. In the Indian Ocean in the last century there were reports of a 150-ton schooner, the *Pearl*, being capsized by a giant squid. The *Pearl* was becalmed in the Bay of Bengal and the report came from the crew of a steamer, the *Strathowen*, who said they had seen the giant tentacles simply pull the ship over with all hands lost.

Such a feat would certainly not be beyond the capacity of the monster that drifted ashore on the long dunes of St Augustine's Beach in Florida in 1896; an enormous, though mutilated, corpse washed up in the winter tides. Fortunately it attracted the attention of Dr DeWitt Webb of the local Scientific and Historical Society, who tenaciously fought off curious souvenir-seeking bystanders, fishermen wanting to cut it up for bait, and a travelling showman who wanted to take it away to the fair. The good doctor thus preserved what is to this day the sole physical evidence that giant octopuses, of Jules Verne proportions, really do roam the ocean floor. Dr Webb relayed the details of his find in meticulous letters to Professor W H Dall of the National Museum in Washington. The corpse had lodged itself in a shallow pit in the sand and the doctor first tried to turn it over. 'Judging from the

De Witt Webb's photograph of 'the remains of an enormous monster that came ashore' on St Augustine Beach, Florida, in 1896

difficulty of moving it,' he wrote 'it must weigh six or seven tons, for twelve men with a block and tackle ought to move anything less.' Later Dr Webb returned with four horses, six men, three sets of tackle, a rigger, and a lot of heavy planking which were all very much required to get the carcass 40 ft higher up the beach.

By now he was able to relay to Professor Dall that his find was clearly an invertebrate with no sign of a beak or any of the other characteristics of a squid. The body was 21 ft (6.4 m) across and 7 ft (2.1 m) thick, the skin alone up to 3½ in (89 mm) thick and almost impervious to axe blows. For all that, the conscientious doctor managed to carve up large chunks to be sent to Washington.

The experts, after wavering for a while, finally dismissed Dr Webb's invertebrate as a whale, the Smithsonian Institution deciding that it could 'scarcely afford the expense' of sending anyone all the way to Florida to view it. They did, however, preserve some bottled bits of the St Augustine phenomenon in their cellars and there,

seventy-five years later, two scientific sleuths Joseph Gennaro and F G Wood unearthed them, after reading of them in some old papers. Stinking foully, but intact, were several pieces, about the size of a Sunday joint. Gennaro, Professor of Cellular Biology at New York University, prepared slides for histological analysis. He was quickly convinced that the sample was not whale blubber. Nor did the tissue have the characteristic pattern of a squid. As he looked at slide after slide he was forced to the conclusion that it was indeed an octopus. But the implications were almost unthinkable. A body that size implied an octopus 200 ft (61 m) across, each tentacle long enough to reach across Broadway or Oxford Street.

Wood meanwhile went back to the documents in St Augustine. Yes, there had been stumps of arms beside the body, maybe even attached to it, at least five of them. A local man, a Mr Wilson had seen one arm lying west of the body, 23 ft long, three arms lying south; 'one I measured over 32 ft and from appearances attached to the body (although I did not dig quite to the body as it laid well down in the sand and I was very tired.' Mr

To many people, sea monsters are just sailors' tall stories but the evidence suggests otherwise

Wilson's testimony was sober and precise. The slides, the documents, the extraordinary photographs, the opinion of those who saw the corpse, all the facts, suggest that not only are there octopuses ten times as big as the marine biologists admit to, big enough to blanket Piccadilly Circus, but one of them actually came ashore eighty-odd years ago in Florida. Wood himself collected a number of stories, especially in the vicinity of the Bahamas, of large octopuses, far beyond the 20 ft (6 m) that is regarded as the maximum in the textbooks.

Bruce Wright, Director of Wildlife Biology at the North Eastern Wildlife Station in New Brunswick, reported an instance in 1964 when he went to inspect a carcass on a reef off the southernmost Bahama Island, Caicos.

'The wind was blowing right on to the shore and the boat would not land. We had no dinghy and the sight of a big barracuda just before we entered the discoloured water around the carcass discouraged swimming ashore. I observed and photographed the carcass from our nearest approach which was about 20 yd. It was simply a cigar-shaped mass of flesh without any mouth, pectoral fins, tail flukes, eyes or a blowhole. It was over 50 ft long and about 10 ft in diameter.'

In the same year, 1964, Burton Clark of the Miami Sea Aquarium was off the Bimini Islands. 'At a depth of approximately 100 ft there was some large creature which showed up clearly on the fathometer trace paper.' It was in the same area off the Florida coast that a seaman, J C Martin, at the end of the Second World War says he saw an enormous octopus floating right beside his ship. But the hardest evidence for a giant octopus still remains in that small fragment of the St Augustine creature preserved from the last century.

No such relic exists of the most intriguing of all the great sea mysteries, the giant sea serpents and sea monsters. Of these, with one possible Celtic and one Antipodean exception, neither hide nor hair, fluke nor fin, has ever come into man's hands. Yet they have been seen by thousands of people, many experienced seamen, trained naturalists, and oceanographers among them. Sometimes hundreds of people at once have seen a sea serpent, but there are no acceptable photographs, no significant gap in the order of ocean life, to give credibility to the monster of the oceans. Yet so numerous, so precise, so detailed and sober, so similar are the witnesses' reports that it seems possible that at least one, and maybe three or four species of sea monster inhabit our seas. Monsters with humped backs, heads sticking many feet out of the water, often a mane and huge eyes, have been described since ancient times. There are vivid accounts from the Greeks, precise details from the old Scandinavian writers like Olaus Magnus, right through the medieval period, up to modern times. In 1848 there was a sensation when

The sea serpent seen by the frigate HMS *Daedalus* between the Cape of Good Hope and St Helena on 6 August 1848

The Times reported that the captain of one of Her Majesty's frigates, the nineteen-gun *Daedalus*, had actually reported to Their Lordships of the Admiralty seeing a sea serpent on a passage from the East Indies. Captain Peter M'Quhae's dispatch said they had watched the monster quite close for twenty minutes. 'Had it been a man of my acquaintance I should easily have recognized the features with the naked eye. It did not deviate from its course to the southwest which it held at the pace of twelve to fifteen miles per hour, apparently on some determined purpose.' The swift speed, like the other details which M'Quhae provided, were to become a staple of monster sightings: the large head of a snake, 4 ft (1.2 m) out of the water 'which it never during the time it continued in sight of our glasses lowered below the surface of the water'; something like the mane of a horse washing about its back; and a dimension 'comparing it with what our main topsail yard would show in

A 'marine monster' seen from the SS *City of Baltimore* in the Gulf of Aden, January 1879

the water' of at least 60 ft (18 m).

The sea serpent was already old hat in the United States. For a decade from 1817 it appeared every summer off the East coast. Off Nahant it had a 'two-foot egg-shaped head'; in Lynn Bay it had 'the head of a fish or a serpent elevated two feet above the surface followed by seven or eight bunches all about six feet apart, undulating along like a caterpillar.'

The great authority on sea serpents, Bernard Heuvelmans, has catalogued more than 500 sightings in the past 150 years, but inevitably it is the more modern reports in an era of sophisticated marine exploration that have the most fascination.

In 1959 two Scotsmen had a vivid sighting off the Isle of Soay. One was Tex Geddes, who had once crewed for Gavin Maxwell the naturalist, the other was a holidaying engineering inspector, James Gavin. They were out fishing for mackerel together in fine weather. They had already watched some killer whales and basking sharks when Gavin noticed a black shape a couple of miles away. Geddes described what followed:

'When the object appeared to be steaming towards us, we both stood up for a better view. I can't remember exactly how close it was when I heard the breathing, but I certainly could hear it before I could definitely have said that the object was alive. It was not making much speed, maybe 3 or 4 knots. I am afraid we both stared in amazement as the object came towards us, for this beast steaming slowly in our direction was like some hellish monster of prehistoric times.

'The head was definitely reptilian, about $2\frac{1}{2}$ ft high with large protruding eyes. There were no visible nasal organs but a large red gash of a mouth which seemed to cut the head in half and which appeared to have distinct lips. There was at least 2 ft of clear water behind the neck. I would say we saw 8 to 10 ft of back on the water line.'

The animal perused the men and the dinghy at its leisure.

'The head appeared rather blunt and darker than the rest of the body which seemed to be scaly and the top of its back was surmounted by an immense saw-toothed ridge. It seemed to breathe through its mouth which opened and shut with great regularity, and once when it turned towards us I could see into its cavernous red maw. I saw no teeth.'

But monsters are not confined to the North Atlantic. In 1943, Thomas Helm, an ex-US

'Morgawr', the Cornish sea monster photographed in February 1976 near Falmouth

Marine, was out with his wife off the west coast of Florida when they saw a strange creature making straight for their boat.

'It was unmistakably some kind of animal, the head about the size of a basketball on a neck which reached nearly 4 ft out of the water. The entire head and neck were covered with wet fur which lay close to the body and glistened in the afternoon sunlight. When it was almost beside our boat the head turned and looked squarely at us. My first thought was that we were seeing some kind of giant otter or seal, but I was immediately impressed by the fact that this was not the face of an otter or seal. The head of this creature, with the exception that there was no evidence of ears, was that of a monstrous cat. The face was fur-covered and flat and the eyes were set in the front of the head. The colour of the wet fur was uniformly a rich chocolate brown. The well-defined eyes were round and about the size of a silver dollar and were glistening black. Where I judged the mouth should be, was a moustache of stiff black hairs with a downward curve on each side.'

Helm, an experienced game fisherman,

thought it might be some kind of sea elephant or some relative of the West Indian seal which was thought to be exterminated two hundred years ago, but he dismissed the idea. As he said, 'All the seal family have long pointed noses and eyes on the sides of the head. The creature my wife and I saw had eyes which were positioned near the front of the face like those of a cat.'

Canada too has a most convincing monster popularly known as Cadborosaurus, which has appeared regularly off the coast of Vancouver from the turn of the century.

Captain Paul Sowerby of West Vancouver saw it in 1939.

'We were headin' North, and, about 30 miles off-shore, and saw this thing, standing about 4 ft out of the water. So, I headed over towards it and took a look at it. At first I thought, it looked like a polar bear with his ruffles of hair. When we got right up along side of it—and the water was crystal clear—there was just this great long column of this thing going down at least 40 ft and huge eyes. I had an old Newfoundlander as a mate and he said "Do you see the eyes on him?" Mouth and nose I have no recollection at all, just these great big eyes. And the eyes seemed to open from top and bottom.'

Captain Sowerby still recalls the thick,

fatty, wrinkled body stretching as far down as he could see. But then he made a wrong turn, putting the creature between his boat and the sun, and that was the last clear sight he had.

Mr David Webb, a fisherman, saw Caddy once:

'I was fishing out of Cadboro Bay in 1941 over on the east side of the Island, and a southeast gale started blowing, so I decided it was time to go into the harbour. I had a young pilot by the name of David Miller. Suddenly, near where I moored my boat, I saw a strange animal come up out of the water—a thing with about a 5 or 6ft neck on it. It had a head something like a camel. I called Dave Miller and we decided to try and lasso it toward the shore, but that was out of the question, it travelled too fast for us, but we did follow it for about 3 miles.

'It was travelling along at about 7 or 8 miles an hour, and it appeared to have a fish in its mouth that it was feeding on, because all the birds were trying to dive on it and get the fish. It seemed to be a good 6ft out of the water, and judging by the length of the neck, I imagined it to be another 20ft or so in the water, but I couldn't see below the surface. It was something I have never seen before or since . . . I have seen sea lions, basking sharks, whales, but I have never seen anything like this in my life.'

Caddy has been the subject of the most systematic first-hand enquiry yet made about a sea monster. Two marine biologists from Vancouver, Leblond and Sibert, appealed on the local radio and in newspapers for eyewitnesses of Caddy. Of the two dozen acceptable accounts they received, most could not be identified with any known creature and the drawings imply, as the two researchers note, that there is more than one unknown sea creature making appearances off the Canadian coast.

Early in 1980, John Andrews had been

Captain Paul Sowerby

fishing at Sechelt, near Vancouver:

'I saw a head about 1½ft long, about 8 or 9in wide, and it had large catlike eyes and they reflected light like a cat's and they could move in opposite directions. One was looking at me and one at the bottom. It was probably about 40 or 50ft long. It was sort of between a snake and a seal I guess.'

Neither Leblond nor Sibert could categorize the creature.

Elsewhere passengers on liners had seen sea serpents like the 'equine'-looking beast, 60 to 80ft (18–24m) long, which appeared beside the liner *Amerika* off the Virgin Islands in 1934. It has materialized most dramatically in the middle of a U-boat action. The captain of *U28*, Georg von Forstner, gave this account:

'On 30 July 1915, our *U28* torpedoed the British steamer *Iberian* carrying a rich cargo in the North Atlantic. The steamer sank quickly, the bow sticking almost vertically into the air. When it had been gone for about twenty-five seconds there was a violent explosion. A little later pieces of wreckage, and among them a gigantic sea animal, writhing and struggling wildly, was shot out of the water to a height of 60 to 100ft. At that moment I had with me in the conning tower my officers of the watch, the chief engineer, the navigator, and the helmsman. Simultaneously we all drew one another's attention to this wonder of the seas. As it was not in Brockhaus nor in Brehm we were, alas, unable to identify it. We did not have the time to take a photograph for the animal sank out of sight after ten or fifteen seconds. It was about 60 ft long, was like a crocodile in shape and had four limbs with powerful webbed feet and a long tail tapering to a point.'

Vivid, intriguing, mysterious accounts, attested to by the most impeccable experienced witnesses can be duplicated literally hundreds of times. Thousands of people have seen a sea serpent. Yet no proven physical remnant has ever been found. There have been well-attested strandings of monsters going back at least to the Stronsa Beast which was washed ashore on Orkney off Scotland in 1808.

Almost invariably, as with the Stronsa Beast, these turn out to be basking sharks. The dead basking shark decays in the most deceiving manner. First the jaws, which are attached by only a small piece of flesh, drop off leaving what looks like a small skull and thin serpentlike neck. Then, as only the upper half of the tail fin carries the spine, the lower half rots away leaving the lower fins which look like legs. Time after time this monsterlike relic has been the cause of a sea serpent 'flap'.

But there is one case, unknown to most students, which does challenge the assertion that no sea monster has ever come ashore.

It all began in the summer of 1942 when Charles Rankin, a council officer at Gourock on the River Clyde in Scotland, was diverted from cares of war by complaints of an awful stench coming from the shore. He went down with his foreman to be confronted by a most unusual carcass. Rankin was in a dilemma. The nostrils and indeed the health of the folk of Gourock required protection, but at the same time here was something

perhaps unknown to science. As Rankin now testily recalls, he rang the Royal Scottish Museum, but that body was dismissive. Next he thought of photographing it, but it was a restricted area, and the Royal Navy gave him a stiff warning when he asked for permission. So finally the Gourock monster was chopped up and buried in the grounds of the municipal incinerator.

But Rankin was, and is, a precise man and his description cannot lightly be dismissed. He is very clear about what he found:

'It was approximately 27 to 28 ft in length and 5 to 6 ft in depth at the broadest part. As it lay on its side the body appeared to be oval in section but the angle of the

The Stronsa beast, washed ashore on Orkney in 1808, drawn in a letter by Sir Alexander Gibson to his son in Ceylon

flippers in relation to the body suggested that the body section had been round in life. If so this would reduce the depth dimension to some extent. The head and neck, the body, and the tail were approximately equal in length, the neck and tail tapering gradually away from the body. There were no fins. The head was comparatively small, of a shape rather like that of a seal but the snout was much sharper and the top of the head flatter. The jaws came together one over the other and there appeared to be bumps over the eyes—say prominent eyebrows. There were large pointed teeth in each jaw. The eyes were comparatively large rather like those of a seal but more to the side of the head.

'The tail was rectangular in shape as it lay and it appeared to have been vertical in life. Showing through the thin skin there were parallel rows of "bones" which had a gristly, glossy, opaque appearance. I had the impression that these "bones" had opened out fan-wise under the thin membrane to form a very effective tail. The tail appeared to be equal in size above and below the centre line.

'At the front of the body there was a pair of 'L'-shaped flippers and at the back a similar pair, shorter but broader. Each terminated in a "bony" structure similar to the tail and no doubt was also capable of being opened out in the same way.

'The body had over it at fairly close intervals, pointing backwards, hard, bristly "hairs". These were set closer together towards the tail and at the back edges of the flippers. I pulled out one of these bristles from a flipper. It was about 6 in long and was tapered and pointed at each end like a steel knitting needle and rather of the thickness of a needle of that size but slightly more flexible. I kept this bristle in the drawer of my office desk and some time later I found that it had dried up in the shape of a coiled spring.

'The skin of the animal was smooth and when cut was found to be comparatively thin but tough. There appeared to be no bones other than a spinal column. The flesh was uniformly deep pink in colour, was blubbery and difficult to cut or chop. It did not bleed and it behaved like a thick table jelly under pressure. In what I took to be the stomach of the animal was found a small piece of knitted woollen material as from a cardigan and, stranger still, a small corner of what had been a woven cotton tablecloth — complete with tassels.'

Against such exactness and circumstantial detail, it is hard to maintain that Mr Rankin's monster was a shark or any other known species.

It was thirty-five years later before another such intriguing find turned up.

In the South Pacific and off the coast of New Zealand the Japanese organize squid fishing on a considerable scale. Satellite pictures have shown the lights of the fishing fleet, brighter than any other light source on earth, including the illuminations of New York City. And it was in that area that the Japanese fishing boat *Zuiyo-maru*, in September 1977, hauled up an unwanted catch.

Five key photographs were taken of the decaying monster that they pulled aboard. Along with the measurements and the evidence of the assistant production manager of Taiyo Fisheries, Michihiko Yano, and crucial pieces of flesh from the fin, they represent an unsolved riddle. For the crew of the *Zuiyo-maru*, fearful that their rotting monster would contaminate their catch, threw it back overboard. The creature was 33 ft (10 m) long, apparently devoid of a dorsal fin, and certainly baffled the experienced fishermen on board. The pictures, portions of flesh and descriptions that they brought back were to baffle Japan's best marine scientists too. Some still thought it was a basking shark, too far putrefied to be easily recognized. But Dr Fujio Yasuda of the Tokyo University of Fisheries, and one of the world's leading marine biologists, disagreed. He noted first: 'In no known species attaining a large size is the trunk so elongated.' The body plan of the animal, the location of its fins, he declared to be quite different from that of a shark. He concluded: 'We are not able to find any known living fish species which agree with the animal trawled off New Zealand. If it is a species of shark, it may represent a species unknown to science.'

Two other Japanese were of similar opinion. Obata and Tomoda of the Tokyo National Science Museum said: 'Whether the animal belongs to a group of sharks or whether it is a marine reptile, we do not know any genera or species that agree with it.'

It is, however, likely that some at least of the sea-monster sightings have an explanation which, though still extraordinary, falls within the bounds of conventional biology. After a report from a trawler in 1962, the Russians are now speculating that Steller's sea cow, the four-ton 'dodo' of the Arctic which was supposedly exterminated in the nineteenth century, may still survive in the Bering Sea. The huge creature, which lived off seaweed and went to sleep on its back, is also being sought by the English explorer Derek Hutchinson who is mounting expeditions to the Aleutian Islands off the coast of Alaska. Steller's sea cow, vast and walrus-like, would fit many a good monster identi-kit. Researchers in the far north received some unexpected encouragement in early 1980 when the Russians reported seeing the Greenland whale, thought to be on the verge of extinction, herding in large numbers near Cape Stoneheart. More than 150 were counted and N Doroshenko of the Pacific Scientific Research Institute of Fisheries and Oceanography, Vladivostok, said: 'Perhaps they know of a patch of open water in the winter ice, and have been able to keep out of sight by not migrating south in the autumn.'

The world of the elephant seal, manatee, and walrus, all known creatures, already offers marine apparitions to terrify and confuse any innocent who has never seen one before. The leathery sea turtle, greatest of the turtles, can be up to 10 ft (3 m) long, and travels remarkably widely. The Soay beast certainly has a hint of the turtle about him.

But all these put together can hardly account for the hundreds and hundreds of first-hand, detailed reports by respectable individuals of many nationalities, who had nothing to gain but derision, and yet who have persisted in recording their sightings of the sea serpents.

Perhaps more than any of the contemporary mysteries which intrigue the modern imagination, we can be sure that the sea serpent will one day surrender a final proof of his existence.

Arthur C Clarke comments:
Whether or not life began in the ocean—and as we have seen some scientists are now doubting this—there can be no question but that the largest, and most bizarre, of living creatures are to be found in the sea. No man in his right senses could have imagined the sperm whale, or the giant squid—or the hideous little dragons of the abyss. Compared to them, there is nothing particularly remarkable about the 'Great Sea Serpent'—except for its success in eluding us.

Probably it isn't a serpent—but a fish or even a mammal. Still more probably, it isn't an 'it'—but a 'them'.

In any event, the game of hide and seek cannot last much longer. The two most powerful nations on the planet are straining their resources to make the ocean 'transparent'—so that they can detect each other's nuclear submarines. One day their vast undersea sonar arrays and other secret devices will turn up some surprises for the biologists. . . .

5

Circles and Standing Stones

Stonehenge and Avebury

On a fine Midsummer morning dawn breaks slowly over Salisbury Plain. For a full hour before sunrise, Stonehenge and the barrows of the great prehistoric cemetery which surround it stand out eerily in the first yellow-green light of the day.

In the shadow of the stones, the Druids, hooded and robed in white, have begun their annual ritual of fire and water, celebrating the advent of the year's longest day. Inside the circle itself are the lucky few with official passes: journalists, photographers and the villagers of nearby Amesbury. Outside, beyond a protective barbed-wire fence, a small crowd has gathered.

The sight they have all come to see begins a few seconds after 5 am, when the first rays of the sun appear over the long lip of the horizon. It is the start of an event precisely planned by the people who built Stonehenge almost 4,000 years ago. Only at Midsummer can watchers in the centre of the circle see the sun rise in line with the Heel Stone, 40 yd (37 m) outside the ring.

As the first rays appear, the Druids' celebration reaches its climax with the cry: 'Arise, Oh Sun! Let the darkness of night fade before the beams of thy glorious light!'

But the drama of their ceremonies, so fitting to the time and place, masks the authentic mystery of Stonehenge: for these Druids have no true place here.

There is no doubt that Druids did exist in Britain before the Roman Conquest. Julius Caesar described them as men of great learning 'given to discussions of stars and their

movements, the size of the universe and of the earth'. Some of their activities were less refined, as their rituals included human sacrifices in which they would use 'figures of immense size whose limbs, woven out of twigs, they fill with living men and set on fire, and the men perish in a sheet of flame.' However, historians and archaeologists have found no hard evidence to link the Druids with stone circles, and although very little is known about the Druids at all, what evidence there is in ancient texts suggests that they were at the height of their influence a thousand years after the completion of Stonehenge, when its original purpose may have been long since forgotten.

Modern Druids, arriving for the summer

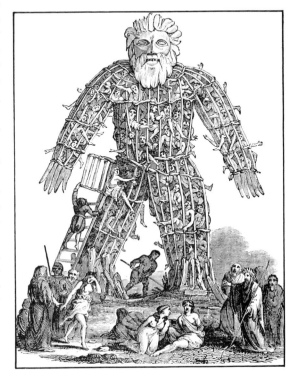

Left: Stonehenge
Right: Julius Caesar described a human sacrifice in which figures of immense size, filled with men were burned to appease the Celtic gods

Modern Druids continue to celebrate an annual ritual even though modern scholars believe Stonehenge to have been built long before Druidic times

solstice ceremonies by car and luxury coach, owe their place at Stonehenge to the romantic theories of seventeenth- and eighteenth-century antiquarians like John Aubrey (1626–1697) and William Stukeley (1687–1765). They read Julius Caesar's description of the Druids, and, quite without evidence, associated them with the standing stones and stone circles they came across in the course of their travels through the British countryside. So today, visitors to these 'Druid Temples' imagine that they were built by the mysterious priests of the cruel and ancient Druid faith.

In fact, no one knows for certain who erected the stone circles or why, and the reason is simple: the builders had no writing. The architects of Stonehenge could therefore not leave behind them any documents or inscriptions to explain why they chose to build this extraordinary construction on Salisbury Plain; why they mixed local stones with others quarried more than 200 miles away in southwest Wales; why they demolished and rebuilt it several times in the

course of a thousand years; or why they balanced great stones on top of each other in a style more suited to building in wood. Above all, they left no clues to the function of Stonehenge, and, therefore, to the reason why the circle is aligned to the sunrise at Midsummer.

Stonehenge is no isolated mystery, for it is just one of a thousand prehistoric stone circles scattered throughout the British Isles and northern France. They were built, archaeologists believe, between 3250 and 1500 BC. The circles that remain have survived because they were built in what are now remote and sparsely inhabited regions: perhaps thousands of others have not stood the test of time and have been deliberately destroyed or absorbed into the landscape.

In almost every respect, stone circles present a puzzle to archaeologists. Firstly, their size varies enormously. Keel Cross in County Cork, for instance, is only 9 ft (2.75 m) in diameter, whereas Avebury in Wiltshire encompasses a whole village.

Avebury, alone, is an incredible undertaking. It covers $28\frac{1}{2}$ acres (11.5 ha) and its original ditch was higher than a two-storey house. It is difficult to imagine just how hard it must have been for the builders to cut the chalk upland, using 'picks' made of discarded deer antlers.

To make the main circle, stones weighing as much as 60 tons were transported many miles, perhaps on wooden sledges secured by leather ropes. Before the sledge could move, hundreds of trees would have had to be cut down to give a clear path in what was then a heavily forested area. In 1938, when a small 8-ton stone was restored to its original position in the circle, it took twelve men five days using steel hawsers. The building of Avebury must therefore have been the work of many generations of people whose equipment was primitive and whose life was a short brutal fight for survival.

Avebury from the air: by far the largest stone circle in Great Britain

A look at the map raises more questions: there are no stone circles in southeast Britain—perhaps because these people preferred to build in wood, while in northeast Scotland there are often several circles in a very small area.

Baffling, too, is the style of their construction which varies from area to area. In the west of England the circles are spacious and open while sites in northeastern Scotland are smaller with an extraordinary arrangement of stones as their focal point: a mighty rock on its side flanked by two uprights.

Furthermore, archaeologists have found almost nothing to help them explain the purpose of the circles. Professor Richard Atkinson, of University College, Cardiff, who began digging at Stonehenge in the 1950s, says:

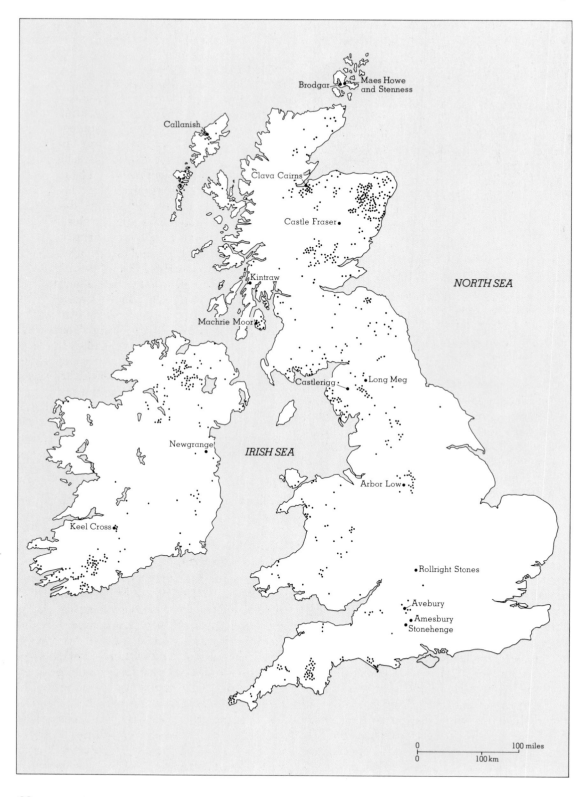

Above: Avebury's 'Barber Stone' was re-erected in 1938. Standing beside the stone is Mr W E V Young, assistant to Alexander Keiller who was responsible for the operation
Left: Distribution of standing stones and stone circles in the British Isles

'You have to settle for the fact that there are large areas of the past that we cannot find out about. Stone circles are barren archaeological sites. There is almost nothing in them to suggest what went on there, and absolutely nothing has ever been found which has enabled us to know with certainty what they were for.'

The finds at Stonehenge bear out this view. There are antler picks used to dig the stone holes, mauls for dressing the stones, pieces of flint and axe, fragments of pottery from different periods, bone pins, and the occasional skeleton. But neither separately nor together do they tell us what went on there or what was in the minds of the people who placed or dropped them within the circle. This is all the more surprising since we know the site was used for about a thousand years. The only clue may lie in the very scarcity of the finds: there is no trace of 'litter' that you would expect to find where there had been houses and settlements. 'It is as though the people who built the circles treated them like we treat church,' says

Atkinson. 'They were clearly special places where you didn't drop litter.'

Prehistoric geometry

While archaeologists flounder, mathematicians and engineers have discovered an additional mystery. They say that many circles were deliberately designed to be anything but circular. This strange property was first pointed out by Professor Alexander Thom, a former Professor of Engineering at Oxford University, who has been surveying megalithic sites since the 1930s. From measurements made in circles all over the British Isles and northern France, Thom has found several types of design. Some, like Machrie Moor on the Isle of Arran in Scotland, are ellipses; others, like a circle surrounding a tomb at Clava Cairns near Inverness, are egg-shaped; while others like the spectacular Long Meg and Her Daughters in the English Lake District, are flattened rings. 'In fact, so many stone circles aren't circular that my father and I no longer refer to them as circles. We call them stone rings,' says Professor Thom's son and collaborator, Dr Archie Thom. If the Thoms are correct, their conclusions suggest that the people of prehistoric Britain worked out geometry for themselves a full 2,000 years before Pythagoras.

Although this is quite possible, Dr John Edwin Wood, who has spent many years studying the layouts of stone circles, believes that all that was required was not so much mathematical geometry as we know it, but a highly developed sense of shape. Castlerigg in Cumbria, for example, may have been laid out with a few lengths of rope and some pegs. The circle builders would have laid out a series of equilateral triangles. Then, in a series of movements in which one main line would have swung round some pegs and free of others, the designers would have been able to describe the arcs that create a flattened ring or an ellipse. It still leaves the question why should the circle builders have gone to such lengths to make circles that are not circular? Since the patterns

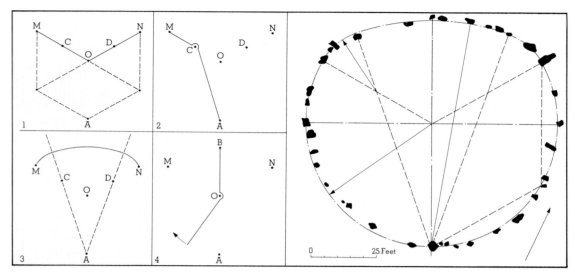

How Dr John Wood thinks Castlerigg was set out:
(1) A peg is placed in the intended centre of the ring. Three ropes cut to equal length are used to construct four equilateral triangles. Pegs are placed at the corners and then pegs *C* and *D* are put halfway between the centre peg and the corner pegs. (2) A rope is tied to peg *A* and taken to *M* via *C*. The rope is then cut at *M*. (3) The rope is swung round in an arc from *M* to *N*, rotating about *C* until it goes free then letting it catch on peg *D* at the other side (but not snagging on peg *O*). (4) Sight along *AO*. When the rope is in line add peg *B* at the end of the rope. Unhitch the rope from *A*, tie an end to *B* and allow rope to pivot round *O* to draw the rest of the ring.

are repeated, and about a third of all stone circles in Britain fall into one of the half dozen categories, the people must have deliberately decided to draw these shapes. Moreover, egg shapes, flattened rings and ellipses are late developments: the earlier the circle, the more likely it is to be truly circular, so there is ample evidence that ancient man had perfected the art of laying out accurate circles.

This raises yet more questions. What prompted the circle builders to make their layouts more and more complicated? How were they able to transmit their ideas throughout prehistoric Britain where in many places the forests were so dense that, it is said, a squirrel

Castlerigg, near Keswick, in the English Lake District

could run from Chelmsford to Anglesey without breaking cover once?

Astronomical alignments: Newgrange

Nothing about stone circles is more mysterious or magical than the question of their astronomical alignments. In recent years theories about these have overshadowed all other discussion.

The idea that some circles were aligned to the sun, moon or even the stars is not new. It certainly dates back to the eighteenth century when William Stukeley noted in his book on Stonehenge that the stones were aligned to the Midsummer sunrise. At the beginning of this century, the astronomer, Sir Norman Lockyer, published a set of alignments which he had discovered during a survey of Stonehenge.

The simplest and most dramatic evidence that prehistoric man studied and exploited the movements of celestial bodies comes not from stone circles but from two magnificent chambered tombs—one in Ireland, the other on Mainland in Orkney.

Newgrange Tumulus is sited on the banks of the River Boyne, a few miles down narrow country lanes from the city of Drogheda in the Irish Republic. Since being restored, its great curving mound, faced with brilliant white quartz and inset with oval granite boulders, reveals it to have been one of the architectural wonders of ancient times. Although it is little known outside Ireland, Newgrange has a special significance: it was built in about 3250 BC, about 500 years before the Pyramids of Egypt. It is therefore the oldest existing building in the world.

Five thousand years ago, the people who farmed in the lush pastures of the Boyne Valley hauled 200,000 tons of stone from the river bank a mile away and began to build Newgrange. At the foot of the mound, they set ninety-seven massive kerbstones and carved many of them with intricate patterns. Inside, with 450 slabs, they built a passage leading to a vaulted tomb, and placed a shallow basin of golden stone in each of its three side chambers.

Newgrange, constructed as early as 3250 BC, one of the largest megalithic tumuli in the British Isles

By the time one of Ireland's leading archaeologists, Professor Michael O'Kelly of University College, Cork, came to excavate and restore Newgrange in the 1960s, the tomb had been a tourist attraction for more than 250 years. (It had been discovered by chance in 1699.) So it was hardly surprising that he was able to find only a handful of the bones which the tomb and its stone basins must have been designed to hold. But despite the visitors who had walked up the stone passageway into the corbelled chamber for more than two centuries, the most spectacular secret of Newgrange still awaited discovery.

As O'Kelly's team of restorers removed the grass and weeds from the mound, they came across a curious rectangular slit above the door. It was half-closed by a square block of crystallized quartz, apparently designed to work as a shutter. There were scratches on the quartz: clearly it had often been slid to and fro, providing a narrow entrance to the tomb above the main door, which was firmly sealed with a 5-ton slab of stone.

But what was the slit for? It was too small and too far from the ground to be an entrance for people. Professor O'Kelly remembered a local tradition which said that the sun always shone into the tomb at Midsummer. Perhaps the 'roofbox', as it came to be known, was designed to admit the summer sun to the

Newgrange at Midwinter: the light passes down the passageway into the back of the chamber

tomb without the entrance stone having to be moved. 'But it was quite obvious to us that it couldn't happen at Midsummer because of the position of the sun' says O'Kelly. 'So if the sun was to shine in at all, the only possibility would be in Midwinter.'

In December 1967, Michael O'Kelly drove from his home in Cork to Newgrange. Before the sun came up he was at the tomb, ready to test his theory. 'I was there entirely alone. Not a soul stood even on the road below. When I came into the tomb I knew there was a possibility of seeing the sunrise because the sky had been clear during the morning.'

He was, however, quite unprepared for what followed. As the first rays of the sun appeared above the ridge on the far bank of the River Boyne, a bright shaft of orange light struck directly through the roofbox into the heart of the tomb.

'I was literally astounded. The light began as a thin pencil and widened to a band of about 6 in. There was so much light reflected from the floor that I could walk around inside without a lamp and avoid bumping off the stones. It was so bright I could see the roof 20 ft above me.

'I expected to hear a voice, or perhaps feel a cold hand resting on my shoulder, but there was silence. And then, after a few minutes, the shaft of light narrowed as the sun appeared to pass westward across the slit, and total darkness came once more.'

Every year since 1967, O'Kelly has returned to Newgrange for the midwinter sunrise, and every year, from his vantage point lying on the smooth sandy floor of the tomb, he has seen the bright disc of the sun fill the roofbox and the shaft of light pass down the passageway, across his face, into the recess at the back of the chamber. Its precision makes him certain that the effect was deliberately engineered.

'The builders must have sat here on the hillside, perhaps for a number of years, at the winter solstice period, watching the point of sunrise moving southward along the horizon, eventually determining the point where it began to turn back again. Having established this, they could then have put a line of pegs into the ground and laid out the plan of the passage.'

However, there was one more problem to resolve. The roofbox would have had to have been precisely aligned to the horizon and, as each of the stone slabs weighs about a ton, the position of the slit would have had to have been determined before the building began. Add to this the fact that the tomb was built on a hill, with the chamber 6 ft (1.8 m) above the entrance, and the achievement of the builders of Newgrange is all the more astounding.

Astronomical alignments: Maes Howe

On Mainland in the Orkney Isles, stands Maes Howe, another passage grave built about 2670 BC, 600 years after Newgrange. Set at the edge of a loch, flanked by the gaunt stones of the Circle of Stenness on one side and by the raked Ring of Brodgar on the other, Maes Howe is probably the least visited of all the architectural wonders of the ancient world. Here, a passage leads from its low entrance to a chamber 16 ft (4.9 m) high. The walls are

Maes Howe in Orkney: the tomb chamber; the walls are built of tightly wedged dry stones

built of dry stones, so tightly wedged together that it is impossible to push a knife blade between them.

Maes Howe is also a place of pilgrimage at the winter solstice. Every year, on 21 December, members of old-established Orkney families call at the farm across the road for the key to Maes Howe, and are let into the tomb at three o'clock in the afternoon. They come to its dark chamber to watch not the dawn but the sunset.

A local schoolmaster, Magnus Spence, first recorded the alignment in 1893. He noticed that when he stood in the middle of the tomb's chamber 'the view is very limited, not extending farther in breadth than a few yards. Strange to say, *in the centre of this contracted view*, and at a *distance of forty-two chains* stands the Monolith at Barnhouse. ... The alignment formed with this long passage of Maes Howe and the Standing Stone of Barnhouse indicates directions too remarkable to be merely accidental.'

Spence was right: at the winter solstice, when the sun sets over the Barnstone 22 yd (20.1 m) away, its last rays light up the dark chamber of Maes Howe for the only time in the year. Just as at Newgrange, the sun can penetrate the chamber through an 18 in (46 cm) 'letter box' above the tomb's blocking

slab. This also may explain another mystery of Maes Howe—a strange bend in the entrance passage, which could have been designed to admit the sun after the tomb had been extended.

It is thought that stone circles were built many years after chambered tombs like Newgrange, and may recall their shape. This theory is reinforced by the fact that Newgrange is surrounded by the beginnings of a circle, and Maes Howe by a low earth bank. Whole 'complexes'—consisting of a tomb and a circle for each family—like the Circle of Stenness and Maes Howe tomb in Orkney were built at the same time and this suggests that a tradition of incorporating astronomical alignments into engineering projects may have arisen among prehistoric people. Certainly, there are clear alignments at many stone circles. One of the most spectacular of all is at Long Meg and Her Daughters in Cumbria. Here, at Midwinter, the sun sets over Long Meg herself, a stone more than $9\frac{1}{2}$ ft (2.9 m) high, standing outside the circle and, significantly, of a different geological type to her fifty-nine 'Daughters'.

Astronomical alignments: Kintraw

The many mysteries of stone circles—their geometry, their barrenness and their alignments — have given birth to countless theories about their use. Many cannot be taken seriously, but others have stimulated violent controversy, not least theories about the purpose of astronomical alignments. Once again, the main contribution to the debate has come from the meticulous Professor Alexander Thom. In papers first published in academic journals, he put forward the idea that prehistoric man had built the circles as astronomical indicators and that the alignments to the sun, moon or stars helped him to determine key dates in the year. One way of doing this was, Thom believes, to align stones with distinctive geographical features on the horizon and he has been able to put his theory to the test.

In a lonely field in Kintraw in the Scottish Highlands stands a single stone. Here the skyline is dominated by the island of Jura and its range of hills, the Paps, 26 miles (42 km) away. Professor Thom calculated that, at the winter solstice, the last rays of the setting sun would appear in a cleft between the hills if an observer were standing exactly in line with the standing stone. But, although the theory looked good on paper, there was a snag: a nearby ridge, now covered in trees, would have prevented the ancient calendar-makers from actually seeing the sun from the stone, and would also, therefore, have prevented them from fixing the position of the stone in the first place. Undaunted, the Thoms searched for a place from which both Jura and the stone could be seen. They found it high on a gorge above: a long, narrow ledge, which they thought might not only have been used to make observations but might have been specifically designed for the purpose.

The idea captured the imagination of one of Scotland's leading archaeologists, Dr Euan MacKie of the Hunterian Museum, Glasgow. Here was a unique opportunity to test an astronomical theory objectively by excavation. In the summers of 1970 and 1971, MacKie excavated the ledge at Kintraw, and soon his digging revealed a layer of stones just below the turf. When a soil expert was called in to decide whether the stones had been placed there or had merely rolled down the hill, MacKie's hopes and the Thoms' hunches were justified. Using a well-established technique known as Petrofabric Analysis, the orientation of the stones on the ledge was plotted, and it was found that the pattern they made corresponded not to that usually made by falling scree, but to ancient pavements known to have been made by man.

The final test occurred in December 1978 when Dr Archie Thom, in his fieldwork kit of kilt and jacket, climbed to the platform at Kintraw and lined up his surveyor's theodolite on the Paps of Jura. For the first few minutes of sunset the cleft in the hills was masked by cloud. But then, in triumphant vindication of his family's theories, the clouds parted and revealed the last arc of the sun as it slid behind the hill, in the cleft, exactly as predicted.

The Thoms have found many other sites which, like Kintraw, have significant lunar or solar alignments, although none of them has provided evidence as convincing as the man-made platform. They believe they can show Stone Age people to have been accomplished astronomers, studying the sky for its own sake and making calculations like their successors today.

It is an attractive theory: the idea of wise men waiting for the sunset at Kintraw, or standing on specially built mounds at the Ring of Brodgar to watch the moon, is beguiling and not unreasonable. Few people who have studied the achievements of ancient man believe that he was any less intelligent than modern man. Professor Atkinson, in the early days a passionate opponent of the views of 'astro-archaeologists', now believes there is much in the theories of the Thoms and their followers. 'The statistical evidence is such that you can't dismiss it out of hand,' he says. 'There is certainly a case for close analysis. Thom has no axe to grind. He says "Here are my theories and my inferences. Go and do some more work and see if you agree with me."'

Thom's followers have taken up the challenge with zeal, formulating theories of an élite group of astronomers travelling the country to spread their knowledge of the skies. In one brave experiment, an American schoolmaster risked his neck by walking along the lintels of Stonehenge to test a notion that ancient astronomers used pits in the lintels to identify directions of the rising moon at significant points in its cycle.

A house of the dead
The problem is that theories based on astronomy cannot provide the whole answer to the mystery of the stone circles, because most circles do not have precise astronomical alignments. Moreover, some archaeologists criticize the exclusively astronomical interpretation claiming that it relies too

An aerial view of the Ring of Brodgar in Orkney. This huge circle may have been a lunar observatory

heavily on statistics and too little on the actual evidence on the ground, and that many of the sites described as observatories have changed out of all recognition since the time when they were built. It is far more likely that alignments provide *part* of the answer and that they were an important element in the ceremonies and religious ritual of ancient Britain.

Professor O'Kelly believes that this is what the builders of Newgrange intended when they aligned their tomb to the mid-winter sunrise. He believes that the people whose bones were placed in the stone basins in the chamber had qualities especially valued in their society — perhaps they had the gift of prophecy or the 'evil eye' — and that Newgrange was designed as a temple for the spirits of the dead. As he waits in the tomb for the sun to rise on the shortest day of the year, O'Kelly is fond of speculating about the ceremonies which may have gone on there five thousand years ago.

'I think that the people who built New-grange built not just a tomb but a house of the dead, a house in which the spirits of special people were going to live for a very long time. To ensure this, the builders took special precautions to make sure the tomb stayed completely dry, as it is to this day. Sand was brought from the shore near the mouth of the Boyne ten miles away, and packed into the joints of the great roof stones along with putty made from burnt soil. And to make absolutely sure that there would be no possibility of rainwater percolating through, they cut grooves in the roof slabs to channel it away. If the place was merely designed to get rid of dead bones, there would be no point in doing all this.'

On the day of the solstice he envisages a group of people gathered in front of the tomb's decorated entrance stone in the pre-dawn darkness. He believes that as sunrise approached, someone climbed up to the

Professor Michael O'Kelly of University College, Cork, a leading archaeologist whose work at Newgrange and elsewhere has contributed greatly to our understanding of standing stones and circles

roofbox and removed the blocks of quartz which temporarily closed it. What then went on is pure speculation. Perhaps the people made offerings to the spirits of the dead. (There is evidence of such a practice at a similar tomb in Denmark where the remains of 4,000 food vessels were found in front of the kerbstones.) Or perhaps they wished to ask the spirits of the dead for their help in the year to come.

If O'Kelly's interpretation of the magical phenomenon at Newgrange is on the right lines, it is tempting to imagine similar ceremonies in the circles, triggered off by celestial events.

Energy transmitters

But there are stranger theories to explain the purpose of the circles. Stonehenge, for instance, has been imagined as an ancient racecourse, a bullring, a war memorial, the tomb of Boadicea, and a base for UFOs. While few people now take those ideas seriously, another theory has caused much excitement in recent years (though not among archaeologists). Its adherents believe that the stones of ancient circles may harness and transmit energy from the earth and sun, and that they were erected in places where this energy could be tapped. This, they say, would explain the ancient belief that the stones have magical powers of healing, a claim recorded by the twelfth-century historian, Geoffrey of Monmouth. Writing of Stonehenge, he says '. . . in these stones there is a mystery and a healing against many ailments . . . for not a stone is there that is wanting in virtue or leech-craft.'

It is a fascinating idea, and in many ways just as reasonable as the vague legends of dancing virgins and human sacrifice. In 1979, one group of investigators, instigators of an experiment they call the Dragon Project, published some intriguing preliminary results of a study undertaken at the Rollright Stones—a circle of seventy-seven weather-beaten stones in the Oxfordshire countryside. The team, led by a scientist, reported that around dawn it had detected ultrasonic pulses emanating from the stones. They made the same experiment at more modern versions of standing stones such as concrete Ordnance Survey Trig Points and detected no such pulses.

So were stone circles ancient transmitters of energy, electrical spas for the sick and lame? It will sound preposterous to many people, and the burden of proof undoubtedly rests upon the advocates of 'earth energies' but scientists have seen stranger theories proved correct. However, the likelihood is that the true purpose of stone circles is less exotic. The few people who have made an intensive study of stone circles see them as centres of religion and celebration for the families and communities scattered throughout the deep forests of prehistoric Britain. 'You have to reckon with dancing in stone circles,' says Stuart Piggott the former professor of Archaeology at Edinburgh University and one of the leading authorities on stone circles. 'There are, after all, two basic kinds of dance—in a line or in a circle. Did they perhaps dance round the stones or along the avenues leading to the great circle of Avebury?'

At one related site a musical instrument was found: a whistle carved from a swan's leg bone. At a site in Wales, an archaeologist found that the surrounding earth had been impacted by constant marching or dancing. 'They may be enclosures for the gods,' says Piggott, 'and the scarcity of finds may be due to ritual cleaning or to the possibility that people rarely invaded the sacred territory within the stones.'

Religious rituals

Religion needs a theology and the man who has done more than anyone to reconstruct it is Dr Aubrey Burl, an archaeologist and the author of the standard work on stone circles. He has made the most comprehensive study ever of the evidence gleaned from past excavations of stone circles and of the theories advanced to explain them. As a result, he believes the circles were the churches, chapels and cathedrals of ancient times and is prepared to speculate on what went on in them.

To explain his theories he chose the rugged but romantic setting of a small circle set in a golden barley field at Castle Fraser near Aberdeen in North East Scotland. This circle, like the others in the area, has a feature which, until Burl began to study it, was unexplained: a stone on its side, lying to the southwest, flanked by two upright stones. Even today, the precision of the circle's ancient builders is breathtaking. A spirit-level placed on any of these recumbent stones, in any circle, shows it to be exactly level after four thousand years.

'Now lots of people have tried to explain this,' says Burl, 'and they have looked to see whether recumbent stones were directed towards where the sun would set at midwinter or where the moon would set. Or even with those circles that are at the south-southeast, whether they were in line with the rising of the moon or the sun, but these don't work.' Others tried to find alignments with planets like Venus or stars like Capella,

The Rollright Stones – a circle of seventy-seven weathered stones in Oxfordshire, 34 yd (31 m) in diameter

Aubrey Burl, a principal lecturer in Prehistory at
Hull College of Higher Education and a leading
authority on stone circles

but also without success. Then, as Dr Burl
studied plans of the Aberdeenshire circles,
he realized why the recumbent stone and
its flankers had been placed in the southwest corner of the circle. The answer was
surprisingly simple. At night, when the
moon is out, and passes across the sky
on a line between the southeast where it
rises and the southwest where it sets, at
one point in that journey it seems to pause
above the recumbent stone and hover between its two flankers. Burl believes that
since this could not have helped to establish
points in a calendar, it must have been designed to play an important part in rituals,
just as the sun may have dominated rites at
Newgrange and Maes Howe.

At this remove it is impossible to say what
importance the moon had for the circle-
builders. Burl speculates: 'It could have
been the place where people thought the
dead went to, or where the living came from.
It could have been the giver or the taker of

life. It could have been the place from which
good harvests or spirits came.'

Support for the idea that these Scottish
circles, at least, were laid out for moon
rituals comes from a curious discovery made
in some of them: hundreds of quartz pebbles,
which Burl says may possibly have represented miniature moons and almost certainly reflected the moonlight.

From the discoveries made at places like
Castle Fraser, Aubrey Burl can evoke the
rituals which may have been practised
there.

'These are places of dread [he says]. The
people who built those circles were
people who had very insecure lives. They
had no knowledge of what caused a
blizzard or drought or an epidemic. They
saw their children dying; they saw their
crops failing: not every year, but, when it
did happen, they had no means of stop-
ping it, because they had no understanding of it. Now, if you're in that sort of
situation, you either take an attitude of
Che Sera, Sera—what will be, will be—
or else you try to do something about it.'

What the circle builders tried to do, Burl
believes, was to pray to the spirits of the
dead to intercede for them. The recumbent
stones may symbolize the entrance to a tomb
—there is a magnificent carved stone which
may have inspired them at the entrance to
Newgrange—and the deposits of bone suggest rites of death. Indeed, at Loanhead of
Daviot, another recumbent stone circle
near Castle Fraser, 5 lb of tiny bones were
found: the pitiful remains of many different
children. There are traces, too, of fires
which could have been funeral pyres. The
ceremonies may have reached their height
when the moon stood over the recumbent
stone, framed by the flankers, and every
nineteen years, because of the strange way
the moon moves in the sky, its orb would
have been so low on the horizon that it would
have seemed to have rolled along the top of
the stone itself: a miraculous event indeed.

Although Burl's theories seem far more

plausible than tales of ancient astronomical élites or mysterious sources of energy, there can be no final answer to the question: Why were these great circles erected? After so many thousands of years, we can never know for certain anything about the people who left behind these mute stone testaments to their beliefs except that they were our ancestors, and that the stones are therefore part of our heritage and culture.

'The mystery will always remain powerful because archaeology can only recover a remnant of the past [says Aubrey Burl]. We deal with broken pottery and broken human bone; we deal with silent stones, with the moon passing over the stones. That is all silent evidence, and we will never see the people dancing, or hear them singing, or hear children crying or see the crops laid waste. We can only reach out a little way into the darkness.'

Arthur C Clarke comments:
Only one thing can be stated with certainty about such structures as Stonehenge: the people who built them were much more intelligent than many who have written books about them.

It cannot be too firmly stressed that the ancient architects—our ancestors of *only two hundred* generations ago! — were men exactly like us. If they had been snatched up by a time traveller as infants, and carried forward to our age, they could have been astronauts or scientists or newspaper editors—or *you*, gentle reader . . . There is no need to invoke any magical or mysterious powers, still less the intervention of any 'superior' beings, to explain their achievements.

What we *cannot* explain—and may never be able to—is: why did they do these things? Yet throughout history men have engaged on vast enterprises which were often meaningless to later generations. We can no longer recapture the mentality of those who built the great cathedrals, even though we have good written records of the Middle Ages and often know the very names of the master masons involved. How much more difficult, then, to understand the motives of men who had no way of sending their thoughts and beliefs into the future—except by the mute evidence of their labours?

It is only very recently that clear-headed archaeologists—as opposed to woolly-minded mystics—have accepted the view that 'primitive' men may have known much more about astronomy, geometry, and surveying than—well, the average city-dweller of today. Just *how* much more is still in dispute, and likely to remain so until many more of these ancient circles have been investigated and measured.

It is always very dangerous to say 'there are some things that can *never* be known'. We can now measure the temperature of long-vanished seas, the strength and direction of the earth's magnetic field ten thousand years ago, and recapture much other information locked up in bones, clays, tree rings, and sedimentary rocks . . . So perhaps some day we may be able to open up a window on the past, as H G Wells dreamed long ago in his short story 'The Grisly Folk':

'A day may come when these recovered memories may grow as vivid as if we in our own persons had been there and shared the thrill and the fear of those primordial days; a day may come when the great beasts of the past will leap to life again in our imaginations, when we shall walk again in vanished scenes, stretch painted limbs we thought were dust, and feel again the sunshine of a million years ago.'

Creatures of Lakes and Lochs

At the last count, ninety-one people had seen Champ the monster of Lake Champlain in North America. He seems to have a long neck, a rather serpentine body up to 30 ft (9 m) long and dark skin. On the other hand, Manipogo, the monster of Lake Winnipegosis, Manitoba, in Canada is almost always seen as slate grey with humps and a single horn sticking out of the back of his head 'like a telescope'. Furthermore, he is supposed to have had his picture taken and has been seen swimming around with a baby monster. Issie, Japan's favourite in Lake Ikeda, has two humps and has already earned a Mr Matsubara 100,000 yen when he won the money offered by Ibusuki City Council for the first photograph of Issie. The most famous of them all, the Loch Ness monster has now clocked up his 3,000th witness. He has been filmed, photographed and subjected to sonar scans and has scared divers and boat parties. Other monsters adorn lakes in Sweden, Ireland, New Zealand, Africa and Russia. Australia has its own, presumably marsupial, version, the Bunyip. There is even the Lágarfljótsormur in Iceland.

The 'Monster of the Lake' is one of the most witnessed, probably the most photographed, of all the unexplained phenomena of our time. Most of the people who have seen lake monsters are highly respectable and sane, yet always the monsters have remained elusive even though their territories are relatively confined. Serious evidence of their activities is submerged under hoax and hilarity. Issie, after allegedly surfacing near a resort in southern Japan

Left: the Loch Ness monster: the famous Rines photograph of 1972

much favoured by honeymoon couples, was awarded a special observatory in 1978, opened by the reigning Miss Hibiscus. Enthusiastic supporters then poured saké into the lake in the hope that Issie would become inebriated and come up to gambol on the surface. The Swedes, less festive, have built a giant trap for the lake monster of Storsjön and baited it with a pig, so far without bringing home the bacon. Ogopogo, who materializes in Lake Okanagan in western Canada, got his name from a 1920s musical. It goes:

> His mother was an earwig
> His father was a whale
> A little bit of head
> And hardly any tail
> And Ogopogo was his name

Indeed there has always been a music-hall quality to stories of Monsters of the Lakes, ever since the great Loch Ness bonanza that began with the sightings and photograph of 1933. The people who actually report seeing the monsters are rarely so amused, however. When Erin Neely was out water-skiing on Lake Okanagan in 1977 she apparently almost ran over Ogopogo. She was so shocked she dropped the tow line, fainted and almost drowned.

Ogopogo gave Mrs Lillian Vogelgesang a nasty moment that same year. Her nine-year-old daughter suddenly let out a yell while she was playing on the beach. 'I couldn't believe what I was seeing,' said Mrs Vogelgesang. 'I screamed, it's him, it's him.' She saw a 50 ft (15 m) creature, 'at least 5 ft in diameter', twisting and turning, apparently chasing fish, close by the shore. It was olive-green in colour with 'a shiny and smooth skin', and what looked like flippers or paddles. The water round its humps was frothing and churning. 'It really shook me up', she said. She thinks her screams scared the creature off and, as it moved away, each hump left a trail, and in no time at all it was halfway across the lake towards Casa Loma. Mrs Vogelgesang had no doubts about the extraordinary dimensions of the creature she saw, for she was able to judge it against the length of the dock at Sarsons Beach. 'If I hadn't had the children', she added, 'I would have run down to the edge of the dock, for I could have actually touched it, it was so close in.'

The monster of Loch Ness too is not totally benign. Constable John Fraser of Inverness was out one night with the water bailiff, Alex Campbell, looking for poachers when there was a great surge of water. 'What in the name of heaven is that?' enquired the constable. 'It's Nessie,' said the bailiff. The next ten minutes would have matched any late-night spine-chiller. While the two men sat motionless in the rowing boat in the middle of the dark loch, for it was past midnight and there was no moon, the great surging and swelling of the water continued around them. Though there was no wind, their little boat started to rock and pitch. For two or three minutes, it seemed certain that they would be overturned; then, as it subsided a little, the two men heard something resembling the noise a horse makes when breathing heavily after a canter. The panting continued, apparently very close to the boat. The two men sat petrified. Then slowly the breathing faded away and they were left once again with total silence, in the darkness of a flat calm loch. 'We finished our journey with no trouble,' said the bailiff, 'but we had had a bad scare.'

More usually, the monsters of the lakes seem to inspire awe rather than fear. Father Matthew Burke was fishing with two other priests on Lough Ree in Ireland on the calmest of evenings in May 1960.

'Lo and behold [he recounted], there was this object on the top of the water, a couple of humps and a head. Now I have been on the loughs and rivers and lakes and all that and I have seen all the usual things in Ireland, but this was nothing that I could place at all. I'm afraid I was then guilty of saying a stupid thing. I said, "Let us pull over towards it." As we pulled the oars a bit, it went down and I remember feeling a terrible consternation that it was gone for ever. But lo and behold, up it comes again, and stayed there on top of the water for, I suppose, five minutes. We stayed the three of us wondering. Finally it went down and that was the last we saw of it.'

Even more frightening, it would appear, is meeting a monster face to face in the water. Two skin-divers from New York, Fred Shanafelt and Morris Lucia, reported that they were diving, looking for a sunken cabin cruiser at Maquam Bay on Lake Champlain when Lucia signalled to Shanafelt. 'From his actions, I knew we were in some kind of danger,' said Shanafelt, 'I surfaced about 10 ft out from the shore, looking back to see what had given Morry such a fright. That's when I saw this thing.' The two men judged the monster to be at least 40 ft (12 m) long. It had a head like a horse which eventually rose 8 ft (2.5 m) out of the water, and the colour was mushroom grey. Lucia said: 'It did not make any effort to harm us. Once it cocked its head as if it was curious about our appearance. I think we could have gone right back into the water without being hurt. Of course, I would not have done that for a million dollars!'

Perhaps because there are so many witnesses, such a proliferation of photographs, and such challenging evidence, the lake monsters and their supporters get the shortest possible shrift from the world's conventional scientists. Dr Denys Tucker incurred the disapproval of the Natural History Museum in London for wasting time on the Loch Ness phenomenon. Similarly an enquiry addressed to the Icelandic Museum of Natural History about the Lágarfljót monster and the bones which had supposedly been found by a distinguished Icelander produced a very vinegary response to the effect that the Lágarfljótsormur has never been anything but a legend. According to the museum, this monster was just leaves, tree branches and other vegetative remains brought together by the strong currents in the Lágarfljót river.

For all that, eminent naturalists, zoologists and research scientists have been sufficiently persuaded of the strength of the evidence to run the risk of academic obloquy and recommend at least further investigation. Sir Peter Scott, the celebrated British naturalist, writing in the leading British science journal, *Nature*, gave a scientific name to the Loch Ness creature: *Nessiteras rhombopteryx*. 'Those who have worked over the years to identify the Nessies', he said, 'have produced a hard core of evidence. Now that their existence seems closer to being established, giving the species a name will focus greater attention on further studies which must in due course lead to more detailed knowledge of the animals' anatomy, biology and phylogeny.'

Peter Scott's painting of the Loch Ness monster, *Nessiteras rhombopteryx*, done in 1975

In Canada, Dr James A McLeod, head of the University of Manitoba Zoology Department, led the investigation into Manipogo, using nets and skin-divers to scour Lake Winnipegosis. He pointed out that the many witnesses clearly saw something. 'Until we can identify what they saw as something commonplace or otherwise, we cannot call them liars.'

Ogopogo

Canada's other famous monster, Ogopogo, provides as intriguing a challenge as any in the world, perhaps even including Loch Ness.

Lake Okanagan lies in appropriately serpentine form along 80 miles (128 km) of southern British Columbia. It is never more than a couple of miles wide and is deep and cold—carved, like Loch Ness, by Ice Age glaciers out of the bedrock. The shores of the Lake are quite heavily populated and roads run very close to the water. Ogopogo-watching is almost an armchair activity. In 1976, a girl claimed to have seen him from a Kelowna City Park parking lot. In 1977, he materialized in front of the Westbank Yacht Club. The same year, two men from the Pandosy Trailer Park were sitting chatting on a log when they caught sight of him. Along the lakeshore roads it was reported in 1978 that people, in chilly weather, did not even bother to get out of their cars when Ogopogo surfaced, but just parked and watched in comfort.

Ogopogo has an ancient lineage. The Okanakane Indians called him Na-ha-ha-itkh and used always to carry a dog or chicken when they crossed the lake by canoe. If Na-ha-ha-itkh came too close the sacrifice got thrown overboard and the Indians could safely proceed. The monster was soon occupying the attention of the early settlers. At Westbank in the 1870s a missionary's wife, Mrs Susan Allison, saw what she thought was a log which suddenly started to swim up the lake against the wind and current. It was the start of a series of sightings that have continued unabated to the present day.

In 1976, Ed Fletcher from Vancouver was

out on Lake Okanagan when a USO, or Unidentified Swimming Object, as they are known in Canada, cut across his bow. 'If I had not shut the engine off I could have run him over or jumped on his back, for the boat drifted to within 15 or 30 ft of him.' Fletcher and his daughter, Diane, who was with him in the boat, were close enough to the shore at Gellatly Bay to turn back and fetch their camera. They came back out with another passenger, Gary Slaughter of Kelowna, and, almost on cue, says Fletcher, Ogopogo surfaced again.

'I saw his whole length this time, about 70 to 75 ft. I shut the engine off when we got near him and the boat coasted to within 50 ft of him when I shot the first picture.' For an hour the three had a private showing. 'He would submerge, swim at least two city blocks, then surface and all the while we chased after him.' Fletcher's technique was to accelerate his boat towards the animal then cut the engine and hope to coast as close as he could. More than a dozen times the creature surfaced and submerged and Fletcher got five photographs. The beast swam coiled up and then stretched out, but even coiled up the party reckoned its length to be 40 ft (12 m). Diane Fletcher described the skin as smooth and brownish like a whale's skin, with small ridges on its back. Just like Mrs Vogelgesang, who was to be so frightened by it the following year, she was struck by its girth, 4 ft (1.2 m) at least. It swam in an undulating corkscrew sort of motion. Both she and Gary Slaughter thought the head was 2 ft (0.6 m) or more long, flattened like a snake's and with 'two things standing up from the head like the ears of a Dobermann Pinscher'.

The following July, the Fletchers who had patrolled the area of the previous sighting throughout the summer, again saw a strange wave. Then their boat received a sudden bump and a great bubble appeared which burst leaving a dreadful odour. Only a couple of days later, the water-skier, Erin Neely, had her encounter with Ogopogo. She believes it was the wave from the monster

that upset her, but she says the creature was within arm's length of her as she trod water. When she was brought ashore she had to be treated in hospital for shock.

Between April 1977 and August 1978, the *Kelowna Daily Courier*, the *Penticton Herald* and the *Vernon Daily News*, newspapers around the lake, carried a dozen reports often involving confirmed sceptics. 'I did not believe it before, but we circled the thing in our boat, keeping it about a hundred yards away,' said Harry Staines of Westbank. He described it as resembling a long black eel about 35 ft (11 m) long swimming with an up and down motion and leaving 'quite a wake'.

But it was in 1968 that film evidence was secured by a visitor to the lake, Art Folden from Chase, British Columbia. He was driving home on an August evening when he reached a stretch of road quite high above the Okanagan Lake at Penticton. At this point on Highway 97 he was perhaps 300 yd from the water. Suddenly, he noticed an object in the lake below. He stopped his car. For once in the hunt for monsters, whether on land, lake or sea, the circumstances were right. Here was a man not only with an 8 mm ciné camera, a telephoto lens, and some film actually loaded up and left over from a day shooting the family's home movies, but also a man self-possessed enough to conserve his last footage by switching off the camera whenever the object submerged and starting again when it reappeared.

The Folden film has been subjected to the critical examination that is to be expected in any such circumstance. Taking a line on the pine trees that are shown in some frames, most investigators agree that the object was 60 ft (18 m) or more long. There seems little argument that it was moving at very considerable speed. There were no signs of the coils that most previous witnesses referred to. Some viewers claim to discern a head and tail. More certain is that it created a fair wake and had a big girth, 3 ft (0.9 m) or so at the head end, tapering towards the tail.

Mrs Arlene B Gaal, an Okanagan who is

A still from the Folden film of Ogopogo showing a serpentine creature with flipper and tail

the principal authority on Ogopogo, has repeatedly seen the film and has researched the lay-out of the filming site. She has no doubt of the authenticity of the film and that it shows at the very least an unusual 'form of life in Lake Okanagan'.

But to this day Ogopogo eludes all attempts at closer contact. In 1977, sixty volunteer scuba divers took turns to be lowered in a cage 30 ft (9 m) down into Okanagan Lake equipped with cameras and powerful air-craft landing lights in order to trap Ogo-pogo into a night picture but no luck. Then there was a plan to lower electrodes into the water to try and flush him to the surface with electric currents. Lately, Lake Okanagan Investigation Bureau has been set up to col-late evidence, but this still can produce little more than the constant stream of eye-witness accounts. These are written off by the Federation of British Columbia Natur-alists as 'an optical illusion produced when an observer views obliquely a bow wave mov-ing across flat water under certain lighting conditions'. Leaving aside the Folden film, however, it is difficult to fit such a thesis into the context of many eyewitness reports without doubting not only the eyesight but also the honesty of perfectly respectable Canadians. The publisher of the *Kelowna Daily Courier* himself, Mr R P Maclean, was in his own lakeside garden when he saw something with three humps like car tyres, no visible scales, only 50 ft (15 m) away. It went down in the water in an undulating motion. Seven Red Cross workers described him off Penticton—a dirty brownish green, 25 ft (7.6 m) long and riding high out of the water with three large humps trailing be-hind. Another water-skier, Sherri Campbell, had something huge surface beside her and dropped the tow in fright. After she was picked up, the boat, which could do 40 mph, chased the wake across the lake, but could not catch up with it. Ogopogo even made an appearance outside the offices of the Kelowna Chamber of Commerce in 1969. But no one had a camera to train on the lake below. Evidently very speedy and with 80 miles

of lake to roam, the only threat that seems to face Ogopogo now is the weedkiller which the state government is pouring into the clogged waters in some of the bays. Chemis-try may get him if guile cannot.

Manipogo

Canada is well supplied with monsters, many with impressive credentials. Apart from Caddy, the sea serpent off the British Columbia coast, there is the Turtle Lake monster of Saskatchewan whose first sight-ing goes back to 1924, and the black beast of Lake Ponenegamook east of Quebec who was also first sighted in the early 1920s. In 1977, he was tracked for ten days by a three-man team of divers with sonar equipment, who managed an interesting 25 ft (7.6 m) trace from right under their boat and a rather murky black shape on one of their automatic cameras. Manipogo, the creature of Canada's Lakes Manitoba and Winni-pegosis that lie north of Winnipeg and are joined by the Dauphin River, managed to avoid any encounters with white men until at least 1935, but he seems to share many of his fellow monsters' ability to put the 'fluence on all attempts to pin him down. When he arose in front of a large group of picnickers at Manitoba Park on the lake shore in 1960, there was a real Marx Brothers sequence. One woman grabbed her camera, rushed down to the water's edge, raised the view-finder to her eye and promptly fell in. Another lady, camera in hand, rushed back to get her husband and just forgot to take a picture first. Tom Locke, the man who actually designed Manitoba Park had both a still and a ciné camera. With careful self-control he put down the still camera and used his ciné camera. At first the action jammed but he got it going. He followed a good track of the monster, lowered the camera as the creature disappeared—only to find there had been no film in the camera! Indeed Manipogo was a real tease that day. Not only could many people make a good description of what they had seen: a flat snakelike head, dark skin and three big humps, according to Mr A R Adam who chased after it along the lake shore, but it also produced for them a mate and a baby. Steve Rehaluk, of Rorkton, Manitoba, his wife Ann and his two sons all got a good view. 'We were sitting at a picnic table' he recalls. 'There was a ripple in the water. When I first looked there was only one. But when I ran to the shore I could see another beside it and a third trailing behind.' He thought they looked like three big black snakes. At least seventeen people spotted Manipogo and family that day but no one got a picture. It was two years before two fishermen took the one rather fuzzy picture that exists of the monster. The family remain secure in the huge expanse of their northern fastness.

Champ

Further south is Lake Champlain, running down from Canada through Vermont and New York State. The Americans have been equally unlucky with Champ. Joe Zarzynski, the champion of Champ, has already nominated him for the United States Endangered Species list, although he has never actually seen him himself. Champ has the most illustrious history. He was first sighted by Samuel Champlain himself, the discoverer of the lake in 1609; he frightened the cream of New York society on a steamboat excursion in the 1870s; then he had a price of $50,000 put on his carcass by the unfeeling showman, P T Barnum, around the turn of the century. However, his appearances in what is a relatively accessible part of New England are disconcertingly rare. Janet Tyler, a Deputy Sheriff from Westport, whose house faces the lake, saw a dark creature splashing in the cove opposite her porch, its head sticking 3 or 4 ft out of the water, but by the time she got to the telephone to call a 'posse', it had disappeared. In 1947, L R Jones of Swanton was fishing with two companions off North Hero Island:

'The bass were biting really well and we were about to hoist anchor when there was a tremendous splash. It was calm and no other boats were in sight. Then out of the depths reared a huge dark form. Three segments appeared, clearly discernible above the water's surface, separated one from the other by about 5 ft of water, the overall length of the creature being about 25 ft.'

The three men agreed it was certainly a single creature which moved at about 15 mph. It stayed around for two or three minutes before disappearing.

Although a baby monster '20 ft long which propelled itself through the water by the action of its tail and legs' was allegedly captured on the Bear Lake in Utah in 1871, most of the monsters of the United States of America, are, like Champ, decidedly shy compared with their Canadian cousins or even the sea serpents of the New England coast which performed with the zest of vaudeville stars in the early nineteenth century. Many of the lakes which Indians say have monsters have produced the odd sighting by white men. Lake Walker in Nevada produced a sighting of a fast 45 ft (14 m) creature in 1956. The Flathead Lake in Montana has had enough reports for a company to offer a thousand dollars for any creature, sturgeon or other fish or monster which is over 14 ft (4 m) long and taken from the lake. Reports of monsters on Lake Payette, Idaho, many of the Wisconsin Lakes, especially Red Cedar Lake, Lake Ontario and even the Salt Lake, Utah, have not been substantiated by photographs or film.

Issie

Perhaps inevitably, no one in Japan is so foolish as to see a monster without taking his photograph. Mr Matsubara, who got the prize for the first picture of Issie on Lake Ikeda in 1978, had only come for a three-day holiday, away from his shop in Kagoshima City. He said it was about half past one in the afternoon when Issie surfaced. 'Something huge came up from the water and disappeared again in fifteen to twenty seconds. I only managed one shot.' But it was enough to pay for his holiday.

Issie is in fact the subject of a rather touching legend. It is said that there was a beautiful white mare living by the lake. One day a Samurai lord took her foal away. The white horse felt very sad and jumped into the lake,

occasionally surfacing again to look for her lost foal. Today she is a tourist industry, a food: Issie dumplings 'with a slight seaweed flavour', and a pop song which goes:

> Male hump and female hump
> Shining in the sun are
> Calling each other
> In the Romantic lake
> I want to see Issie again
> And also to let you see

Mr M Omagari took a picture of apparently two Issies together in 1978, and later that year more than twenty people saw Issie in the middle of the lake. 'Two big humps each 15 ft long and a couple of feet high were swimming for about two minutes,' said a local builder, Yutaka Kawaji. 'There was another 15 ft between each hump and the skin was very dark.' Mr Kawaji said he had seen the creature three times, the first time when he was at primary school thirty years ago. The Japanese have another

Lake Ikeda's Issie photographed by Mr Matsubara

monster in Lake Kutcharo on the northern island of Hokkaido, complete with photographs, a research programme by divers, and a Kussie Protection Group. Unfortunately, credibility is stretched on this occasion as Lake Kutcharo was virtually poisoned with acid after an earthquake in 1938.

Although many countries around the world have claimed a monster of their own, the classic one remains the Loch Ness monster in Scotland.

The Loch Ness monster

Loch Ness slashes like a great scar north-eastwards, almost severing northern Scotland from the rest of Britain: 24 miles (39 km) long, it can be a daunting place. Sheer mountains rise 2,000 ft (600 m) from the loch side. The water, always dark and murky, can be whipped into impressive storms. The depths reach 900 ft (275 m), perhaps 1,000 ft (300 m). Inverness lies at the northern end, Fort Augustus at the southern. Urquhart Castle stands out as the greatest landmark halfway along on the northern side. It was

here on the northern bank of the loch in 1933 that a monster was not only seen but also photographed.

This photograph, which was immediately reproduced by the Glasgow *Daily Record* and the London *Daily Sketch*, was taken by a Mr Hugh Gray who had worked at the local British Aluminium Company works at Foyers since 1916. Afterwards, when his photograph had been shown around the world, he swore a statement about the circumstances in which the picture had been taken.

'Four Sundays ago, after church, I went for my usual walk near where the Foyers river enters the loch. The loch was like a mill pond and the sun was shining brightly. An object of considerable dimensions rose out of the water not so very far from where I was. I immediately got my camera ready and snapped the object which was then two to three feet above the surface of the water. I did not see any head, for what I took to be the front parts were under the water, but there was considerable movement from what seemed to be the tail.'

Hugh Gray's 1933 photo of the Loch Ness monster

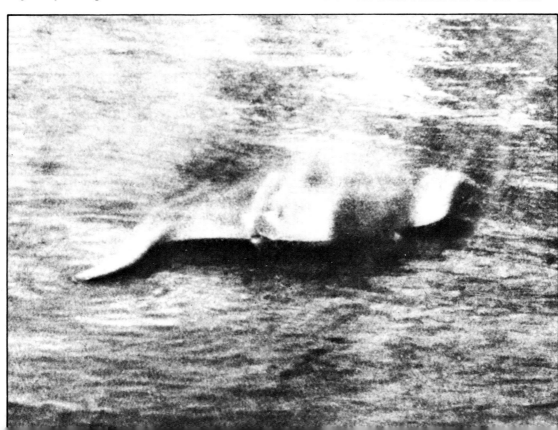

Colonel Robert Wilson took this photograph of Nessie in May 1934; labelled by the newspapers the 'surgeon's picture'

Earlier that year, a flurry of sightings had appeared in the local and national papers. One day in September, the Reverend W E Hobbes of Wroxeter had arrived at Miss Janet Fraser's Halfway House tea shop to find the place empty. All the guests were upstairs looking at the monster. Joined by the new arrival, the group watched the creature disporting itself about half a mile out in the loch. They gave what was to become an almost standard description of the monster: two low humps and a tail which splashed about making a disturbance on the surface, a snakelike head and neck which stood well out of the water and seemed to be looking round, a large shining eye.

This was only one of more than fifty sightings that had the newspapers streaming north for copy to bury the gloomy news of unemployment and depression which was otherwise dominating their pages. Almost everyone noticed the V-shaped wash and the considerable speed which the monster produced when it moved. Some noticed a powerful tail and in August, Mr A H Palmer, who saw it at only a 100 yd range, reported a gaping red mouth, 1 ft or more across and short horns or antennae on the head. All the witnesses that year were sure the creature was large, at least 20 ft (6 m) long.

The worldwide publicity produced a steady stream of monster hunters to the loch, which in almost half a century since has never really abated, though Nessie and her pursuers have had quiet periods such as during the Second World War and the 1950s.

By May 1934 there was another picture, taken this time by a London gynaecologist, Colonel Robert Wilson. The picture has none of the fuzziness associated with many of the monster pictures. It is crystal clear and shows what looks like a head and neck sticking high out of the water. There is a ring of ripples suggesting it has just emerged. By August, the London *Daily Mail*, which had published the 'surgeon's picture', had another photograph of the monster, this time seemingly showing a fin or a flipper as it powered through the water.

The world had to wait until 1951, however, for a picture showing the characteristic humps so many witnesses had reported. These were finally captured on a box Brownie by a woodman working with the Forestry Commission, Lachlan Stuart. By his account, he had got up to milk his cow when he saw something moving in the loch below his croft. He grabbed his camera, shouted to his wife to join him and rushed down to the shore where the animal was now only 50 yd away. It had a long neck and a head as big as a

Captured on a box Brownie in 1951, Lachlan Stuart's photograph was the first to show Nessie's humps

sheep and rather the same shape. It was splashing about and there were three distinct humps sticking up to 4 ft out of the water. Stuart got only one picture, because he had trouble with the shutter of the camera, but he reckoned the object he and his wife saw was over 50 ft (15 m) long, and certainly something very large and distinctive was recorded on that single shot.

Whatever it shows, the Stuart picture is probably genuine, which is more than can be said for several of the photographs that have had a worldwide showing. Zoologist, Dr Maurice Burton, recalls investigating the site from which one picture that is often reproduced was taken. He found the burned remains of four plastic sacks, a stick got up to look like a monster's head, and some rocks tied together with distinctive red and white string which had been thrown into the water. As he delicately puts it: 'these findings lead to certain conclusions, none of which has anything to do with proof of a large unidentified animal in Loch Ness'. Don Robinson, the Yorkshire zoo owner, managed to hoax everyone for a day or so by leaving the body of one of his elephant seals, which had

unfortunately died, beside the loch. Someone else left what were claimed to be monster footmarks, but turned out to be made by a cast from a hippopotamus's hoof. It is not therefore too surprising that the weight of responsibility for proving Nessie's existence has now moved away from still photographs to two other elements. First there is the sheer size and respectability of the eyewitness evidence, much of it at close quarters from people like judges, soldiers, doctors. Secondly, there is the evidence of movie film, which is much less easy to fake even if it is just as difficult to interpret.

Undoubtedly the champion eyewitness is Alex Campbell, the water bailiff of Loch Ness, who has now had eighteen encounters with the monster and even had it jostle his boat and scare his dog under the seat.

'My best sighting [says Mr Campbell] was in May 1934 right off the Abbey boathouse. That morning I was standing at the mouth of the River Hawick looking for what we call a run of salmon. I heard the sound of two trawlers coming through the canal from the West. Suddenly there was this upsurge of water right in front of the canal entrance. I was stunned. I shut my eyes three times to make sure I was not imagining things—the head and the

Eyewitnesses of the Loch Ness monster: (right to left) Mrs Robertson, Mr Wilkins and son, Mr and Mrs Macnab, Alex Campbell, Gwen and Peter Smith, Dick Raynor

huge humped body were perfectly clear. I knew right away that the creature was scared because of its behaviour. The head was twisting about frantically. It was the thud, thud of the engines that was the reason for its upset. As soon as the bow of the first trawler came within my line of vision, that's when it was in its line of vision too, and it vanished out of sight, gone. I estimated the length of the body 30 ft at least, the height of the head and neck above water level as 6 ft, and the skin was grey.'

Mr Campbell met the monster regularly until his last sighting just before his recent retirement. He was passing Cherry Island on the road to Inverness when he saw it.

'There was just one huge hump probably 8 ft long and 4 ft high. Then without any preliminary cavorting about it just shot off to the other side of the loch. I was staggered at the speed. I had a wonderful view of the body. It did not alter course, but kept up this great pace leaving a wash about 3 ft high.'

Certainly Nessie sightings in no way eased off in the 1970s. Mrs Robertson in 1975 saw two of the monsters at once:

'A friend of mine, a German nun, came to visit us and we went for a walk. She asked me to take a picture of her. While I was handing back the camera I noticed this object, a terrific huge thing with two humps swimming from the river mouth opposite. It was between two big trees so we could afterwards measure its whole length. We reckon it was 40 to 45 ft long. It was grey with two humps and a long neck sticking out of the water, I should think 9 to 10 ft. I could not keep my eyes off its head. It was a very peculiar shape. It had no dome. It was squarish with a big black spot in the middle and it was white all round it. The same white occurred along its neck.'

As early as 1933, just before Christmas, the first ciné film of the monster was captured by Malcolm Irvine, who was subsequently to get another sequence in 1936. Then a South African, G E Taylor, claimed the first colour film—three minutes of the monster's hump at a distance of about 200 yd. Then in 1960 came the most celebrated film, taken by Tim Dinsdale. This was the film that was to revolutionize the hunt for the monster. It certainly turned Dinsdale's life upside down. This aeronautical engineer promptly gave up his job and devoted the next twenty years to the search for the Loch Ness monster. He fitted out and camouflaged a little boat called *Water Horse* on which he spent weeks eating and sleeping in the vain hope that definitive proof would come within range of his cameras.

It was Dinsdale's film that also inspired the establishment of the Loch Ness Investigation Bureau, which introduced an element

Veteran of forty expeditions, Tim Dinsdale has seen the Loch Ness monster on three occasions

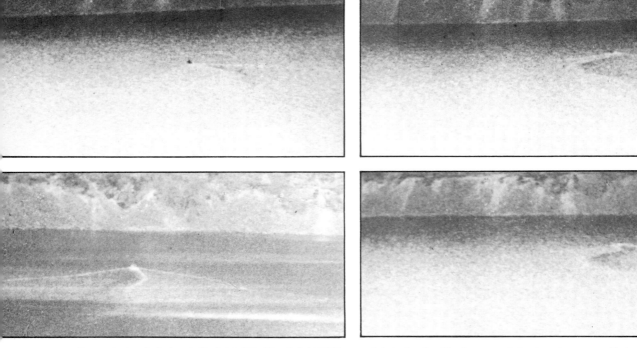

A sequence of photographs from Tim Dinsdale's 1960 film when he saw the monster moving at about 10 mph with the hump clearly visible. The film was judged to be genuine by the RAF's Joint Air Reconnaissance Intelligence Centre

of science and system into the search. The bureau collated and codified all the sightings, pursued Nessie's history which went all the way back to St Columba in the year AD 565, and organized its own long-term vigil at the loch. In its wake have come enthusiasts with all the paraphernalia of the age—in 1970, Wing Commander Ken Wallis in his autogyro plane; then Dan Taylor from Texas with his yellow submarine *Viperfish*, which had many a hair-raising moment as it penetrated as deep as 820 ft (250 m) and got caught in whirlpools, but saw neither hide nor hair of its quarry. Britain's Independent Television News came to Loch Ness with sonar searching gear, and Bob Love with the Honeywell company's version of the same equipment. Love did have a sonar contact for two minutes in 1969 that was interpreted as a large animal. But all this activity failed to add materially to the films,

which had all shown objects at some distance, insufficiently distinct to be proof positive but intriguing enough to attract all but the most sceptical.

Despite all the organized effort the best evidence still seemed to turn up by chance. Peter and Gwen Smith from Luton were holidaying round the loch. Gwen was idly gazing across at Urquhart Castle with a view to taking some shots for the family movie. 'Suddenly,' she recounts, 'this thing came vertically up out of the water, more or less where I was looking. I started filming and of course, I caught it just as it was going down. We stood for a minute and then it came up again and I started filming again. And then a third time.'

Her husband watched the whole thing through binoculars.

'The head rose up at least the height of a man [he said]. It was a good foot thick across the neck. The head seemed to me strangely rectangular. I watched it actually turn its head through ninety degrees as though it was looking directly at us or directly away from us. The last time it came right next to a youth who was in a boat. It came up very confidently as before, then, suddenly, seemed to change its mind and withdrew very quickly as it perceived the boat. I am convinced, if only because of the enormous length of the neck that it was no animal we are familiar with.'

The film, though clear enough, adds little to earlier photographs of the animal.

Throughout the forty years since the bonanza of the 1930s, there have been occasional but enticing suggestions that the Loch Ness animal might occasionally venture ashore. The affair of the hippopotamus's hoofprint hoax has rather discredited this idea but in 1934 a local veterinary student, Arthur Grant, making his way home by motorbike after midnight and apparently perfectly sober, had a terrifying experience. Suddenly just ahead of him in the moonlight an enormous object appeared.

'I had a splendid view [he said later]. In fact I almost struck it with my motorcycle. The body would be 15 or 20 ft in length and very hefty. I distinctly saw two front flippers and there seemed to be two other flippers behind, which it used to spring from. The tail would be 5 to 6 ft long; the curious thing about the tail was that the end was rounded off, it did not come to a point.'

More than a quarter of a century later, in February 1960, Mr Torquil Macleod on a private monster-hunting expedition saw, through binoculars, a monster laid up on the beach at the remote Horseshoe. He wrote to Constance Whyte, the historian of the monster, that he had watched it for nine minutes before it flopped back into the water. 'I had a clear view of its left fore flipper which is grey in colour and spade shaped . . . I confess to being rather appalled at its size, somehow the descriptions have never quite sunk in, but there is no doubt that this individual was of the order of 40 to 60 ft in length.'

With that the animal seems to have abandoned any rash excursions on dry land and stuck to water.

It was there, in the 1970s, that it was subjected to the most sophisticated, sustained assault on its privacy by the American, Dr Robert H Rines, a wealthy and successful patents lawyer who had his first sighting on a June evening in 1971 when a lump scooted about for him in Urquhart Bay. Rines, through his Academy of Applied Science, decided to devote the full power of American money and inventiveness to the search. The following year, he appeared with the Edgerton underwater camera, as used by Jacques Cousteau, and linked it to a Raytheon sonar scan. They were quickly rewarded. On the night of 7 August, the sonar scan was showing a lot of fish when, suddenly the fish took off out of the area and a big black trace appeared on the screen. One of the observers in the sonar boat, Peter Davies, set off to summon Dr Rines who was in another boat.

'I don't mind telling you that it was a rather strange feeling,' said Davies, 'rowing across that pitch black water knowing that there was a very large animal just 30 ft below. It was the sheer size of the echo trace that was frightening.'

Dr Robert Rines with an underwater camera during his search for the Loch Ness monster

As soon as possible, the Rines team flew back to America with the film from their camera which had been linked to the sonar. When the pictures came back from Kodak, there was the famous flipper picture and Rines felt he was in reach of his great goal. It was to be another three years before he got the celebrated pictures that have been claimed as proof that a monster, much like the traditional picture, truly inhabits Loch Ness.

Rines believes that the monster actually bumped into the Academy's underwater rig in 1975. Certainly something set it swinging wildly, but when the team got back to New York it turned out there was nothing on the main camera and they did not bother to get the back-up camera's film processed for nearly a month.

'Then about three o'clock in the morning,'

This photograph of Nessie was taken on 21 May 1977 by Anthony Shiels

says Rines, 'I got a call from my colleague, Charlie Wycoff, "My goodness", he said, "we've got it." I rushed over that early morning and that was the first time I saw the head and neck picture and the picture of the whole body. I'm bound to say I thought that would clinch it, but as you know, it didn't at all.'

Indeed Rines had the galling experience of seeing the pictures leaked before their official release, hearing them denounced in scathing terms by the staff of the Natural History Museum in London, and finding the academic seminar, which Sir Peter Scott had set up for him, collapse in disarray as the guests scuttled for cover for their reputations.

The two pictures, allegedly of the head and the body, certainly seem something less than positive to the casual viewer. In fact, they might be dismissed as showing nothing but the pervading murk of Loch Ness. However, given the careful calibrations of the Rines team, it does seem likely that they represent something extremely large which drifted in and out of range of their cameras.

Rines, disconsolate, gallantly persists.

'We're going to stick to it until we get a definitive enough set of pictures for the so-called experts to identify what these animals are and then I think the world will love us.'

To that end, he is now training a pair of dolphins to try and pursue Nessie instead of waiting for her to come to him.

In the meantime, the sightings continue and so do the 'rational explanations'. The most effective critic of monster theories is the British zoologist, Dr Maurice Burton, if only because for nearly thirty years he was one of the few academic believers in the monster. After his apostasy in 1961, he devoted himself to opposing the monster thesis. He was reinforced in his new scepticism one Sunday afternoon when, as he tells it, almost the whole village of Foyers turned out to watch the supposed monster swimming in the loch. Burton says, however, that he had previously seen a small motor boat set out from the shore, had kept it in view of his binoculars and had taken a series of photographs of the craft, and knew from subsequent questioning of witnesses at Foyers that this was what they had mistaken for the beast. Burton thinks motor boats account for a lot of the sightings, especially where it is alleged that the monster exhibited great speed. Many others, he thinks are otters, pointing out that an otter, 8 ft (2.4 m) long, was captured in the Shetland Isles in the last century. He believes particularly that there was probably a very large otter loose in the loch in the 1930s. Another monster illusion he suggests is caused by the wash from vessels which can come ten minutes or so after the ship has passed. Then there are hoaxes, of which he personally uncovered one. Also there may be seals that get into the loch from the sea, and gaseous rubbish floating up from the loch bed.

Other doubters besides Burton have suggested that there may be a giant eel. A red deer has been caught in a beguiling series of photographs swimming across the loch and looking in the distance far more like a monster than some of the usual pictures. The magazine, *New Scientist*, was even persuaded to carry an article suggesting that one of the classic photographs, the surgeon's picture, was actually of an elephant swimming along with its trunk in the air!

Whatever the plausibility of these various explanations, it is hard to believe that literally thousands of observers, many of them experienced naturalists and fishermen, could have been so wildly mistaken as to misinterpret even an 8 ft (2.4 m) otter for a 40 ft (12 m) monster, to mistake a motor boat for a creature with two humps and a 6 ft (1.8 m) long neck, or the most unexpected of waves for a gambolling pair of Nessies. If many of the pictures can be explained away, what about the sonar readings? In the mass sightings, can everyone be deceived in the same way? And what of Rines' photographs?

Among the believers in some unidentified animal in Loch Ness there are various schools of thought. Some suggest a new species of long-necked seal, remembering

the heavy breathing that has been heard, while others espouse the giant eel. But the favourite is undoubtedly a plesiosaurus, a giant fish-eating reptile supposed to have died out seventy million years ago. Certainly museum reconstructions of the plesiosaurus accord uncannily closely with the descriptions of the Loch Ness monster given by eyewitnesses and also, it has to be conceded, with the underwater blur recorded by Robert Rines' camera. But could it have survived the freezing over of the loch in the last Ice Age? Moreover, any creature in the loch presupposes a breeding population of at least a dozen animals. Can there really be that many monsters in the loch?

On the other hand, the sceptics must explain away not only the films, the still pictures, the eyewitnesses, but also Rines' pictures, and perhaps most difficult of all, sonar traces.

Of all the monsters around the world, Nessie always seems the closest to discovery. If she is finally corralled it should give new heart to the bands of optimists who are camped round other lakes in Scotland, Ireland, North America, Japan, Sweden and the Soviet Union intent on proving that the chimaera of the water do have real earthly substance.

Arthur C Clarke comments:

Almost everything I have said about sea monsters (Chapter 4) also applies here. The only additional point worth making is that the probability of large unknown creatures existing in lakes seems very much less than in the ocean. To give a land analogy—I could believe a dinosaur in, say, the Matto Grosso, but not in Central Park or Kensington Gardens. . . .

In fact, if it were not for Loch Ness, I would not take this subject very seriously. The evidence for *something* in the Loch is overwhelming; whether it is an animal new to science is another matter.

If you want my personal opinion—on Mondays, Wednesdays and Fridays I believe in Nessie. . . .

7

Figures in a Landscape

One hot summer's day in 1932, George Palmer, a civil pilot, was making a leisurely flight from Las Vegas, Nevada, to Blythe, California, a small town inland from Los Angeles. As he neared Blythe, Palmer scanned the desert 5,000 ft (1,500 m) below, looking for emergency landing sites as pilots do in difficult country. Suddenly, as he neared the winding Colorado River, about 18 miles (29 km) from his destination, the giant figure of a man swam into view.

Palmer had only seen it for a moment, and was well aware that the desert sun can play tricks on the most experienced of pilots. So he turned and made another run across the stony bluffs near the river's edge. And there it was, a giant lying on his back, drawn in stones upon the desert pavement. Palmer guessed that the body was about 100 ft (30 m) long. And nearby, the astonished pilot could see another vast figure: a four-legged animal like a dog or horse.

Alerted by Palmer, the Los Angeles Museum sent its Curator of History, Arthur Woodward, to investigate, and when he reached the plateaux or *mesas* near Blythe, Woodward found not one group of figures, but three. This was a major archaeological find on his own doorstep, and Woodward's report barely conceals his excitement:

'The first one we visited consisted of a "trinity" of a man (spread-eagled and lying partly in a huge circle, which from its nature appears to have been used as a dance ring), a long-legged, long-tailed animal, and a small serpentine coil which may have represented a reptile. The man in this case was ninety-five feet long from

Left: Jim Woodman's photograph of the Giant of Atacama in Chile

the crown of the head to the bottom of his feet. The dance ring was a hundred and forty feet in diameter. The animal was thirty-six feet in length from the tip of its nose to the base of its tail. The serpentine coil was twelve feet in diameter.

'The next mesa we visited had a single figure, that of a man upon it. The outline was ninety-eight feet long. The torso was over seventeen feet wide. The arms were outstretched over a span of seventy-four feet. The third mesa had a "trinity" similar to the first one, save that here the artists had outdone themselves as creators of Herculean monsters. The man in this case was a hundred and sixty-seven feet in length. Each hand had the normal number of fingers and each foot the requisite number of toes.'

But the strangest thing about the desert giants was that no one had reported them before, despite the fact that the area had been 'fairly well covered', as Woodward puts it, 'by hundreds of wandering prospectors, surveying crews and many others afflicted with the *Wanderlust*.' This was mainly because the Blythe figures, drawn on the desert before the age of aircraft, were almost impossible to detect on the ground, and were clearly designed to be seen *from the air*.

More than 4,000 miles (5,400 km) further south, pilots in southern Peru had made a similar puzzling and spectacular discovery. As the local airline began to open up the country, aircrew and passengers were amazed to discover that the desert between the Ica and Nazca valleys, more than 200 miles (320 km) south of Lima, was crisscrossed with a vast 'picture book' of lines, geometrical figures and drawings of birds, insects and animals. Not only was their scale extravagant—some of the lines ran for miles, unswervingly straight over plateaux and mountains, others formed giant enclosures like runways — but they too seemed to have been laid out to be viewed from the sky.

In the face of these discoveries, American archaeologists of the 1930s began to ask questions: who had drawn the pictures, what did they depict, and what were they for? It was easy to ask the questions, but it would prove to be far more difficult to arrive at any satisfactory answers. In Britain, archaeologists and amateur antiquarians had been tackling similar problems for at least two hundred years.

The white horses of Britain
On the green hillsides of England, there are at least fifty landscape figures. The reason for this is quite simple: in the downland areas, a layer of white chalk lies just beneath the turf. It can easily be exposed with no more than a spade. Conditions are especially suitable in the West Country, where there is plenty of chalk and where the hillsides tend to be steep and prominent enough to be seen from a great distance. In Wiltshire alone, there are seven white horses, at least half a dozen regimental badges, a kiwi (once maintained by a shoe-polish company), and a panda.

Unlike the strange giants of southern California or the Nazca lines, the origins of most of these figures is known and so are the intentions of the people who cut them. The regimental badges near Salisbury, for example, were made by soldiers stationed nearby during the First World War. The first was cut by men from the London Rifle Brigade, and was such a success that other regiments followed suit, often having to do the work in the early morning before practice began on the nearby rifle ranges. Many of the white horses are also relatively modern: the New Pewsey Horse in Wiltshire was designed to celebrate the 1937 Coronation by George Marples, an expert in leucippotomy,

as the art of cutting white horses is infelicitously called. Likewise, the Marlborough White Horse, also in Wiltshire, was made by a party of schoolboys from Mr Greasley's Academy in 1804, and the Kilburn Horse in Yorkshire, instigated by a returned native, a London grocer called Thomas Taylor, was cut in 1857.

We know too how the figure was cut. The Reverend Plenderleath was told of the construction of his local white horse, at Cherhill, by 'a very intelligent old man, who was born in the year 1786—only six years after its completion'. The horse's creator, a doctor called Christopher Allsop, first marked out the outline with white flags.

'Then [says Plenderleath], he took his position at a spot exactly on a line between the Downs and Calne, about two hundred yards above the top of Labour-in-Vain Hill, and, from thence, by means of a speaking tube, directed the removal of the stakes one way or the other, until he was satisfied with the result. The turf was then pared off, and the hollow levelled up with chalk. . . .'

The white horse at Cherhill completed in 1780

Many of the white horses do present minor mysteries. George Marples, for example, found it so difficult to ascribe precise dates to many of them that he incorporated the year, 1937, into his design for Pewsey. The origins of the horses at Woolborough and Hackpen are unknown, and the Osmington White Horse at Weymouth Bay in Dorset is attributed to three separate sources: a soldier who cut it to commemorate visits to the town by George III and his brother, the Duke of Gloucester; some engineers, expecting a Napoleonic invasion; or some navvies who, according to Thomas Hardy in *The Trumpet Major*, designed it to celebrate victory in the Battle of Trafalgar. And then there is the white horse that turned up suddenly in the summer of 1948 when a field was ploughed at Rockley Down near Marlborough. A magnificent, prancing figure, it measured 126 ft (38 m) from nose to tail, but no record of its cutting has ever been found. Now the horse itself has returned to obscurity beneath the farmland from which it so briefly emerged. The fact that no one can clearly remember who, in 1925, cut the white horse at Littlington in Sussex illustrates how quickly a small mystery can arise from the largest of landmarks.

However, major mysteries, comparable to the riddles of the Californian giants and the Nazca lines, exist in the case of four British hill figures: two chalk giants and two horses, one white, the other red.

The white horse is at the village of Uffington in Berkshire, and is such a local landmark that the whole area, the Vale of the White Horse, takes its name from it. Most of the other British white horses were inspired by it, but the Uffington horse differs from them in one crucial respect: it is the only truly ancient white horse now in existence— all the other horses look as modern as the thoroughbreds stabled in the racing establishments at nearby Lambourn. This is because they are in the style of the eighteenth-century painter George Stubbs, whose equine pictures were popular with the clergymen, doctors and farmers who cut

The only known photograph, taken in 1948, of the Rockley Down horse

many of the hill figures. The Uffington White Horse is a strange, stylized and disjointed creature, its head is skeletal and beaked, its body thin and elongated, with only two of its galloping legs attached to its flanks. It looks more like a dragon than a horse and the nearby Dragon Hill where St George is said to have killed the dragon has led some people to identify it as that mythical creature. But the earliest reference to it, in a twelfth-century *Book of Wonders*, clearly describes it as a horse with a foal—though what has become of the foal remains one of Uffington's many mysteries.

There are many other references to the White Horse of Uffington in ancient documents. In a cartulary or book of monastic documents relating to the Abbey of Abingdon in the reign of Henry II, a monk named Godrick is said to own land *juxta locum qui vulgo Mons Albi Equi nuncupatur* (near to the place which is popularly known as the Hill of the White Horse.) A fourteenth-

Perhaps the most famous of white horses, at Uffington in Berkshire

century manuscript classes it as a marvel second only to Stonehenge. In more modern times, Thomas Hughes, author of *Tom Brown's Schooldays*, wrote a novel set in Uffington and containing much folklore about the White Horse, and G K Chesterton an epic poem full of rolling cadences and rather muddled history. But none of these writers can solve the mystery of White Horse Hill: the horse is certainly ancient, but no one knows exactly how old; it gallops across the Berkshire Downs, but no one knows why it is there.

There have, of course, been many theories. In the seventeenth century John Aubrey and the topographer, Thomas Baskerville (1630–1720), believed the horse was cut by the Anglo-Saxon leader Hengist (his name means 'stallion') twelve hundred years before. Others thought it was commissioned by Alfred the Great, in whose kingdom of Wessex Uffington is situated, to celebrate his victory over the Danes in AD 871. More

recently, archaeologists have suggested it was the totem of a horse cult. It has even been 'identified' as an ichthyosaurus.

Certainly, the inhabitants of the Vale of the White Horse must have held it in high esteem, for chalk figures must be regularly cleaned or 'scoured' if they are not to disappear again beneath the encroaching turf. From the seventeenth century onwards, historians recorded the curious ceremonies that accompanied the scouring. Known as the Uffington 'Pastime', it was a festival intended to celebrate the horse after a hard day's work of restoration. Thomas Hughes describes the last 'pastime' held in 1857, which was a colourful country fair visited by lords and ladies, gypsies and mountebanks. It suggests that earlier ceremonies may have had a more serious ritualistic purpose, with the horse, perhaps, as an object of worship.

In the face of all this conjecture, one noted archaeologist, Professor Stuart Piggott, has analysed the problems of establishing at least one fact about the White Horse. Piggott has a special interest in the problem:

his family came from the Vale and he now lives there himself. His great-grandfather farmed at Uffington; his grandfather, as a boy of ten, was taken to the 1857 'pastime'.

In 1931, in a review article in *Antiquity*, Piggott discussed attempts to set a date for the cutting of the White Horse. One was a very simple technique which had first been suggested in 1740 by a writer who called himself Philalethes Rusticus. Rusticus, and others after him, noticed a stylistic similarity between the Uffington Horse and horses portrayed on coins from the early Iron Age. These early Iron Age horses shared many of the peculiarities of the White Horse, notably the disjointed legs and the beaklike jaws. The coins were minted in Britain sometime in the first century BC and they imitate a coin of Philip of Macedon, who had died two centuries earlier. On one side of Philip's original coin is a chariot drawn by two horses and driven by a charioteer. It had long been noted that the design was copied again and again, with the result that 'the chariot degenerated on the British examples to a wheel. . . , the charioteer to a group of pellets and the horse (in the latest stages) to a jumble of dumbbells and crescents'. Halfway through this process of degeneration, the horse on the coins begins to bear a striking resemblance to the Uffington White Horse. There are several such coins from the Uffington area preserved in the Ashmolean Museum in Oxford and elsewhere. And, to reinforce the point, Piggott also recalled how horses on two early Iron Age buckets were in the same artistic tradition. The coins, particularly, allowed him to agree to a fairly precise date for the horse: it was unlikely that so massive a work would have been undertaken during the Roman occupation of Britain, and therefore suggested it was cut in the Celtic Iron Age during the first century BC.

The Cerne Giant

An equally puzzling figure stands on a hillside above the picturesque village of Cerne Abbas in Dorset. He is called, quite simply, the Cerne Giant, because, as with the White Horse of Uffington, nothing is known about his origins, and even his name is lost. Yet he is an imposing fellow, 180 ft (55 m) long from head to foot, brandishing a knobbly club 120 ft (37 m) long in his right hand, as he marches across the hillside away from the village. Unlike the white horses, the Giant is drawn in outline only: his body is made of the hillside turf and the shape and anatomical details are marked out by trenches 1 to 2 ft (30–60 cm) wide.

The most striking feature of the Cerne Giant is that he is the most blatantly sexual of all the British hill figures. Indeed, his phallus is 30 ft (9 m) long, and is so prominent that he has been nicknamed 'The Rude Man of Cerne'. Inevitably, there have been many attempts to bowdlerize him over the years: one of the first was in Hutchins' *History of Dorset* of 1774, where the engraver has stripped him of his manhood. More recently, one letter to *The Dorset Magazine* said 'Propriety demands that he don a loincloth', and there was even an attempt to

The Uffington 'Pastime'—the ritual scouring

provide him with a figleaf of sacking and paper. Fortunately, the Giant has survived in all his glory, much to the delight of archaeologists, small children, and old ladies who, apparently, always seem to be standing in the most embarrassing place on the figure when they ask their guide exactly where they are.

Not surprisingly, the Cerne Giant has been taken to be the symbol of a fertility cult, but the few clues to this are vague. One curious phenomenon is that at dawn on 1 May the sun rises directly in line with an observer standing at the base of the Giant's phallus. Whatever this may mean, plenty of legends are associated with him, some of which suggest the vestiges of fertility rites. Girls who fear they may lose their husbands or boyfriends walk round him, hoping his

influence will help them prolong their relationship, and others visit the Giant for luck in the week before their marriage. People who live in the Cerne district think that if a barren woman sleeps or makes love on the Giant's phallus she will bear children. It may also be significant that maypole dancing was a regular feature of the village's May Day celebrations, and that the site of the maypole was a rectangular enclosure called the Trendle or Frying Pan a few yards up the hill, above the Giant's left arm. May Day frolics were certainly associated with fertility; indeed, one sixteenth-century writer, Philip Stubbs, wrote: 'I have heard it crediblie reported by men of great gravity that, of an hundred maides going to the wood, there have scarcely the third part of them returned home again as they went.'

But folklore is a notoriously unreliable guide, and modern theories about the Giant's

The Cerne Giant nicknamed 'The Rude Man of Cerne'

identity depend on one crucial factor: the date when he was first drawn. The village of Cerne Abbas lies in an area scarred with the remains of ancient forts, henges and camps, and this has led some scholars to claim that the Giant must be a very old man indeed, cut perhaps in prehistoric times. But others think differently, and suggest that, by archaeological standards, he may be quite 'modern', dating from the seventeenth century. They have come to this conclusion by sifting through the reports of the surveyors, tax collectors and topographers who have chronicled the changing landscape of Britain over the centuries.

It is odd, if the Giant is ancient, that he is not mentioned in any document written before 1751. In that year, the Reverend John Hutchins, author of a guide to Dorset, wrote to Dr Lyttleton, Dean of Exeter, about a 'gyant delineated on the side of the Hill, facing the town, of vast Dimensions. . . .' It is stranger still that detailed surveys of the area, notably in 1356 and 1617, should have missed him. There is also nothing in the one set of documents that could hardly have ignored his presence, the parish records. Another telling argument advanced by the modernists is that it is hardly likely that so phallic a figure could have survived in a place like Cerne where there was an important monastery established in the sixth century AD.

Hutchins was certainly convinced of its modernity. In his letter to Dr Lyttleton he wrote: 'I have heard from the Steward of the Manor it is a modern thing. . . .' Moreover, both Hutchins and local legend agree that the Giant is, in fact, a lampoon, but they are divided on the question of his identity. The locals say he was cut in 1539 when the monastery was dissolved, and that he depicts Thomas Corton, the corrupt last abbot. The Giant's obscene appearance represents his lust, the club his desire for revenge, and the direction of his feet shows he is on his way out of the area. Hutchins, on the other hand, though he later decided the Giant was ancient, said that it ridiculed a local landowner,

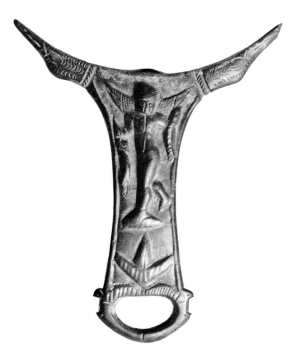

Bernard Pickard's skillet handle depicting Nodens

Lord Holles, whose servants rebelled against him, killed his son, and cut the figure on the hillside to mock him. However, there is no real evidence to connect either the abbot or Lord Holles with the Giant. The eighteenth century delighted in follies, and drawings of primitive men in early seventeenth-century books look very like the Giant, all of which reinforce the case for his modernity.

If, however, the Rude Man of Cerne is ancient, then he may portray a god. The question is, which one?

The first candidate is Nodens, a Celtic god thought to have been worshipped by the Durotriges, the tribe that inhabited Dorset before the Roman invasion of Britain in AD 43. The theory stems from a remarkable discovery made just 13 miles (21 km) from Cerne during the Second World War. A ploughman was ploughing a Celtic fort called Hod Hill near Blandford Forum when he discovered a hoard of objects, including a bronze handle, probably from a skillet or bowl, depicting a naked man. No sooner had the handle been identified by experts as Celtic and the man as Nodens, than the handle's then owner, Bernard Pickard, realized that he had seen him, or someone very like him, before: on the hillside at Cerne. Certainly there are marked similarities: the man on the handle faces forward but his feet are in profile, his nipples are clearly delineated, and in his hand he carries a knobbly club. There are differences too: the figure on the handle has wings and he holds a hare to symbolize his role as god of hunting, and his club is in his left hand, while the Giant's is in his right. Despite this, Bernard Pickard claims the handle provides enough evidence to say that the Cerne Giant may be Nodens.

The rival candidate from the ancient world is Hercules, and his champion is Professor Stuart Piggott. Part of the evidence Piggott cites is very circumstantial indeed, consisting of two cryptic quotations from old documents. The first comes from a statement by the antiquarian William Stukeley in 1764 that 'the people there give the name of Helis' to the Giant. The second crops up in a twelfth-century account of a famous visit to Cerne made six hundred years before by St Augustine. The visit did not go well, for Augustine and his followers, who had come to convert the villagers to Christianity, were chased from the place and cows or fish tails were tied to their clothes. The débâcle was reported by a later chronicler, Walter of Coventry, who mentions in passing that the god Helith was once worshipped in the area. Piggott points out the obvious similarity between the names Helis and Helith, and claims that they may have derived from the name Hercules, by way of the ancient version, Helethkin.

There is good reason for believing that Hercules was an important god in Roman Britain. Roman emperors had an egotistical tendency to identify themselves with great mythical heroes, and, in AD 191, the Emperor Commodus managed to establish a cult that worshipped him as the incarnation of Hercules. The cult flourished in Britain, and portrayals of Hercules on an altar found at Whitley Castle, Northumberland bear a close resemblance to the Cerne Giant. Furthermore, Stuart Piggott goes on to speculate that the Trendle, the curious earthwork above the Giant, may have served as a country sanctuary for the Hercules cult. The giant would therefore have been cut in about AD 191 as an icon or as a sign to summon the faithful to the hillside temple.

With so many theories, and so little evidence to go on, only new information will help provide the key to the identity and function of the Cerne Giant. One useful step may be to establish whether the Giant looked different when he was first cut. Although he was apparently scoured every seven years, the ravages of the weather or the encroaching grass can soon change or obliterate parts of chalk figures. Indeed, before the most recent scouring in 1979, the Giant had become overgrown and indistinct, and could have disappeared in a few years if its owners, the National Trust, had not called in a firm of building contractors to restore him.

There is a new scientific technique for discovering whether ground has been disturbed in the past. It is called resistivity surveying, and has already helped archaeologists in their search for lost features of hill figures. To conduct a resistivity survey, a scientist walks over the area he wishes to examine, carrying a set of electrodes on a frame. At regular intervals, he sticks the electrodes into the ground and passes an electric current through them. With a meter, he measures the soil's resistance to electricity. The basic principle is that soil which has been disturbed is looser and drier than the undug ground beneath, and is more resistant to the electric current. As a result, the disturbed areas give a high resistance, while that of untouched land is low.

The exciting part comes back in the laboratory: now the points where resistance is high can be plotted and joined up, as in a child's puzzle book, to see if they form a recognizable pattern. The technique is still in its infancy, and may do no more than pinpoint rocks or rabbit holes just below the surface, but it can also yield remarkable results.

The Long Man of Wilmington, near Eastbourne, Sussex

The Long Man of Wilmington

An early resistivity survey revealed some intriguing 'lost' features of Britain's other great chalk giant, the Long Man of Wilmington near Eastbourne in East Sussex. Like the Cerne Giant, the Long Man is cut in outline, in trenches 2 ft 4 in (71 cm) wide. He is 231 ft (70.1 m) tall, his legs look rather athletic, but his face is blank and his body quite sexless. The most striking thing about him is that he holds a staff about 240 ft (73 m) long in each hand. Even less is known about his early history than the Giant's, because no document before 1799 mentions him. A sketch made in that year shows the Long Man with a rake in his right hand and a scythe in the other, like a labourer setting out for the fields. But by 1825, if a local guide-book of the time is to be believed, the Long Man merely carried two staffs, suggesting that if they existed in the first place the rake and scythe-blade had been obliterated.

Certainly, the detailed shape of the Long Man may have been changed over the years, notably by a restoration in 1874, when he was given a permanent outline of 7,000 bricks. Mr K W E Gravett of the Sussex Archaeological Society decided to carry out a resistivity survey to discover whether the tops of the staves had in fact disappeared. Gravett and his companions, working on the steep slopes of Windover Hill, found it an arduous task, but the results of their two-day survey were unexpectedly rewarding. Their meter registered points of disturbance, not only at the tops of both staves, but also above the Long Man's head. When they joined up the points, the outline of something very like a rake appeared on the right-hand staff, a 'scythe-blade' on the other, and, on his head, a 'feather' or 'plume'. It is a fascinating discovery, suggesting the 1799 sketch may be the most accurate portrayal of the Long Man, but, even if the resistivity findings are verified by excavation, they fail to solve the central question of his purpose. In the hope of establishing whether the Cerne Giant's appearance has altered, we commissioned a resistivity survey from Anthony Clark of the Ancient Monuments Laboratory in London's Savile Row. Clark was the first full-time geophysicist to be employed in British archaeology, and was therefore uniquely qualified to do the work. If the Giant turned out to be carrying a hare, then the case for identifying him as the Celtic god Nodens would be strengthened; if, on the other hand, something like a lion skin were to emerge, Professor Stuart Piggott's theory that he is Hercules would win the day.

The survey began in July 1979 and, after two days' work, Clark and his assistant, Alister Bartlett, were already excited: their instruments showed that the ground round the Giant's arm and left hand had been disturbed, but the exact pattern of the disturbance must wait for computer analysis.

Many experiments and tests will have to be carried out before it will be possible to say with any certainty what, if anything, is there. Even if there is something by the Giant's arm it may be difficult to say it is definitely the shape of a hare or a skin but, in time, the mysterious Cerne Giant may, reluctantly, yield up part of his secret.

The Red Horse of Tysoe

The final mysterious British landscape figure is the Red Horse of Tysoe, which, at the moment, can be seen neither from the ground nor the air. It was once so prominently situated above the village of Tysoe in Warwickshire that the whole area was known as the Vale of the Red Horse, and the creature itself was dubbed 'The Nag of Renown'. The Horse was red because it was cut, not from

Graham Miller's photograph of October 1964 from which he discovered the Red Horse of Tysoe

chalk, but from the loamy soil. Now it has vanished, and the search for it has become something of a personal crusade for two local men, Kenneth Carrdus and Graham Miller, both retired schoolmasters.

Carrdus and Miller spent long hours in libraries and record offices before establishing, to their satisfaction, exactly where the Red Horse had been before its destruction by a pub landlord in 1800. The documents they had consulted led them to a slope near Tysoe called The Hangings. After several years and a dry summer, Miller photographed a patch of vegetation on the Hangings that had turned a different colour from its surroundings. The patch formed the head, neck and back of a gigantic horse. Later, aerial pictures revealed not only the ears, legs and tail, but also the outlines of two other horses: clearly there had been a succession of Red Horses cut at different times. Carrdus and Miller also chanced upon a map drawn in 1796 with the symbol of a horse on the spot they had found. According to their measurements, the Red Horse of Tysoe measured 200 ft (64 m) long and 250 ft (76 m) high. The problem was that many people could not clearly see the Horse's outline in the photographs and, despite a resistivity survey commissioned by Carrdus which confirmed his findings, some, though by no means all, archaeologists remain unconvinced. Carrdus and Miller, however, are satisfied that they have found what they believe to be the largest Anglo-Saxon work of art in Britain. Until they can convince everyone that it is there, the Red Horse of Tysoe will remain 'lost' beneath the young larches and Scots pines that today cover The Hangings. In the meantime, Carrdus and Miller, undaunted, are searching for another vanished giant, said to have been cut on Shotover Hill near Oxford.

Blythe's figures

With so many of the riddles of the British hill figures still unresolved after more than 200 years, it was perhaps too much to expect that archaeologists in the Americas would come to definitive conclusions about the drawings on their own landscape in a mere half century. The figures at Blythe in California are still a puzzle, although members of an expedition to them from the National Geographical Society in 1951 did, at least, come up with a theory. To the expedition leader, anthropologist Frank M Setzler, the presence of four-footed animals at two of the Blythe sites was a clue to their date. They looked like horses, and horses meant the figures were either very ancient or relatively modern, since the native American horse died out 10,000 years ago and its successor had not been introduced by the Spaniards until 1540. There was little erosion of the figures so Setzler opted for their modernity, and turned to Indian folklore for an explanation. He found a legend of a strange child called Ha'ak who grew to maturity in three or four years. When she began to eat their children, the Indians tried to kill her, and this deed was finally done by another strange figure called 'Elder Brother'. In Arizona, Setzler discovered a shrine depicting the overthrown Ha'ak, and concluded that the tradition had passed from tribe to tribe, and that the giants had been drawn between 1540 and 1850 by local Indians as a similar shrine. But this is one man's theory, and no one has explained why the Indians should have designed figures which, as Setzler graphically put it, 'only Gods or birds could grasp'.

The Nazca lines

In the Nazca desert in Peru, there are far more drawings and far fewer clues. The first person to make a detailed study of them was an American, Paul Kosok, who heard of the lines in 1940 while researching ancient irrigation systems. Like everyone who has since visited the area, Kosok was astonished by what he saw: thousands of lines fanning out across the desert, some ending on cliff tops, others heading for miles straight over mountains; there were gigantic triangles, trapezoids and rectangles. They had been made by clearing the top layer of dark-brown stones from the desert, revealing the lighter-coloured soil beneath. That was the only easy part of Kosok's investigation. After trying to trace the lines from the ground, he flew over them in an aircraft. Only then was he able to appreciate their true extent; as well as lines, there were giant drawings including birds, fish and even a monkey. Amazingly, each figure had been drawn with one continuous line, starting and finishing at the same point.

In the late 1940s, Kosok teamed up with Maria Reiche, a German mathematician and astronomer. She had come to Nazca to pursue a theory of Kosok's that the lines were astronomically aligned. Kosok had hit upon the idea when, late one afternoon, he and his wife saw the sun setting exactly at the end of one of the lines. It was 22 June, the day of the winter solstice in the southern

The mysterious lines stretching across the Nazca desert in Peru

hemisphere, and, struck by the coincidence, Kosok designated Nazca 'the largest astronomy book in the world'. He and Reiche postulated more alignments, believing they formed a calendar by which the local farmers could calculate when to plant their crops. The giant drawings, according to theory, represented the constellations.

Kosok died in 1959, but Maria Reiche has devoted her life to the study of the lines, living rough in the desert, tracing new alignments, and preserving them against the inroads of tourists.

But the key to the Nazca mystery was not as easily found as Kosok believed. In 1968, Gerald S Hawkins, the American astronomer who had used a computer to work out alignments at Stonehenge, came to Nazca to test the astronomical theory. He started with an assumption that had guided him in his work at Stonehenge. This was that the alignments would have to point consistently to one type of event like the rising or setting of the sun, moon or particular stars to have any real meaning. The purpose of all the lines must be explained in terms of the astronomical theory, because it would be unsatisfactory to explain the purpose of only some of them.

Hawkins first asked the computer to work out how many of the lines 'hit' extreme positions of the sun or moon. The answer— 39 out of the 186 included in the sample—was not a great deal better than would be expected by chance alone, and meant that far too many of the lines were left unexplained; moreover, only a few of the 39 alignments were along an apparently significant line. So Hawkins turned to the stars, feeding into the computer a catalogue of star positions dating back to 10,001 BC. Once again, the number of alignments with stars at any one period in ancient history was statistically too small to justify the claim that the Nazca lines formed an astronomical calendar. Hawkins had apparently proved that the Nazca lines were not a calendar. What, then,

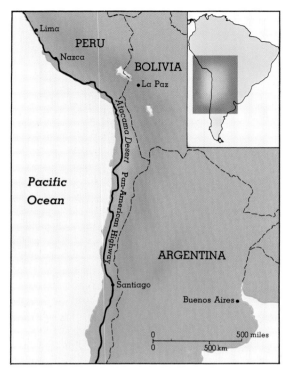

are they? Who built them and when? Could it all have been done without means of flight?

With the exception of Maria Reiche, no one has studied the Nazca lines with greater intensity than the English explorer and film maker, Tony Morrison. Since 1961, he has visited the area more than a score of times, and his travels in South America have given him a deep insight into the psychology and philosophy of its people. Morrison believes the lines are essentially religious in purpose, and from old documents and people who live in the Andes, he has established that there is a tradition of wayside shrines linked by straight pathways. The shrines, or *wak'as*, are often no more than a pile of stones, the paths, or *siq'is*, may be indistinct or even imaginary. Morrison thinks that the Nazca lines are sacred pathways linking shrines in the desert, and indeed evidence has been found of piles of stones which may represent these. The extraordinary pictures may have been icons and the great geometrical 'enclosures' places for religious meetings.

Above: Nazca and the Atacama Desert
Below: Maria Reiche cleaning 'Kosok's bird'

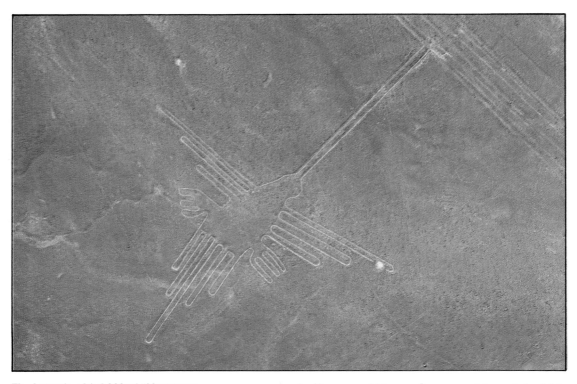

The humming-bird 100 yd (90 m) long

A religious interpretation of the Nazca lines provides a simple answer to the question of why they can only properly be seen from the air, as they would have been designed to be seen not by man but by the gods. If that were the intention, then the line builders succeeded admirably; the Pan-American highway was constructed right through the middle of the lines without anyone realizing. Morrison has shown that it is possible to construct straight lines over many miles, using a series of ranging poles, so the method of their construction is no mystery, and the birds and insects could have been made by scaling up small drawings. As it is, a great deal of nonsense has been written claiming that the lines were created by ancient astronauts who used the clearings as runways: an idea that deserves to sink into obscurity as quickly as spaceships would slump into the soft desert surface if they ever attempted to land at Nazca.

Yet one man has shown that the Nazca Indians could have flown, and has risked his life to prove it. Jim Woodman, a writer and publisher from Miami, is an old-style adventurer with an imagination to match his flamboyance. He spends much of his time in South America and, in 1973, decided to investigate the Nazca lines. As he flew over Nazca in a small plane, he set his compass on one line and followed it for 6 miles (9.7 km) without a single deviation even when the line passed over a mountain range. The experience convinced him the ancients had been able to fly. In the desert below, Woodman discovered the Nazca Indians had possessed two things that could have made flight possible: rope and finely woven textiles. With them, they could have built a hot-air balloon, powered by the heat from bonfires, traces of which Woodman believes he found among the lines, along with wood for fuel. The Indians could have used the balloons to supervise their handiwork.

Woodman's balloon, *Condor 1*, was made of cloth and rope copied from samples which had once been wrapped round the bodies of

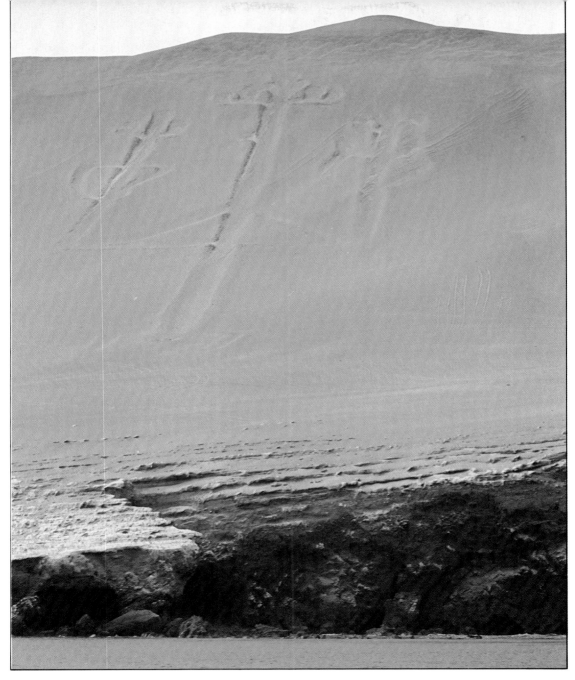

The candelabrum on the coast of Peru photographed by Tony Morrison

dead Indians buried nearby. The gondola was built of reeds from Lake Titicaca on the Peru-Bolivian border. At dawn on 28 November 1975, *Condor 1* rose into the clear blue sky above Nazca with Jim Woodman and the intrepid British balloonist, Julian Nott, sitting astride the gondola. At 300 ft (90 m), the 80,000 cu ft- (2,260 m³-) balloon levelled off, and Nott and Woodman ditched ballast and began their descent. Landing was the most dangerous moment, and the crew undid their safety harnesses 20 ft from the ground and jumped smartly off the gondola as it hit the desert. The flight had been short, but it had proved Woodman's point.

The Nazca lines are far from being the only drawings on the South American landscape. When the Spaniards first sailed down the coast of Peru, they saw a giant 'candelabrum' engraved on a place overlooking the bay of Pisco, and other explorers have found many other lines and figures in the Andes foothills. Soon after his balloon flight, Jim Woodman heard of a mountain, far to the south of Nazca, in the Atacama Desert in Chile, where, it was said, there was a mountain covered with lines, dominated by the giant figure of a man. The giant had been photographed only once from the air by a Brigadier-General of the Chilean Air Force. The photograph was indistinct, but it was enough to inspire Woodman to investigate further.

The vast geoglyphs in the Lluta Valley photographed by Jim Woodman

In the summer of 1979, Woodman journeyed through the glittering Atacama, a desert where it has hardly ever rained in all recorded history. On his way, he had stopped on the Pacific coast to see figures of warriors 300 ft (90 m) high staring out to sea, and a mountain covered with vast geoglyphs— figures outlined with stones—of llama trains, condors, spirals, circles and a flying man. The name of the mountain is Sierra Pintada —the Painted Mountain—and local archaeologists think the geoglyphs were signposts for Inca traders.

Finally, Woodman came to a mountain in the Atacama Desert known as Sierra Unica, the Solitary Mountain. On its slopes he saw the Giant of Atacama, 393 ft (120 m) long, staring at the sun. It is the largest representa-

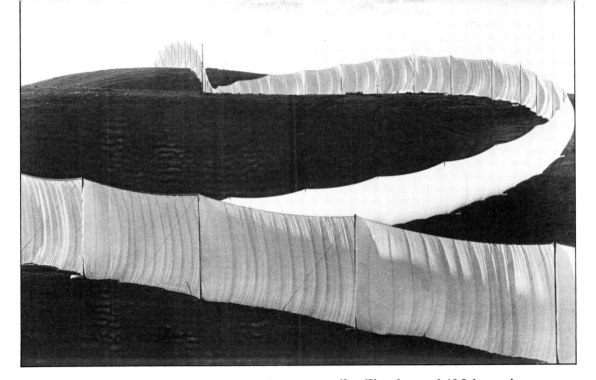

The artist Christo's contemporary counterpart to the drawings in the desert: 'Running Fence'

tion of a human figure in the world. On his head he wears a crown, his hand is an arrowhead, and there are boots on his feet. He is surrounded by a vast complex of lines and 'runways'.

Atacama is 850 miles (1,370 km) from Nazca, but it is the same desert. The lines, runways and even the giant may stem from the same culture, one which experts believe may have flourished at Nazca around the birth of Christ. It is too early to say whether they are related, but once again the questions posed in the green downlands of Britain, in the dusty deserts of California and in the foothills of the Peruvian Andes will be asked: what made people wish to draw so extravagantly on the landscape? Why did they do so, and when?

As for Jim Woodman, veteran of Nazca and now the Atacama, he knows the impossibility of finding real answers. Instead, when people ask him, as they often do, why men have laboured to make great pictures which only the gods can see, he replies with a smile: 'I'm damned if I know.'

Arthur C Clarke comments:

My earlier comments on circles and standing stones apply even more strongly here. The 'Nazca Lines' are certainly puzzling and impressive, but they may represent not much more than man's age-old desire to leave some record of his existence—'Kilroy was here' on a landscape-filling scale. The contemporary artist, Christo, has been doing exactly the same sort of thing with his 50-mile-long constructions.

And as for the figures of animals which can only be appreciated from an aerial vantage point—why should there be any mystery about this? Men have always peopled the sky with gods, and seen all manner of strange beasts in the patterns of the stars.

From this, it is only a short step—and a good deal of tedious but not difficult labour —to reproduce those patterns on the ground, perhaps in the hope of receiving celestial benefits.

Sorry, Herr von Däniken. The simplest explanation is often the right one. . . .

Of Beast and Snake

8

How tantalizing are the animals that still elude the traps and cages, the tranquillizing darts and the scientific classification of man. There is surely, still undiscovered, a great maned wolf which prowls the Andes mountains of South America, for we have just one magnificent pelt. Is there, too, a great ape in the Amazon forests? One extraordinary photograph suggests there is. Do those most dark and daunting jungles also hide giant anaconda snakes 100 ft long and as thick as a man's body? Twice the proprietor of the Bazar Sportivo in Manaus, Brazil, arguably the world's remotest photographic dealer, has processed film of such monsters.

The Tibetan blue bear, so strong that he can break the neck of an ox, has never fallen alive into the hands of Western man. But to see his mighty and luxuriant fur stretched out on a frame in a London saleroom conjures up as fearsome a picture as any of the wildest tales of the Himalayas.

Much closer to civilization, perhaps even on the outskirts of the cities of Australia, may lurk a great cat, call it the Queensland tiger or the Victoria panther. It would be as mythical as England's Surrey puma were it not that, in 1964, a sober lady from Melbourne produced a vivid snapshot of a striped and tigerish-looking creature, allegedly taken beside a road in the state of Victoria. Its ferocious antipodean cousin, the Tasmanian tiger, now extinct, certainly did exist, and there are those, including the London *Daily Telegraph*'s Melbourne correspondent, who claim to have seen it in recent years.

Nunda

Africa, still the dark continent, has the most chilling stories of fierce and aggressive animals unknown to the zoologist. Captain William Hichens, a British administrator at Lindi in Tanzania, told of an experience that would ordinarily summon up visions of lion-men and witch-doctors rather than a beast of the jungle. He writes:

'It was the custom for native traders to leave their belongings in the market place overnight, ready for the morning's trade and we placed a local constable there to keep watch. Going to relieve the midnight watch, an oncoming native constable one night found his comrade missing. After a search he discovered him terribly mutilated underneath a stall. The man ran to his European officer, who went with me at once to the market. In the victim's hand was clenched a matted mass of greyish hair, such as would come out in a violent fight. We found it obvious that the askari had been attacked and killed by some animal. Next morning a native governor of the district hurried into our office with two scared-looking men at his heels. They said that the previous night they had been at the market place when they were horrified to see a gigantic brindled cat leap from the shadows and bear the policeman to the ground.'

The men told Hichens it was the 'nunda' or 'mngwa', not a lion or leopard, but 'a big cat as big as a donkey and marked like a tabby'. The animal got another askari some nights later and then attacked other villages along the coast. Hichens, convinced it was a man-eating lion, made every attempt to kill it, without success. But when he sent the tufts

Right: the controversial photograph of the 'ape' taken by Francis de Loys in 1929

The elusive king cheetah photographed in 1975

of what he thought was mane for examination, it was returned with the remark: 'not hair but fur, probably cat'. Hichens was later to see an experienced native hunter brought in badly mauled by what he said was a mngwa. Another Englishman, Patrick Bowen, tracking a supposed mngwa after it had carried off a little boy, found that the spoor was not a lion's, but similar to that of a huge leopard.

All this might be dismissed as the heated tales of colonial Africa were it not that we now know there is, roaming the bush of Botswana and South Africa, but never captured, a king cheetah—living proof that we have not yet confined all the great cats of that continent. Paul Bottriell and his wife, Lena, are testament to the dedication needed in the quest for unknown animals. They have sold their house, staked their livelihood, in the pursuit of the king cheetah.

Huge, striped down his back like a tiger, and feared by the Africans as dangerous to man, unlike the ordinary cheetah, the Bottriells have proved their quarry exists. They possess vivid film and stills of a vigorous young male. They have identified his range along the Mozambique border. They have lain in wait for weeks, even quartered the country in a hot-air balloon, but they have been unable to pin the king cheetah down.

The pygmy elephants

Nor indeed is it only the cats which are elusive. The pygmy elephant has played hide-and-seek with the white hunter for more than half a century. An unfortunate Belgian officer, Lieutenant Franssen, became obsessed with the natives' assertions that beside the huge bush and forest elephant there was a tiny elephant that lived mainly in the rivers and marshes, indeed was almost aquatic, and hid on land in the thickest forest, where its small size allowed it to move freely. He set off with only some local helpers and disappeared into the jungle. Months later he emerged, already sick with the fever that was shortly to kill him, but bringing the hide and tusks of a miniature bull elephant. It stood just over 5 ft (1.5 m) high, though Lieutenant Franssen said it was one of the biggest in the herd, but it had the most impressive tusks, 2 ft 2 in (0.66 m) long. It could not have looked less like the massive elephants, more than twice that size, which roam the rest of Africa; the lieutenant died, that same year, confident he had found a new species of elephant. But although diminutive elephants have actually lived in the Bronx Zoo in New York, and in Antwerp, both were put down as freaks or dwarfs. The pygmy elephant remains a chimaera of the Congo forest.

The great dense green forests of Africa still taunt any zoologist bold enough to assert that they hold no more secrets. The traveller who flies in comfort to the capital

Kinshasa, of the old Belgian Congo (now the Republic of Zaire) takes a taxi into the city, and is overwhelmed with skyscrapers and office blocks, might be forgiven for imagining that Africa has surrendered to the urban onslaught of the twentieth century. Though across the river in Brazzaville, to go, to this day, on the witch-doctors' stalls within a mile of the Presidential palace you can buy gorillas' hands, monkeys' skulls and the venom of snakes. The price of crocodile steaks is controlled, and the adventurer is on the threshold of 1,000 miles of virgin forest. From Brazzaville in the Congo there are no metalled roads, not even to Pointe Noire, the country's port on the Atlantic coast. Only the extraordinary railway, built at the cost of thousands of lives by the French in the early years of the century, still makes a track through the jungle. It wends its way on one branch up to Gabon. The other line goes for 800 miles (1,290 km) to the Congo border and then across into the primitive forests ruled until recently by Emperor Bokassa. Bangui, the ramshackle capital of

The okapi

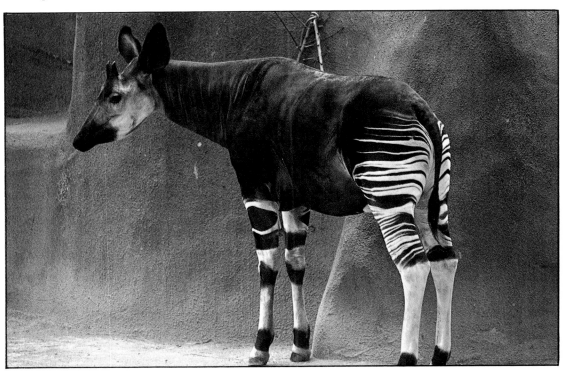

The giant panda discovered in 1937 by Mrs William Harkness and brought to Chicago

the Central African Republic, keeps the trees at bay, but beyond, until the forest fades into savannah and then desert, there is unexplored jungle. The traveller realizes it would be hopeless vanity to assume that no creatures could still be hiding where such large and unlikely animals as the okapi were found only recently.

The okapi, indeed is living proof that tales from the Africans of strange beasts in the forest cannot be ignored. For years their stories of a sort of giraffe that lived in the forest were dismissed until the okapi emerged to vindicate them.

South America has, if anything, even more unexplored terrain. True, the Trans-Amazon highway is now slashing its way across the continent, but for the animals, their retreat lies open all the way to the Andes. In the north, where Venezuela and Colombia meet, there are whole archipelagos of Lost Worlds, islands of rock and ravine rising up sheer for 3,000 ft (900 m) or more from the jungle floor. Here is the world's highest waterfall and almost perpetual clouds. So nearly impassable are these great outcrops with their crevasses and thick vegetation, so cut off by their steep cliffs from the jungles below, that it seems quite distinct species may well survive from the earliest times.

Across the world, this century has thrown up surprises for the zoo keepers of the West. In 1912 a pioneer airman made a forced landing on an island off Malaya, to be confronted with a huge real-life dragon: 10 ft (3 m) long or more with great jaws and a powerful tail, it killed and ate pigs, deer, even donkeys. This was to be identified as the Komodo dragon, a reptile preserved it seems from the era of the dinosaurs. Nor was it till this century that the biggest ape, the mountain gorilla, 700 lb (320 kg) and with a 9 ft (2.75 m) reach, was discovered. Only a few years before that, the biggest bear, the 10 ft tall 1,600 lb (725 kg) Manchurian brown bear, first faced a white man. The giant panda, known from a skin and pursued by all the most dedicated hunters and zoo collectors

in the Western world, still managed to elude them for more than half a century. It was not until 1937 that Mrs William Harkness, whose husband had died in the unsuccessful quest for the panda, finally found a baby one asleep in a tree in northern China and shipped it back to the Chicago Zoo, to the accompaniment of a ticker-tape welcome and the excited attention of the newsreel cameras.

In the last decade there have been finds, if less picturesque, then certainly as scientifically surprising. It is at least 8,000 years since a piglike creature called the Chacoan peccary, or, to give it its palaeontologist's name *Catagonus wagneri*, was thought to have become extinct. Its fossils had been found in North America among the bones of giant sloths and mastodons. But in the summer of 1975, Dr Ralph Wetzel of the University of Connecticut was in the scrubland of the Gran Chaco in Paraguay classifying the wildlife, and collecting specimens, when unknowingly he acquired evidence that the 'extinct' peccary still lived. For back home, as he went through the collection of skulls and

Wetzel's Chacoan peccary—a fossil come to life

skins brought back from Paraguay, he discovered the head and pelt of an outsize peccary, brought in by the locals. Wetzel soon established that his Chacoan peccary, which stood over 3 ft (0.9 m) high and weighed 100 lb (45 kg), was indeed a 'living fossil' identical to the extinct peccary. Back the following year in the Chaco, Wetzel found whole herds of his peccary which the Paraguayans were cheerfully shooting for the pot. Indeed it was to transpire that the hide of Wetzel's peccary had been on sale for years in Fifth Avenue furriers in New York, used for trimming coats and hats.

In Australia, also in 1975, a new little marsupial, a hamsterlike animal which brought up its young in a pouch like a kanga-roo, was discovered living in substantial numbers on the ranches of South Australia. But the challenges to conventional zoology are far more dramatic than either Wetzel's fossil or the marsupial from Down Under.

Great snakes

It is not without reason that the great snakes that squeeze their prey to death and then swallow them whole, the python, the boa constrictor and the anaconda, inspire a very special niche in our pantheon of terror. The dread scene in *Swiss Family Robinson* when the boa constrictor swallows the donkey has chilled many a child's bedtime reading: still more terrifying are the true stories of these reptiles consuming men. Only in 1972, an eight-year-old boy was eaten by a 20 ft (6 m) python in Burma. And it was from Burma in

A marsupial mouse discovered in Australia in 1975

A huge snake measuring 8.75 yd (8 m) and weighing 220 lb (100 kg)—a photo in a Pernambuco newspaper

1927 too that there came the most authentic tale of a jeweller called Maung Chit Chine who was out hunting in the Thaton district. During a rainstorm he sheltered, away from his companions, under a tree. He did not reappear. His friends eventually found just his hat and his shoes beside a gorged 20 ft (6 m) python. They killed the snake and opened it up. Inside was Chine's body, apparently swallowed whole, and feet first.

In 1979, a South African shepherd boy, Johannes Mokau, aged 14, was out with the sheep on a farm north of Johannesburg. Suddenly a python seized him by the leg and then coiled itself round his body. The boy was already dead and partly swallowed by the time farmworkers got to the scene and attacked it with axes and pitch forks. That python was a mere 15 ft (4.5 m) long, a tiddler compared with one reportedly killed by a group of Frenchmen and Brazilians in the Araguaya area of Brazil.

Zoologist Bernard Heuvelmans records their encounter with an anaconda as told to him by one of the Frenchmen, Serge Bonacase. They saw the snake asleep in the grass and fired at it.

'It tried to make off all in convulsions but we caught up with it and finished it off. Only then did we realize how enormous it was, when we walked along the whole length of its body it seemed as if it would never end. What struck me most was its enormous head, a triangle about 60 by 50 cm [24 by 20 in]. As we had no measuring instruments, one of us took a piece of string and held it between the ends of the fingers of one hand and the other shoulder to mark off a length of 1 m. We measured the snake several times and always made it 24 or 25 times as long as the string. The reptile must therefore have been nearly 23 m [75 ft] long.'

Even allowing a margin for error, this is immensely bigger than the largest snake ever captured and brought back to civilization, dead or alive. The Bronx Zoo in New York has had a reward of 5,000 dollars, now raised to 15,000 dollars, on offer since the 1920s for anyone who could produce a snake longer than 30 ft (9 m).

The measurement of snakes is a tendentious subject, for the skins can be stretched impressively when parted from their owners. On the other hand, making accurate assessments of living specimens is uncommonly difficult as they do not submissively stretch out along a tape measure and it is notorious that the well meaning observer can greatly exaggerate the size of snakes. The longest known living python of which there is a precise measurement has attained 27 ft (8 m), is called Cassius and resides at Knaresborough Zoo in Yorkshire, England.

Few experts will grant the possibility of snakes over about 35 ft (11 m). Even so it is hard to discount the evidence of some of the most respectable witnesses that true

141

A boa constrictor devouring an antelope

Another Amazon traveller George Gardner once found a dead boa in a tree, apparently carried down by floods. One of his friends Senhor Lagoeira had lost his favourite riding horse from a nearby pasture and when the boa was opened up, they found the bones of a horse including its intact skull. It seemed the horse had been swallowed whole. This boa was 37 ft (11.3 m) long, according to Gardner.

In the 1920s and 1930s priests were among the most intrepid of South American venturers. Father Victor Heinz twice saw truly gigantic water snakes. The first, on 22 May 1922, was on the Amazon. 'Coiled up in two rings the monster drifted quietly and gently downstream. Thunderstruck we all stared at the frightful beast. I reckoned that its body was as thick as an oil drum and that its visible length was some 80 ft.'

Seven years later he was again on the river when his crew gave a shout and another monster appeared, but this time it avoided them and crossed to the other bank. In 1930, one of Father Heinz's friends, Reymondo Zima, saw a snake that made such a wave in the river that it almost capsized their motor boat. It rose out of the water and performed what Zima calls 'a St Vitus dance' around the boat before departing 'at fabulous speed, leaving a huge wake larger than any the steam boats make at full speed.' But it was not until the 1940s that the first pictorial evidence appeared of a truly giant snake.

The *Diario*, the newspaper of Pernambuco in Brazil, of 24 January 1948 published a photograph under the headline 'Anaconda Weighing 5 tons'. The snake in the picture certainly seems to be of monstrous proportions, and the paper carried an account of its capture. A band of Indian halfbreeds was moving along the banks of the Amazon when they saw the snake engaged in its siesta. It had just swallowed a steer, the horns of which were still hanging from its mouth. The Indians got a rope round it and towed it down the river by tug to Manaus. It was there that Senhor Miguel Gastão de Oliveira, manager

gargantuans capable of swallowing a horse or overwhelming large boats survive in the South American jungle.

The famous Captain Fawcett, who was to disappear without trace up the Amazon river, himself killed an anaconda on the River Negro. He saw the head almost underneath the bow of his boat:

'I sprang for my rifle as the creature began to make its way up the bank and smashed a .44 bullet into its spine. At once there was a flurry of foam and several heavy thumps against the boat's keel, shaking us as though we had run on a snag. We stepped ashore and approached the reptile with caution. As far as it was possible to measure, a length of 45 ft lay out of the water and 17 ft in it, making a total length of 62 ft. Its body was not thick, not more than 12 in in diameter, but it had probably been long without food.'

of the local Banco do Povo, got hold of the photograph which he sent to the paper. Incredibly, he said, the snake measured 131 ft (40 m) and its body was nearly a yard across. Only four months later the paper, *A Noite Illustrada*, of Rio carried another photograph of a snake which had come out of the River Oyapock. The terrified locals had called the Militia, who had eventually slaughtered it with a burst of machine-gun bullets. The corpse was said to measure 115 ft (35 m).

But no skin or skull, let alone any live specimen, even approaching these dimensions has ever reached civilization. But then, as Serge Bonacase said: 'Who could prepare and carry such a huge skin through the jungle when it is hard enough to carry supplies for one's own survival?'

Loys' ape

Another photograph from the fastnesses of South America is at the centre of perhaps the most celebrated controversy in the zoological world. It was taken in the 1920s by a man of undoubted credentials, Francis de Loys B.Sc., D.Sc., F.G.S. He gave his own account in the *Illustrated London News*.

'I was exploring at the time the untrodden forests in the neighbourhood of the Tarra

Another great snake caught recently near the Amazon

River, itself an affluent of the Rio Catatumbo in the Motilones districts of Venezuela and Colombia, and I came across two animals the nature of which was new not only to myself but to the native woodsmen of my party. At a bend of a western minor affluent of the Tarra River these two animals broke upon the exploring party then at rest and, owing to the violence of their attitude had to be met at the point of a rifle. One of the two was shot dead at very close range; the other one, unfortunately wounded, managed to escape and disappeared in the jungle, the great thickness of which prevented its recovery. The animal shot dead was examined, sat into position on a packing case, measured, and immediately photographed from a distance of 10 ft. Its skin was afterwards removed and its skull and jaws were cleaned and preserved. The hardships met with by the party on their long journey across the forest, however, prevented the final preservation of either the skin or the bones.

'At first examination it was found that the specimen was that of an ape of uncommon size, whose features were entirely different from those of the species already known as inhabiting the country.'

Loys measured it as over 5 ft (1.5 m) high

A spider monkey. Sir Arthur Keith, FRS, identified Loys' 'ape' as a spider monkey

and estimated it to weigh well over 112 lb (50 kg). He said the ape was an adult female, covered in long greyish-brown hair, and, most importantly, it was 'entirely devoid of any trace of a tail'. The animal walked on hind legs on the ground.

The report and the photographs were sent by Loys to the famous French anthropologist, Dr Georges Montandon, who immediately declared to an astounded scientific world that it was an ape and called it *Amer-anthropoides loysi*. Hitherto no trace of an anthropoid had ever been found in the New World but Loys' find fitted neatly into the prevailing theories of the day—one of the missing links between the monkeys and the men of the Americas.

Since that day there has been unending dispute about what Loys shot. Almost immediately, in 1929, Sir Arthur Keith, Fellow of the Royal Society, went into print denouncing Loys' specimen with that refined venom of the English academic. After noting sardonically that Loys had contrived to lose the evidence and had omitted to take notes of the animal's characteristics or photograph it either from behind or with some object that allowed comparison, Sir Arthur picks on the *grand guignol* aspect of Loys' tale: 'The two animals advanced arming themselves with branches, and, I am sorry to relate, behaving shamelessly,' he advises readers of *Man* for August 1929, 'for they defecated into their hands as they advanced and threw their excrement at the invaders.' Sir Arthur's view that it was merely a large spider monkey, with the long tail either cut off or hidden, is still the opinion of primate experts like Dr Geoffrey Bourne. 'If it was genuine there would have been a man in the picture for comparison,' he says. Nettled by English scorn at his gullibility, Dr Montandon responded with Gallic vigour and produced what remains, fifty years on, a challenging case for his identification of Loys' monkey as a South American anthropoid ape.

First, Dr Montandon remembered that he had a cousin who worked for the Standard Oil Company in Tulsa, Oklahoma and demanded to be sent a petrol tin packing case similar to the one that Loys' monkey was propped upon. Cousin Montandon obliged and affirmed that such cases were absolutely standardized and were in use in South America. Then Dr Montandon got two stuffed spider monkeys and a compliant Frenchman and sat them on the packing cases at what he judged to be the same angle and distance as the original picture and took their photographs. The resultant quartet of portraits goes a long way to establish that whatever Loys' monkey was, it was not far off man size and appreciably bigger than its rivals. Montandon, displaying as much conservatism in the accompanying calculations as he could muster, reckoned the creature's height at 4 ft 2 in (1.27 m), the height of a seven- or eight-year-old boy and with proportions that made it more 'anthropoid' than a chimpanzee. The number of teeth too, he maintains—32 as reported by Loys—argues against the spider monkey. Unfortunately,

in the following half century, no other specimen has surrendered itself in the South American jungle to rescue Dr Montandon from his lone stand or Francis de Loys from the suspicion of a 'Piltdown Man'-style hoax.

The Queensland tiger

Perhaps the most unlikely of all the world's unknown animals seems to prowl the settled, almost suburban, areas of eastern Australia, Queensland and New South Wales. This is the Queensland tiger. He has certainly startled and indeed terrified a good many Australians. Mr George Moir, in 1972, saw two creatures rounding up his sheep. At first he thought they were dogs, but as he got nearer he realized that they were completely strange to him. He chased them in his pick-up truck. 'They did not run like dogs. They loped along with the front feet coming down alternately. It was like a canter. They were black all over, at least 2 ft high, with a long slender body, and a tail the same length. My fastest speed was 45 mph and I couldn't catch them. When we came to a fence one took it in his stride and the other, which was lagging crashed into the wire. It recovered quickly and climbed over like a cat.' Moir gave up the chase. Another farmer, Clive Berry, lost hundreds of sheep in the 1950s but failed to capture the predator. 'I am convinced this animal is some sort of cat. Dogs and dingoes grab a sheep anywhere and they don't mind roughing up the wool a bit. This animal's habit of cleaning the meat from the neck bones is similar to a domestic cat. It takes a big animal to clean the sheep right out as mine have been.'

There have been lots of eyewitness accounts. Mr L G Rentsch of Byaduk was mending a fence when he saw an animal some yards away. 'It was 3 or 4 ft high, a cat-shaped head and the coat was very long, about 6 to 8 in.' The animal stared at him, and then loped away.

A Queensland naturalist George Sharp, saw a 'large and dark animal with the stripes showing very distinctly'. Two film makers from Sydney, Dietrich and Patricia Strehle, were working in the McIlwraith Range.

'We had been virtually making our own road through sandy deep gulleys and stopped to inspect a washout ahead. Suddenly a black-looking beast leaped onto the track. Powerfully built, it was about the dimensions of a medium-sized dog, predominantly black, with a very long tail and distinctive catlike head. Bewildered, we watched as the creature made its way up a lightly timbered hill and disappeared over the crest. After twelve months of filming in Cape York we had never seen anything like it and it took a reference book to show that it could only have been the Queensland cat.'

As almost always seems to happen to film makers, they did not have their cameras ready.

One amateur, Miss Rilla Martin, did however, produce a picture of the Victorian tiger in 1964. The stripes, the tiger's head, the cast of the animal's action are undoubtedly reminiscent of the big cats. Certainly it resembles nothing among the known fauna of eastern Australia. Miss Martin says she noticed how fast the creature moved: 'It bounded off into the scrub at a tremendous pace.' Besides the photograph and the sightings, there are frequent reports of clawed-paw marks in many parts of the territory. In 1977 the Australian *Sunday Telegraph* published two pictures, said to be of animals from a pack of Australian 'tigers', eight or more, which were being kept under observation by conservationists along the New South Wales–Victoria border. One seemed to show a male and the other a female with a baby cub with its paws hanging out of her pouch.

A hint of an explanation for the Australian phenomenon is that such an animal might be related to the thylacine or Tasmanian tiger, which existed until after the settlement of Tasmania. The last known thylacine died in a zoo in the early part of the century,

but there are persistent reports that a pack still survives on the island and Dr Eric Guiller of the University of Tasmania has organized a series of searches. In 1979, two policemen near Derby in the northwest corner of the island joined the growing number of Tasmanians claiming to have seen the tiger. But they have been understandably apprehensive of going too close. The Tasmanian tiger, actually more wolf than cat, but with pronounced stripes, was a fearsome animal and certainly will be a dangerous beast to trap. Sir Richard Owen, the English anatomist, examined a skull and pronounced it, 'One of the fellest and most destructive of predatory beasts', for the teeth and jaws were awesomely powerful. It was about the size of a leopard or panther and, like so many Australian animals, was marsupial, carrying its young in a pouch on its stomach. It had two extraordinary teeth at the side of the jaws, 2 in (51 mm) long and apparently working across each other like the blades of a pair of shears. At one time the thylacine ranged most of Australia as well as Tasmania.

The Siberian mammoth

But perhaps the most enticing of all the prospects held out by the unexplored tracts of our earth, the impassable marshes of Africa, the remote tundra and forest of Arctic Russia, the isolated plateaux of South America, is that somewhere there may be some great undiscovered survivor of the prehistoric beasts that once stalked the world, a dinosaur, a pterodactyl, a brontosaurus, a hairy mammoth. In some ways their survival would be more credible than the bizarre and still unexplained story of their sudden extinction. What catastrophe could possibly have wiped out beasts so armoured and adapted for survival as the mammoth, especially in a region where man can have been at best a sporadic threat? Dr Wetzel found his three-foot-high peccary running round Paraguay in quite large numbers when the world thought it had been extinct since the last ice age. So too the coelocanth.

The 'extinct' Tasmanian tiger, perhaps a relation of the Queensland tiger

Crocodiles and many reptiles seem to have survived unchanged from the remotest eras. The Komodo dragon, 12ft (3.6m) long, voraciously consuming pigs, goats, whatever comes its way, and looking for all the world like a dinosaur, lived unknown to Western man on islands in the Indian Ocean until 1912, a true relic of prehistory. In the Pacific, John Blashford Snell's 1979 expedition found traces of the New Guinea dragon, probably even larger than Komodo.

The mammoth is a provocative case. This large prehistoric elephant inhabited Siberia in enormous numbers until certainly no more than ten thousand years ago. We know exactly what it looked like, for complete corpses have been disinterred from the ice in immaculate deep-frozen condition. When Professor N K Vereshchagin took a baby mammoth back to Leningrad in 1977 he was even able to tell what it had been eating when it had the misfortune to tumble down a ravine and be fatally trapped. The tusks of maybe as many as 100,000 mammoths have been quarried from the ice of Siberia in the last two or three hundred years, sufficient to provide a thriving ivory trade for the Yakuts and other tribes of the north. Whenever a whole frozen body emerged from the ice, the Yakuts' dogs would eat the ten thousand-year-old flesh, fresh almost as the day it died, while the Yakuts extracted the great curved tusks. The Yakuts certainly believed that the mammoths still lived, though they thought of them as gigantic moles that burrowed under the earth. The enigma of the mammoth's sudden extinction is put down by Professor Vereshchagin to an 'ecological catastrophe', a radical change in climate which turned the cold, dry and almost snowless weather of northern Siberia into a treacherous combination of heavy snow covering the vegetation in winter and warmer summers, creating swamps and thin river ice, cutting off small islands of land and leaving holes in the ground from melting ice to trap the animals. Certainly they died in their hundreds of thousands as the great mammoth graveyards of the north testify.

But there are those who cling to the hope that the mammoth might survive somewhere in Siberia. And there are two compelling stories of mammoths in historic and recent

The Komodo dragon discovered by Westerners on islands in the Indian Ocean in 1912

times. In the sixteenth century, a Cossack leader, Ermak Timofeyevich, sent to subdue the tribes beyond the Urals, reported that one of the first things his men saw were 'large hairy elephants' which the natives killed and ate and knew as the 'mountain of meat'. This was a hundred years or more before anyone had ever heard of the mammoth. Then in 1918 the French consul in Vladivostok, M. Gallon, met an elderly hunter with an extraordinary tale. Gallon questioned him closely and recorded his story:

'The second year that I was exploring the taiga, I was very much struck to notice tracks of a huge animal, a long way larger than any of those I had often seen of animals I knew well. It was autumn, not freezing yet. In one of these big clearings I was staggered to see a huge footprint pressed deep into the mud. It must have been about 2 ft across the widest part and about 18 in the other way, oval. The track went into the forest. Where it went in, I saw a huge heap of dung. Some 10 ft up the branches were broken, it seemed by its head.'

The hunter claimed to have followed the track for several days, until it was joined by another one and there was a trampled-down area as though of a romp or a fight. The hunter had only five ball cartridges left, when he seemed to be gaining on the animals.

'One afternoon it was clear enough from the tracks that the animals were not far off. The wind was in my face which was good for approaching them unaware. All of a sudden I saw one of the animals quite clearly. It had stopped among some saplings. It was a huge elephant with big white tusks, very curved; it was a dark chestnut colour. It had fairly long hair on the hind quarters, but it seemed shorter on the front. I must say I had no idea that there were such big elephants. I've only seen elephants in pictures but I must say that even from the distance of 300 yards I could never have believed any beast could be so big. The second beast was around.

I saw it only a few times among the trees, it seemed to be the same size.'

The description of a mammoth could hardly be bettered. Certainly, coming from an illiterate hunter it is uncannily accurate, particularly as it describes the mammoth as a forest creature at a time when conventional research still pictured it as exclusively a creature of the tundra and the snows. But, according to Professor Vereshchagin, the nearest thing to a mammoth in Siberia in this era were the elephants which, he regretfully recalls, were turned loose on the steppes by Genghis Khan after the capture of Samarkand. Left to fend for themselves they seem to have succumbed with great

rapidity. If modern man is ever to confront a mammoth it is more likely to be the result of the bizarre but feasible ambition of Russian scientists to 'clone' a mammoth from a cell taken from one of the frozen beasts and grow it to a mature live animal in the laboratory.

It is from those other impenetrable areas, the swamps of Africa, that such hints as there are of a living dinosaur have emerged.

The brontosaurus

The newspapers of Britain and the United States have had plenty of fun at the expense of dinosaur hunters, the most celebrated of whom was Captain Leicester Stevens who set off from Waterloo Station, London, in 1919 accompanied by his First World War trench dog and Mannlicher rifle in search of the brontosaurus and a million-dollar reward from the Smithsonian Institution in

The baby mammoth ten thousand years old, disinterred deep-frozen in 1977

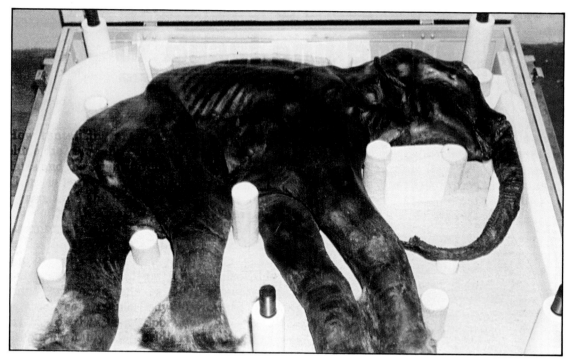

Dima, the baby mammoth, in the Leningrad museum

Washington. The captain disappeared into the Dark Continent and out of the newspaper columns never to reappear.

In 1932 a Swede, J C Johanson, an overseer in the Congo, published an account of a shooting trip in the Kasai. His boy had suddenly called out: 'Elephants!'

> 'There were two bulls, but about 50 yards away from them I saw something incredible, a monster, about 16 yards in length with a lizard's head and tail. Suddenly the monster vanished with an extraordinarily rapid movement. After my boy recovered, we set off across a big swamp. There the huge lizard appeared once more tearing lumps from a dead rhino. I could plainly hear the crunching of bones; I was only 25 yards away. Then it jumped into deep water. The animal's phenomenally rapid motion was the most awe-inspiring thing I had ever seen.'

Tallish as this story in the *Rhodesian Herald* appears, it is typical of a whole series

of stories about such a creature in and around the Congo basin. Carl Hagenbeck, the great Hamburg zoo collector, heard many stories of a creature of the swamps 'half-elephant, half-dragon'. An Englishman, Robert Young, was reported to have shot a 'chipekwe', as the monster was known, but it disappeared into the lake. Also in 1932, a Swiss, Dr A Monnard, took an expedition into Angola to look for the 'brontosaurus'. He came to the conclusion that there was indeed a very large reptilian creature, but it was probably just a very big crocodile. Such unpromising experience still does not deter a new generation of monster hunters. In 1980 Professor Roy Mackal of Chicago University was sufficiently convinced by the stories of a dinosaur-like creature in a lake in the northern reaches of the Congo to brave the new Marxist bureaucracy of Brazzaville and launch an expedition to cross-examine the pygmies, and persuade them to identify the creature from the flash-card pictures of different animals, living and prehistoric, which he had prepared, or even to lead him to the dinosaur's lair. Of such indomitable optimism is the coterie of 'unknown animal' hunters founded.

Arthur C Clarke comments:

An ancient philosopher was once asked the question: 'What is the most cunning of all the animals?' He replied: 'That which no man has yet seen.'

In this age of telescopic cameras, infra-red nightscopes, and aerial surveys, any large land animal must be cunning indeed to remain undetected. The remaining hideouts are the remoter mountains (see Chapter 1) and the dense tropical forests—now in full retreat from the bulldozers. There *must* be myriads of still unknown small creatures (insects certainly) in such places; and there may be some quite large ones. Yes—even 100-ft snakes . . . and there may be plenty of unknown animals in full view—but as they are taken for granted by the locals, no one has bothered to report them.

I have learned not to be sceptical about unlikely creatures. Many years ago, my mother (a lady with a rather vivid imagination) reported that one of the nearby farms boasted a flock of *four*-horned sheep. We all hooted in derision, so she promised to show them to us.

Mounting our bicycles, we made our way through the winding Somerset lanes and came to a hillside on which the flock was browsing. I can still recall walking up that hill, quite certain that mother would turn out to be mistaken. . . .

Well, when we got closer I saw to my astonishment that the sheep *did* have four horns—two large ones, two small ones. I'd never seen such a breed before, and have never seen it since.

I can't remember now if I ever apologized to mother.

9

The Great Siberian Explosion

The civilized world certainly had no excuse for ignoring perhaps the greatest and most mysterious explosion that has ever taken place on earth. In London, on that last day of June 1908, it was possible to read the small print in *The Times* at midnight. In Stockholm, perfectly sharp scenic photographs were taken in the middle of what should have been the admittedly brief northern night. In Heidelberg in Germany, bright shining clouds persisted till morning and in Holland it was quite impossible to take normal astronomical observations because of the brightness. The scientific instruments too gave plenty of notice. Half a dozen traces in London and other parts of England gave gigantic hiccups as first one shock wave and then a second, which had travelled completely round the world, shook the recording pens. Even in America the vibrations were felt. In European Russia, which was even closer to the event, the bright nights went on well into July and an extraordinary photograph was taken of the main street of the town of Navrochat at midnight which looked as though it was exposed in full sunshine.

Certainly some very powerful happening had taken place. A woman did write to *The Times* asking for an explanation; some golfers from Brancaster in southeast England also wrote to say they could have managed a round on the links at 2 am, and the director of the British Association drew attention to the hectic graphs recording the shock waves. But the world then entirely put aside, for nearly twenty years, what had in fact been one of the most cataclysmic events in all its history: an impact

Left: The 'mushroom cloud' of a nuclear explosion. The Tunguska explosion may have looked somewhat similar and it left 'radiation burns' on animals

that, if the earth had been just a quarter of a day further on in its spin, would have wiped out St Petersburg or, at a slightly different angle, London, or, half a day on, New York.

Today, more than seventy years later, it is still far from certain what it was that came hurtling out of the great interplanetary spaces and dashed itself against the earth in the remote and forested regions of far Siberia.

All the exotic phenomena of modern astrophysics have been considered in connection with the mystery. Was it that most demonic of manifestations, a black hole? Could it have been 'anti-matter' which the Nobel prizewinner, Paul Dirac, postulated lay somewhere out in the universe, that would annihilate anything it touched? Was it, as some argue, a crippled spaceship exploding as it entered the earth's atmosphere? Could it, thirty-seven years before the Hiroshima and Nagasaki bombs, have been an atomic blast? But, except for a few notes and reports by local people and papers in Siberia, all investigation had to wait half a generation while Europe fought a war, and Russia divested herself of a tsar, installed the Bolsheviks, and slowly and bloodily removed Admiral Kolchak and the White Russian forces who had taken possession of the vastnesses of Siberia.

Kulik's search
Only in 1921, with Lenin in power determined that the new Soviet Union should be a force in the scientific world, did the first faltering enquiries begin. The new Soviet Academy of Sciences commissioned a remarkable scientist called Leonid Kulik to collect information about meteorite falls on USSR territory. A friend gave Kulik a newspaper

clipping describing the event of June 1908. This said that a huge meteorite had landed near Filimonovo junction on the Trans-Siberian Railway.

> 'Its fall was accompanied by a frightful roar and a deafening crash. The driver of the train stopped in fright and the passengers poured out of the carriages to examine the fallen object but they were unable to approach the meteorite because it was burning hot.'

This one clipping, almost all of it fanciful —though an alarmed train driver had indeed stopped to have his locomotive and carriages examined—was to launch Kulik on a twenty-year quest. But when he died, killed by the Nazis during the Second World War, he had still not come to any clear conclusion as to the cause of the explosion.

Kulik began by gathering eyewitness accounts and collating other meteorologists' reports. The local papers of Irkutsk, Tomsk

Leonid Kulik, commissioned by the Soviet Academy of Sciences to collect information about meteorite falls in the USSR

and Krasnoyarsk had all reported the event. *Sibir*, the Irkutsk newspaper, described it as 'a most unusual phenomenon of nature'.

> 'In the village of Nizhne-Karelinsk in the northwest high above the horizon, the peasants saw a body shining very brightly (too bright for the naked eye) with a bluish-white light. It moved vertically downwards for about ten minutes. The body was in the form of a 'pipe' (i.e. cylindrical). The sky was cloudless, except that low down on the horizon in the direction in which this glowing body was observed, a small dark cloud was noticed. It was hot and dry and when the shining body approached the ground it seemed to be pulverized and in its place a huge cloud of black smoke was formed and a loud crash, not like thunder, but as if from the fall of large stones, or from gunfire, was heard. All the buildings shook and at the same time, a forked tongue of flame broke through the cloud. The old women wept, everyone thought that the end of the world was approaching.'

This village of Nizhne-Karelinsk, Kulik was eventually to discover, was 200 miles (320 km) away from the centre of the explosion.

A local meteorologist named Voznesensky had collected reports of the phenomenon and plotted the likely point of impact. Almost unbelievably, the crash had been heard 500 miles (800 km) away from its centre, and at that distance the seismic instruments in Irkutsk had registered a crash of earthquake proportions.

Kulik read of a 'fiery heavenly body', a 'flame that cut the sky in two' and a 'pillar of smoke'. One eyewitness account by Il'ya Potapovich was sent to Kulik:

> 'One day a terrible explosion occurred, the force of which was so great that the forest was flattened for many versts along both banks of the River Chambe. My brother's hut was flattened to the ground, its roof was carried away by the wind and his reindeer fled in fright. The noise

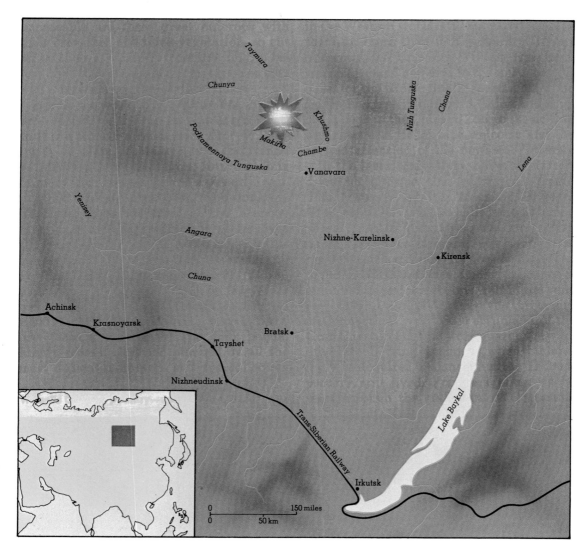

The Tunguska region of Siberia in which the 1908 explosion took place

deafened my brother and the shock caused him to suffer a long illness.'

Kulik's correspondent went on:

'As Il'ya Potapovich told this story, he kept turning to his brother who had endured all this. The latter grew animated, related something energetically in Tungusk language, striking the poles of his tent and the roof and gesticulating in an attempt to show how his tent had been carried away.'

Another witness, like Potapovich a Tungus from the Evenki people, was Vasiley Okhchen. He related how he and his family were asleep when, together with their tent, the whole family went flying into the air. He went on: 'All the family were bruised but Akulina and Ivan lost consciousness. The ground shook and an incredibly long roaring was heard. Everything round about was shrouded in smoke and fog from burning, falling trees. Eventually the roar died away but the forest went on burning. We set off in search of the reindeer which had rushed away. Many of them did not come back.'

A woman of Vanavara, called Koso Lapova, had been on her way to the spring for water.

'I saw the sky in the north open to the ground and fire pour out. We thought that stones were falling from the sky and rushed off in terror, leaving our pail by the spring. When we reached the house, we saw my father Semenov unconscious lying near the barn. The fire was brighter than the sun. During the bangs, the earth and the huts trembled greatly, and earth came sprinkling down from the roofs.'

There were tales of horses bolting with their plough in tow, of a man who felt his shirt burning on his back. Yet, miraculously it was to turn out that an impact which would have killed millions of people had it landed on one of the great cities or inhabited areas of the world, had not caused the death of a single person. Dogs and reindeer, and no doubt much wildlife, died. The local people's flour stores and houses were destroyed. The forest was flattened but no humans were even seriously injured. The event had taken place in one of the few parts of the earth where its effect on humanity could be almost negligible. Had it even crashed into the sea there would have been tidal waves as great as those which followed the Krakatoa eruption of 1883 that swamped huge areas and cost the lives of 36,000 people.

From all these accounts and newspaper reports and the assessment of the local Siberian meteorologists, Kulik still had only a vague idea of where this most awesome of explosions had taken place. And so in 1927, with the backing of the Academy of Sciences, he set out from Leningrad to see if, nineteen years after the happening, he could find the spot where the Tunguska meteorite, as he believed it to be, had fallen.

Kulik's odyssey was to last more than ten years, but, at last, after an epic series of journeys, worthy of the great explorers, he was to find the centre of the Tunguska explosion.

By March 1927, he had left the Trans-Siberian railway at Taishet and set off by horse and sledge over the snow towards the village of Dvorets on the River Angara. After a fortnight he reached Vanavara, the last settlement before he had to plunge into the uncharted Siberian forest, or taiga, as the Russians call it.

The vast, dark, daunting, immense taiga was a fearsome prospect in the 1920s. Even today, when the Russians have set down in the forest whole new cities like Bratsk, where the entire population seems to be under thirty years old, the taiga seems almost untouched. In the summer, paddle boats ply northwards up the River Lena and the Yenisey towards the Arctic Circle, but the settlements they serve cluster along the river banks, never far into the trees. Helicopters and small planes penetrate the isolated places where the Soviets have found minerals too valuable to be ignored. But when, for strategic and economic reasons, the Russians decided to build a new railway through the taiga, it was not mere propaganda that it was officially dubbed a Heroic Labour. The young railway volunteers dropped with tents into the virgin forest and had to start from scratch. Even with modern machinery, the ferocious cold of winter, the dreadful mud of summer, the constant sense that beyond the next 100 miles is another 1,000 miles just the same, debilitates the will and chips away at the courage. In 1927 with only horses Kulik found he could make no progress through the deep snow beyond Vanavara. He bought some reindeer and loaded his supplies onto them, recruited the same Il'ya Potapovich whose brother had been caught in the Tunguska blast, and set off again. Within two days they were having to hack a passage with axes through the dense undergrowth.

Finally, in the middle of April, the men reached the River Mekirta. It was a moment of wonderment. For as Kulik stood on the south bank and gazed towards the north, he saw the first extraordinary signs of the cataclysm that had now obsessed him for six years. On the north bank, there were a number of little hillocks above the general lie of the land. These little knolls stood out starkly against the sky. They had been stripped bare of trees. As Kulik got nearer he could see the great trunks of the fallen pines. Weirdly, they all lay like some annihilated regiment with their tops facing uniformly towards the southeast. Kulik knew that he was seeing the outermost victims of what must have been an enormous blast. Eagerly he climbed the highest of the ridges he could see, the Khladni Ridge as he was to call it. There was the most incredible sight. Stretching as far as he could see, at least 12–16 miles (20 to 25 km), was utter devastation. The huge trees of the taiga lay flat. Pines, firs, deciduous trees; all had succumbed. The sharp outlines of the winter landscape etched it like a plate. And again, this bizarre and unbroken regimentation. Slowly, as he surveyed the scene from the ridge, realization dawned on Kulik. Despite this devastation of almost unimaginable proportions, 12 miles or more of flattened forest stretching to the horizon, the trees still lay in only one direction. The centre of the blast must be even further away. The Tunguska explosion had been vast, beyond even the wildest reports that had filtered back to St Petersburg.

Kulik was anxious to press on to find the point from which the blast had originated but Potapovich and Okhchen, the two Tungus, flatly refused to go on. Kulik was forced to return to Vanavara to find new companions, and it was not until June that, using rafts to transport his equipment along rivers where the ice had melted, he managed to get back to Khladni Ridge. From there, following the line of the fallen trees, he pushed steadily north and west, until one day he came to a natural amphitheatre in the hills and pitched camp in the bottom of its bowl. The bowl was less than a mile across, so the next day Kulik set out methodically to survey the tops of the surrounding hills. He had to work his way almost completely round the circle before he could be certain of what he had found: all the fallen trees

Comet Kohoutek seen from Skylab in 1973. A comet remains the most likely cause of the Tunguska explosion though Kulik believed it had been a meteorite

faced outwards. This 'cauldron', as he called it, was the very centre of the Tunguska blast.

Among all the tribulations that were to follow, this discovery at least was to remain unchallenged. Whatever had caused the mighty Tunguska explosion—and Kulik now knew it had devastated 37 miles (60 km) in one direction alone—this was the epicentre. His own account conveys his excitement.

'I pitched my camp and began to circle the mountains around the Great Cauldron. At first I went towards the west, covering several kilometres over the bare hill crests; the tree tops of the windbreak already lay facing west. I went round the whole cauldron in a great circle to the south, and the windbreak as though bewitched, turned its tree tops also to the south. I returned to camp and again set out over the bare hills to the east and the

The forest flattened by the blast

windbreak turned its tree tops in that direction. I summoned all my strength and came out again to the south almost to the Khushmo River; the tops of the windbreak had also turned towards the south.

There could be no doubt. I had circled the centre of the fall. With a fiery stream of hot gases and cold solid bodies, the meteorite had struck the cauldron with its hills, tundra and swamp and, as a stream of water striking a flat surface splashes spray in all directions, the stream of hot gases with the swarm of bodies penetrated the earth, and both directly and with explosive recoil wrought all this mighty havoc.'

This first account makes almost heart-rending reading. For in his moment of triumph Kulik started to make assumptions that were to involve him in enormous and unrewarded labour and leave him at his death still unaware of the true nature of the explosion, still less what had caused it. For

Kulik took it for granted that a stone or iron meteorite had wrought all this destruction. In the 1920s even that was a brave enough assertion. For it was only a few bold spirits who were maintaining that such vast visitors from outer space could reach the earth and wreak great havoc. Daniel Barringer had bought the great 500 ft (150 m) deep Arizona crater in America specifically in order to prove it was made by an extra-terrestrial impact and was not volcanic as most people assumed. Barringer almost beggared himself in the quest, but he was to be justified. Devil's Canyon, Arizona, is a meteorite crater. But Barringer's discoveries in America led Kulik tragically astray in Siberia.

Almost immediately, in the Cauldron, Kulik thought he spotted places where the fragments of his meteorite must lie.

He wrote:

'The area is strewn with dozens of peculiar flat holes varying from several metres to tens of metres across and several metres also in depth. The sides of these holes are usually steep, although flat sides are also encountered; their base is flat, mossy, marshy, and with occasional traces of a raised area in the centre.'

The expedition's stocks, however, were so low by now that there was no time to investigate further. They set off back, living as best they could off the land. Once or twice they caught a fish, shot three or four ducks, or picked an edible plant called pukchi. Finally they made it back to Vanavara.

On the long journey back along the Trans-Siberian railway to Leningrad, Kulik had only one thought: to organize another expedition to find the meteorite which must, he felt, have been of enormous size. Its fragments must lie at the bottom of the 'peculiar flat holes'. Had he been a Siberian, Kulik would have known that these holes were in fact quite common in the taiga. They are apparently caused by ice forcing its way through the surface peat and then melting in the summer warmth, leaving behind

characteristic marshy depressions. But neither then, nor on his second expedition in 1928, was he accompanied by anyone knowledgeable enough to correct him.

Kulik's second expedition
Kulik had returned to Leningrad after his first expedition with his astonishing news about the size of the great explosion and he had no trouble, even in times of turmoil and austerity in the Soviet Union, in persuading the Academy of Sciences to finance further exploration.

It was this expedition that was joined by the cameraman Strukov from Sovkino and was thus to provide the vivid and engrossing film record we still possess. Strukov seems to have had all the virtues of the great documentary cameraman. When Kulik's boat overturned in some swirling rapids and the leader only just escaped with his life, Strukov kept filming. When the expedition reached its most difficult traverses, Strukov was there first to record it. The small human incidents, the cumbersome struggle to continue scientific work under

Strukov vividly captured on film the difficulties faced by Kulik on his second expedition

mosquito veils through clouds of swarming insects; it is all there. And when the moment came to film the first great panorama of destruction, he gives us epic sweeping shots.

This second expedition was beset with difficulties. Several members suffered from boils and vitamin deficiencies and had to go back. There was Kulik's accident. The magnetic survey seeking iron meteorites was unproductive and the party returned to Leningrad with little to show for their efforts except the graphic and exciting film. This was sufficient, however, to launch a third and much larger expedition the following year.

Kulik's third expedition

Once again the pictures provide an evocative record: the long horse-drawn baggage train, the exhausting task of manhandling boats across swamps and around rapids and shoals, above all the huge labour of cutting trenches and draining the 'peculiar holes', which was Kulik's main objective. The group stayed all the summer of 1929, then through the winter into 1930, saw Krinov, the deputy leader, lose a toe through frostbite while on a trek back for supplies, and another member go down with appendicitis. They put together a much more detailed picture of the devastation without greatly altering the impression gathered by Kulik on his pioneering journey. But of a meteorite they found not a trace. Slowly it was becoming apparent that this site was like no other on earth. Always before, fragments, large or small, often in their thousands, had been recovered from the ground. But at Tunguska there seemed nothing left whatever of the fireball itself. Kulik's team members were already beginning to suspect that their labours in the 'peculiar holes' in the swamp were futile. Krinov took a photograph of the tree stump they found at the bottom of one hole, proving it, at least, could not be a meteorite crater. But he hid the picture from Kulik. For the leader was now utterly dedicated to looking for a meteorite and he would consider no other possible cause of the explosion.

On this third long sojourn the team was also unable to carry out the aerial survey on which so much store had been set. The logistics proved beyond the capability of the Soviet fliers of those days. For more than eighteen months, Kulik and his helpers endured not only deprivation, but, in their principal goal, frustration too.

There now fell on the Soviet Union that dark era, known as the Great Terror. Literally no one was safe from denunciation, from exile or execution, as Stalin liquidated all the old Bolsheviks, almost all the senior officers in the Red Army, thousands of old party members, and sent millions of ordinary Russians to experience for themselves the rigours of the Siberian taiga and tundra in that frightful 'Gulag Archipelago' which Alexander Solzhenitsyn has described.

The fourth expedition

The sole task of any man in the Soviet Union of those days was to survive. For seven years the study of the Tunguska event was buried by more vital considerations. But in 1937, with all opposition to Stalin dismembered, the Terror seemed to ease a little and Kulik set off on his fourth expedition to Siberia

The tree stump that proved the explosion was not caused by a meteorite

with his main task to complete an aerial survey, and to search once again for fragments.

The most careful covering of the ground still produced not a sign of a meteorite, but the aerial survey of 1938 and the close examination of the trees, their burn marks, and the pattern of their fall did at last allow scientists to get some real impression of what had happened on that day in June thirty years before.

First, it seemed that the flying object had entered the earth's atmosphere and become visible somewhere over Lake Baykal and then travelled from southeast to northwest as it plunged downwards, though there was some suggestion that it might have changed direction. Indeed this thought, based on the eyewitness accounts, which now number more than 700, is one of the main planks of those who believe the object was a spaceship. Certainly only a controlled vehicle could have changed direction. No single witness claims to have seen the object actually manoeuvre. But there are sharp contradictions in reports of the flight path as the great bright 'pillar' careered across Siberia. Testimony in the more western area consistently gives a different angle of approach to that from the Baykal area.

What was beyond doubt after the aerial survey was the breathtaking extent of the destruction. More than 770 sq miles (2,000 km²) was devastated, an area as big as Birmingham, England, or Philadelphia. Yet within this enormous blitz, there were some very odd features. Right in the middle quite a large number of trees were left standing, though stripped of their branches.

Furthermore, despite all the diligent surveying, digging, boring, there was absolutely no sign that anything had actually hit the earth. There had been at least two blast waves, an explosion and a ballistic wave, there had been extensive though brief fires and some flash burns. But there was not a trace of impact damage. Curiously too, the new growth of trees seemed to be very much accelerated, compared with other young groups of trees in that part of Siberia.

The puzzle seemed greater than ever. But speculation and enquiry were soon again to be swept away as the Soviet Union was engulfed once more in the fires of war. The Nazi blitzkrieg took Hitler's forces to the very suburbs of Moscow. Kulik, though past fifty, volunteered to fight, was wounded, captured and died. Many others who had worked with him were also killed. The war in Europe ended, and then at the other end of the world came the apocalyptic moment which changed so many things, including in its small way the Tunguska story: the Americans dropped the atomic bomb on Hiroshima.

When a year or two had passed and scientists had time to turn again to the concerns of peace, several of the interested Russian researchers noticed the extraordinary similarity between the pattern of destruction at Hiroshima and the damage caused by the Tunguska blast.

At Hiroshima the first American observers noticed that right in the centre of the blast there was relatively little damage. Similarly, the trees had remained upright in the centre of Tunguska. Also, at Hiroshima the plants seemed to grow more quickly, as had the trees in the blast zone in Siberia. There was the same 'shadowing' effect where favourable contours in the ground seemed to protect people and objects even quite near the epicentre. Above all, that sinister symbol which had entered mankind's nightmare— the mushroom cloud—seemed uncannily like the description that the Tungus had given of a pillar of smoke going up into the sky. The Russian scientists already knew that the Tunguska cloud must have gone very high into the upper atmosphere, for it had been seen from great distances. They also noticed with some awe that the Tunguska explosion had been perhaps a thousand times as powerful as the Hiroshima bomb.

The similarities between Hiroshima and Tunguska were too close to ignore. Yet surely it was inconceivable that an atomic explosion had occurred in Siberia nearly forty

Nagasaki after the atom bomb (1945)

years before the physicists of the United States managed to create the first big bang at Alamagordo? But once the thought was planted other evidence came to mind. The blisters on the Tungus reindeer; were they radiation burns such as the cattle of New Mexico had suffered when the first test dust cloud hit them? Did the tree rings after 1908 show signs of radiation? The American scientist W F Libby thought they did.

As the evidence from scientific expeditions accumulated, from 1958 until the present day, uncanny echoes of atomic and thermonuclear explosions emerged. Dr Vasilieyev of Tomsk University, now one of the leaders of the Tunguska quest, is most emphatic:

> 'There have been the most violent genetic changes, not only in plants but in the small insect life. There are ants and other insects quite unlike anywhere else. Some of the trees and plants just stopped growing. Others have grown many times, many hundreds per cent faster than they were doing before 1908.'

Dr Vasilieyev says no evidence of abnormal radiation has been found. But then the tests were not done until 1960. He points out: What *is* there, is evidence of absolute electromagnetic chaos at the centre of the site. There was clearly an electro-magnetic hurricane of enormous proportions which has shattered, perhaps permanently, all the normal alignments with the earth's magnetic field.

And another strange symmetry with nuclear explosions has emerged. When the Russian, American and British H-bombs were tested in the 1950s it was noticed that they produced on the opposite side of the earth extraordinary bright aurora lights and disturbances in the ionosphere. As it happens, in 1908, the British explorer, Ernest Shackleton, was in the Antarctic at the magnetic opposite side of the earth from Tunguska. He was camped by the volcano Mount Erebus (which brought the Air New Zealand DC10 to grief in 1979) and his team recorded what now seem the most extraordinary display of aurora lights—though they occurred both *before* and *after* the Tunguska explosion. 'It is certainly odd,'

Tunguska after the 1908 explosion

says Dr Vasilieyev. 'I know of no other phenomena than the nuclear explosions which produce these displays at their magnetic opposite side of the world, though it could just be coincidence.'

One thing certainly became clear however. Whatever it was that descended on Tunguska had exploded, like the Hiroshima bomb, not on hitting the ground, but *in the air*. Soon the Doomsday scientists around the world, with the results of both Hiroshima and the H-bomb tests to work on, were even able to work out the height at which the Tunguska object had immolated itself; about 5 miles (8 km) up in the air.

But what could have caused the appearance of a nuclear blast almost before nuclear physics was born? The main material evidence that the new expeditions after the Second World War produced were tiny particles, little magnetite and silicate globules, buried in the soil and embedded in the trees. Both are definitely extraterrestrial. The magnetite contains too much nickel for

our earth. The silicate has little bubbles of gas similar to that known from spectrum analysis of space objects. The magnetic globules contain some very exotic rare earth elements including ytterbium.

These discoveries have done little to curb the enormous variety of speculation that has followed right up to this day. The authors of the 'spaceship' theory, who include eminent scientists such as Soviet Academician Zolotov, assume that the globules are the remnants of the ship, left after it vapourized. They marshal an array of factors in favour of their theory. Eyewitnesses, as well as suggesting the fireball changed course, often describe it as cylindrical or like a pillar. Then there was the odd irregular shape of the ground damage, like an outspread eagle's wings. A 'point' explosion should have been more circular. The outline might be accounted for if it took place in some kind of 'container'. Also it seems from some calculations about the trajectory of the object that it had been travelling in cosmic terms extremely slowly before it exploded—perhaps as little as one kilometre per second, hardly faster than some modern military planes and scarcely the onrush of some body from interstellar space. Above all, if the spaceship was nuclear powered and blew up all the other anomalies would be explained too. The spaceship lobby even have a theory as to what it was doing there. It was short of water and aiming for Lake Baykal, the largest body of freshwater in the world.

Scientists have not been slow to produce other exotic theories of their own. In 1973, A A Jackson and M P Ryan of the Center for Relativity Theory at the University of Texas decided that it must have been a mini-version of a black hole—the newly discovered phenomenon in the universe that seems to suck in and destroy matter that comes near it. With much elaborate calculus they even managed to show that their little black hole would have passed right through the earth and have come out on the other side, somewhere in the Atlantic between Iceland and Newfoundland. The Russians diligently sent for the local Icelandic and Newfoundland newspapers for 1908, even searched ships' logs, but found no trace of the Tunguska-like upheaval in the area which a black hole postulates.

Then some Americans became fascinated with the theory of anti-matter which would destroy ordinary particles if it came into contact with them. Again the scientific world was treated to high-powered calculus, this time from Clyde Cowan and Hall Crannell of the Catholic University at Washington and C R Atluri and W F Libby of the University of California in Los Angeles. They even devised a sophisticated procedure for investigating the enhanced radiation which ought to have followed an anti-matter collision, so far without result. So we are left with the current evidence showing the Tunguska object weighing hundreds of thousands of tons and perhaps 600 yd (550 m) across, exploding at a height of around 5 miles (8 km), causing unequalled devastation, genetic changes and electro-magnetic chaos, yet leaving behind only

tiny little globules of extraterrestrial metals, iron, nickel and cobalt as well as other little balls of silicate. For those scientists who could believe in neither an atomic bomb thirty-seven years too soon, nor a spaceship, there was only another daring thought, floated by an Englishman, F Whipple, and regarded for thirty years as far too fanciful. Perhaps that day in 1908, for the first time in recorded history, a comet had collided with the earth.

Comets are among the most romantic objects in the universe. Coming from the farthest corners of the solar system or even from interstellar space, they appear as magnificent stars with great incandescent tails hurtling across our skies, and have been taken since time immemorial as signs and portents, heralds of great events or looming catastrophes—even the end of the world. Some make their turn round the sun and disappear for ever. Others, like Halley's comet, which caused such a stir in the eighteenth century, return after long intervals. But we know very little about what comets are made of. They may be clouds of frozen gases preserved from the very earliest times of the creation of the solar system. This dirty snowball of gas and dust seems to melt as the comet flies past the sun, producing the characteristic shining tail. They may have much to tell us about the origins of the solar system, and the United States intended to try and fly a space mission to Halley's comet with a probe aimed right at the nucleus in 1986. But perhaps here on earth we already have some fragments of this rare creature—the magnetite globules and the traces of extraterrestrial matter found in the taiga. On that morning in 1908, by some freak of celestial navigation, a comet had perhaps strayed into the earth's gravitational field and dashed itself to death over Siberia.

Two British scientists, John Brown of Glasgow University and David Hughes of Sheffield University, have gone into the comet theory in the greatest detail and particularly into the two strongest arguments against the idea. First, if it was a comet, why did no one see it until the last minute? Secondly, how could a comet produce the appearance of a nuclear explosion? They point out that if it was a comet, coming low out of the dawn sky close to the sun, its brightness would have been hard to detect. They quote the comet 'Mrkos' which was only noticed after it had rounded the sun, passed the earth and was on its way outwards again. The Russians have questioned 120 observatories round the world and not even the two who could—perhaps should—have seen a comet on the Tunguska trajectory, Pretoria and Djakarta, have any record of a sighting.

As for the 'nuclear appearance', Hughes and Brown say that, contrary to what most believe, these nuclear effects can be produced naturally. It happens on the sun with solar flares. They say that a comet would explode when it met a mass of air equal to its own mass. This explosion would be in many ways similar to a solar flare producing radio activity. The great clouds of dust from the explosion, which brought the bright nights

Even in 1953, the effects of the explosion were still clearly visible as this photograph shows

half way across the world as they reflected the sun, may have been radioactive clouds as well—finally dumping their radioactivity as far away as America.

The explanation that a comet caused the Tunguska explosion, vapourizing itself five miles above the taiga, now holds sway among most scientists. Some even claim to identify it with the short-lived comet 'Encke', which is known to have skated across the earth's orbit around that time. A comet indeed seems the most plausible natural solution. But it still leaves some things unexplained. First, if it was a low-density comet, how did it penetrate the earth's atmosphere? All calculations suggest that it should have been stopped on the outer edges of the earth's atmosphere. Secondly, where did the coma, which encloses a comet's nucleus, get to? The tiny globules on the ground hardly account for the debris from a coma which can be 100,000 miles across.

The year 1908 was very strange. Tunguska, the white nights, Shackleton's aurora, the comet Encke, and in Japan, in July, a major meteorite fall.

In 1965 there was a pale hint of something similar over Revelstoke in Canada. Some

The Siberian taiga

cosmic dust was found after the locals heard a loud explosion overhead. But the Tunguska event, comet or no, spaceship, black hole, or anti-matter, remains unique. If it was indeed a comet, it is hardly a comforting thought. If a small comet, too tiny to see in the morning sky, can produce the destructive force of a 20 megaton bomb, what would a big one do? Worse, if the bomb doors of the solar system ever do open again, what chance is there that the great missile would again choose a target so conveniently barren as the remoteness of Siberia? Next time we can hardly be so lucky.

Arthur C Clarke comments:

Unlike many other events discussed in this book, there can't be much doubt that the Siberian explosion really happened. Even the most devout sceptic would find it hard to ignore a few hundred square kilometres of flattened forest.

The Tunguska event is awe-inspiring, and of great scientific importance. But it is no longer mysterious—except for those who prefer romantic explanations to common-sense ones.

The 'spaceship' theory is certainly stimulating, and worth taking seriously; however,

its proponents seldom mention that it is based on a science fiction story by the Russian author Kazantsev, published in 1946. Not that this disproves the theory, of course: and recently the idea has been used again in Donald R Bensen's excellent 'alternative history' novel *And Having Writ* . . . (In which, among other delightful touches, the descent of an alien spaceship off San Francisco leads to the election of Edison as a somewhat Nixonian President of the United States.)

Unfortunately (?), all the evidence in favour of this theory collapses when it is examined in detail. For example, much is made of the fireball's apparent change of course just before impact. However, no eye-witness could possibly give an accurate description of such a terrifying event: for proof of this, see the cases quoted in Chapter 10, where re-entering space vehicles 100 km up were mistaken for cigar-shaped vessels, with portholes, skimming the rooftops!

There is now not the slightest reason to doubt that the Tunguska body was a very small comet, perhaps consisting largely of ice (see comments in Chapter 2). Why wasn't it seen well beforehand, as comets usually are? Because it was in the day sky—on the sunward side of earth—and therefore invisible in the solar glare.

There is a close association between comets and meteors, and as far as I am concerned the Tunguska mystery is settled once and for all by a piece of information I've just discovered in Dr J G Porter's *Comets and Meteor Streams* (1952).

Not until the development of radio astronomy was it found that there are streams of meteors which had never been discovered, because they appear only in the daytime sky. One of the most prominent—the β-Taurids, first reported by Lovell and his colleagues in 1947—meets our Earth as it sweeps along its orbit at the same time every year. And it does so on *30 June*—the very date that the Tunguska object hit Siberia in 1908! It may well be that the daylight hours of every 30 June represent an abnormally high meteor hazard. . . .

But perhaps the most important lesson from Tunguska is that what happened once *will* (not *may*) happen again. Almost all our planetary neighbours bear evidence of repeated bombardments from space. Mercury, Mars, the Moon, the satellites of Jupiter, show meteoric scars sometimes *hundreds* of kilometres in diameter. The only reason why it has taken so long to recognize such stigmata on our own planet is because weathering, and geological processes, have largely obliterated them.

Early in 1980, American scientists produced evidence that the extinction of the dinosaurs, some sixty-five million years ago, was triggered by the impact of a heavenly body far larger than the Tunguska object. Perhaps that gave us a chance to evolve; and perhaps a similar event will open the way to our successors.

It may not happen for a million years. Or it may happen, as I wrote in *Rendezvous With Rama*, much sooner:

'At 09.46 G.M.T. on the morning of 11th September, in the exceptionally beautiful summer of the year 2077, most of the inhabitants of Europe saw a dazzling fireball appear in the eastern sky. Within seconds it was brighter than the sun, and as it moved across the heavens—at first in utter silence—it left behind it a churning column of smoke.

Somewhere above Austria it began to disintegrate, producing a series of concussions so violent that more than a million people had their hearing permanently damaged. They were the lucky ones.

Moving at fifty kilometres a second, a thousand tons of rock and metal impacted on the plains of northern Italy, destroying in a few flaming moments the labour of centuries. The cities of Padua and Verona were wiped from the face of the earth; and the last glories of Venice sank forever beneath the sea as the waters of the Adriatic came thundering landwards after the hammer-blow from space.

Six hundred thousand people died, and the total damage was more than a trillion dollars. But the loss to art, to history, to science—to the whole human race, for the rest of time—was beyond all computation. It was as if a great war had been fought and lost in a single morning; and few could draw much pleasure from the fact that, as the dust of destruction slowly settled, for months the whole world witnessed the most splendid dawns and sunsets since Krakatoa.

After the initial shock, mankind reacted with a determination and a unity that no earlier age could have shown. Such a disaster, it was realised, might not occur again for a thousand years—but it might occur tomorrow. And the next time, the consequences could be even worse.'

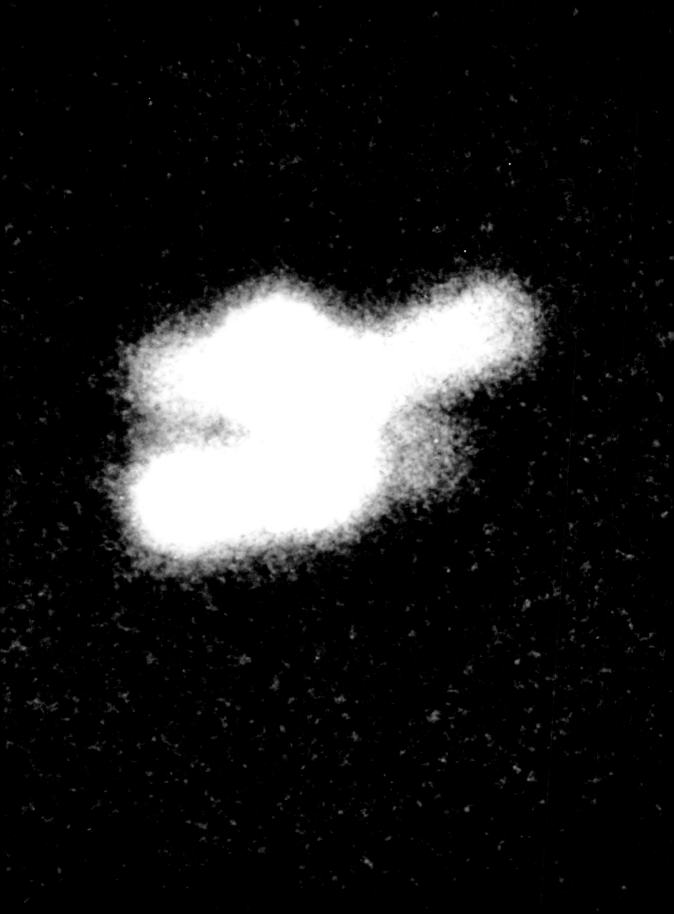

10

UFOs

On 18 January 1979, Britain was experiencing what the newspapers were calling a 'winter of discontent'. A series of strikes coupled with blizzards over the New Year had caused hardship throughout the country. For a few hours that evening, however, the House of Lords, the august but unconventional Upper House of the British Parliament, turned from the depressing affairs of the moment to consider a controversy that had been raging outside its neo-gothic chamber for more than a generation.

At seven minutes past seven that evening, the Earl of Clancarty rose to begin an eagerly awaited House of Lords debate. The subject on the order paper was UFOs, Unidentified Flying Objects.

The timing of the debate was impeccable. All over Britain, strange lights had been seen in the sky on New Year's Eve, and some eyewitnesses had described a flaming spacecraft, complete with brightly lit portholes, flying eerily over the snowy midnight landscape. In Italy, UFO sightings had reached near epidemic proportions, with newspapers and television headlining the 300 yd (275 m)-long fiery craft spotted by naval officers rising out of the Adriatic, and the photograph of a UFO taken by a policeman in Palermo. On the other side of the world, in New Zealand, a shaken Australian television reporter and his film crew described a terrifying night flight alongside a UFO, and, only hours later, the airwaves of the world were alive with their remarkable film of the event.

Lord Clancarty, author of several books on UFOs and well-known in Britain for his

Left: the Russian satellite Proton said to have been reported as a UFO by American astronauts

contention that there are holes at the Earth's poles which could serve as UFO bases, initiated the debate. He had two requests to make of the British government. First, he wished it to prepare its citizens for the coming of UFOs, and to allay what he said were the fears of many people that it was in league with the United States to 'cover up' the truth about Unidentified Flying Objects. Secondly, Lord Clancarty called on the authorities to press for a worldwide governmental study of UFOs, so that the results could be passed on to the public, and he also wanted the Minister of Defence to appear on television to discuss the British government's own assessment of the phenomenon.

It was a provocative start to a debate that had moments of sublime eccentricity. One peer, for example, revealed that he had received a visit from his guardian angel during his childhood, and he also produced this charming explanation for the existence of many of the world's unexplained phenomena:

'I have always thought that just as a mother, when baking bread, leaves a little of the dough over in order that the children may make funny little men with raisins for tummy buttons and put them into ovens and bake them alongside the bread or the cake for the day, so possibly on the day of creation a little of the Divine creative power was left in reserve for the lesser cherubim and seraphim to use and they were allowed to make funny little objects like the Abominable Snowman and the Loch Ness monster. . . .'

There was no lack of jokes, including one described by a speaker as the only known joke ever perpetrated by a Soviet function-

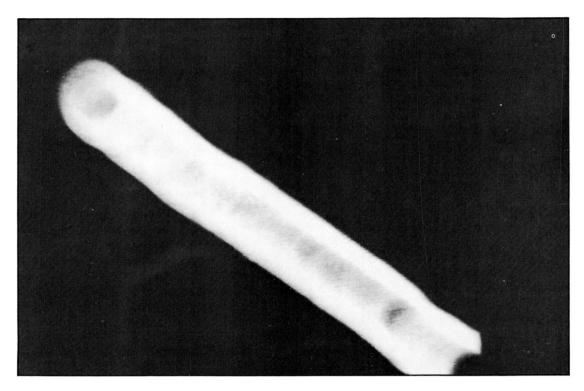

A police picture of a UFO over Palermo, Sicily,
14 December 1978

ary, namely Mr Gromyko, who, when asked what he thought about flying saucers, said, 'Some people say these objects are due to the excessive consumption in the United States of Scotch whisky. I say that is not so. They are due to the activities of a Soviet athlete, a discus thrower, in eastern Siberia, practising for the Olympic Games and quite unconscious of his strength.'

It was, nonetheless, a significant debate, not in the sense that it achieved anything in the way of legislation or that the government of the day agreed to any of Lord Clancarty's requests, but because the speakers who took part in it voiced arguments and counter-arguments which have been echoed on many occasions and in countless books, television programmes and newspaper stories.

Many of the speeches in the House of Lords' debate began with a potted history of the UFO phenomenon. The Earl of Kimberley, for example, maintained that 'UFOs are not products of the twentieth-century imagination. They have been observed here for years—by the North American Indians, by the monks of Byland Abbey in 1290, who were terrified by the appearance of a huge silver disc.' Lord Kings Norton, a self-confessed sceptic, quoted an extraordinary machine which the Prophet Ezekiel claimed to have seen in the heavens, while Lord Clancarty recalled the strange lights, then known as 'Foo fighters' which Allied and German pilots spotted around their planes during the Second World War.

Kenneth Arnold
However, no history of UFOs is complete without mention of a man who now lives in retirement in the American city of Boise, Idaho. His name is Kenneth Arnold, and it was an experience of his that led to the coining of the phrase 'flying saucer' and, thereafter, to the belief held by millions of people today that the earth is being regularly visited by alien spacecraft.

As many peers pointed out in their speeches, Kenneth Arnold earned a kind of immortality because of something he saw on 24 June 1947.

On that day, Kenneth Arnold had finished a job at Chehalis Airport in Washington State. There was time to spare before he needed to return home to Boise, and he therefore decided to spend an hour or so on his return journey searching for the wreck of a Marine C 46 aircraft that had crashed in the area of Mount Rainier in the nearby Cascade Mountains earlier in the year. A reward of 5,000 dollars had been offered for its recovery, and Arnold, a founder member of his local search-and-rescue team, felt he had a good chance of finding it, especially as his own aircraft was specially equipped to fly in mountainous areas.

Just before two o'clock that afternoon, Kenneth Arnold took off from the airport and flew towards the 12,000 ft (3,660 m) mountain. A first sweep over a glacier on the southwest side of the mountain yielded no trace of the lost aircraft, so Arnold turned over the small town of Mineral, Washington, and flew slowly back for a second look:

'A terrifically bright flash hit the sky and it lit up the inside of my airplane, lit up the wings, and it actually lit up all the area around me, almost like an explosion, only it was a bluish-white flash. Now this was in the middle of the afternoon. I'm flying at the mountain with the sun at my back: in other words, I had wonderful visibility and at that altitude the whole world below you looks like a giant swimming pool. It's very distinct, and it was a beautiful bright day. Anyhow, I had assumed quickly—I suppose in a matter of a split-second thought—that some military boy with a P51 had dove over my nose, and the sun was reflecting from his wings back on to me. And I looked all around and couldn't see anybody, and then the flash hit again, and then, of course, I looked off to the left in the vicinity of Mount Baker. And here comes a chain of very peculiar-looking aircraft. They were flying rather erratically, but they were flying, I knew, at a tremendous speed.'

The Earl of Clancarty

Kenneth Arnold

Arnold, an experienced pilot, used to assessing sizes, speeds and distances from his pilot's seat, automatically, tried to establish the main features of the strange craft.

'I estimated their wing-span as being at approximately a 100 ft span at least, and probably a little more. They were flying quite close to the mountain tops, and actually, they were flying at my altitude because they were on the horizon to me, and, being on the horizon, I knew that their flightpath was approximately 9,200 to 9,500 ft. They were approaching Mount Rainier very rapidly, and there were nine

UFOs photographed over Conisbrough, Yorkshire, by Stephen Pratt on 28 March 1966

of them in number. I think there were five in the lead. There seemed to be a little gap between the five and the other four.'

To the mystified Arnold, they certainly did not look like any military or civil aircraft he had ever come across: especially as most of them appeared to be round and without a tail. He saw them clearly against the snow, and they appeared to be silvery coloured on top, and black at the bottom. Their mirrorlike finish would account for the flashes of light which had first caught his attention. The way they flew was also odd: 'They would dip and kind of flutter and sail.' They were in formation, 'in a kind of diagonal chain-like line', but it did not conform to any known military line-ups

Kenneth Arnold knew of. From his knowledge of the topography of the Cascade Mountains, he was also able to make two astonishing calculations: not only was the column of craft 5 miles (8 km) long, but they were travelling at at least 1,200 mph (1,930 km/h), in an era when aircraft were lucky to clock 600 mph (965 km/h).

Fearing that he might have spotted an unknown Russian weapon on a foray into American airspace, he reported his sighting when he touched down at Yakima to refuel. Later, when he got to Pendleton a small crowd was waiting to greet him on the airfield. News had already come through that Arnold had seen something extraordinary, and everyone wanted to ask questions. The story did not leak out to the rest of the world, however, until a local press man, to whom Arnold had told his story, alerted his colleagues, and a press conference began which lasted for three days. When the local UPI bureau chief asked 'How did they fly?', Arnold delivered a reply that, thanks to the reporter's skill in turning a neat phrase, was to add a new term to the English language. 'They flew', Arnold said, 'like you'd take a saucer and skip it across the water, and it would flutter erratically. Only, these things kept going.' When the UPI story appeared in print, the headline splashed the words 'Flying Saucers', and despite the fact that Arnold was keen to point out that he had not applied this description to the craft himself, those two words captured the public imagination and started a worldwide craze.

It is difficult now to say why Kenneth Arnold's story should have caused such excitement. It may be that the public had become well conditioned to the idea of visits from extraterrestrial beings by Percival Lowell's theories of a Martian civilization, or by the books of Edgar Rice Burroughs which they inspired. This certainly seems to have been the case in 1938, when extraordinary panic gripped many Americans in the wake of Orson Welles' radio version of H. G. Wells' *War of the Worlds*. It may be that the success of German rocketry in the Second World War

had convinced people that space travel was now possible. Perhaps the newspaper reports of Kenneth Arnold's sighting and the specific details he gave persuaded people to look at the sky for the first time, and provided a context in which they could discuss anything they saw which they could not easily explain. Where people in the nineteenth century, for example, had 'seen' new planets, comets or even heavenly visitations, they now saw flying saucers.

UFO sightings

Since then there have developed two schools of thought about UFOs: believers, and those who thought there was something strange and unexplained in the sky, but not necessarily alien spacecraft. Thirty years later, when flying saucers had become UFOs and 'Ufology' had, in some eyes, assumed the status of a science, these views were reflected in the House of Lords debate. Although many speakers preferred to occupy the middle ground, the arguments of the believers were advanced by Lord Clancarty in his opening speech. His main concern was that it was impossible to doubt the existence of UFOs because they had been seen by so many sincere and ordinary people. In addition, many trained observers, such as pilots, coastguards, police officers and radar operators had also seen them. So had at least eight astronomers. The UFOs came in all shapes and sizes: sometimes they were like cigars, sometimes they were oval, disc-, sphere-, doughnut-, crescent-, or tadpole-shaped. Many of them were illuminated with very bright lights, which often changed colour and occasionally burned people who came into contact with them. Most significantly of all, he maintained, he could provide examples of many impressive sightings that could not be explained away.

In 1954 the BOAC Boeing Stratocruiser *Centaurus*, on a flight from New York to London, encountered a bright object accompanied by six smaller ones. When the aircrew reported this to the authorities on the ground, fighters were sent up, but the objects disappeared when they got near. Eight members of the crew saw the phenomenon, and fourteen of the fifty-one passengers. On another occasion, UFOs hovered for thirteen days near the missile-stocked Strategic Air Command Bases in the American states of Michigan, Montana, North Dakota and Maine: UFOs which, when interceptor planes were sent to investigate, dimmed their lights and disappeared. Finally, Lord Clancarty told the extraordinary story of the large UFO seen over Tehran, the capital of Iran, in the small hours of a February morning in 1978. It was seen by hundreds of people. When an Iranian Air Force Phantom jet tried to investigate, its communications and instrument systems broke down and it had to return to base. A second jet gave chase, but as it closed on the UFO, a smaller UFO emerged from the original one and headed for the Iranian fighter. The pilot tried to release an AIM-9 air-to-air missile but, once again, none of his instruments worked. As the pilot dived to escape the smaller UFO, it returned to the 'mother ship' and the Phantom's equipment started working again. Eventually, the UFO moved away.

The UFO filmed over Kaikoura in the eastern region of New Zealand's South Island which 'shone with a very bright white light'

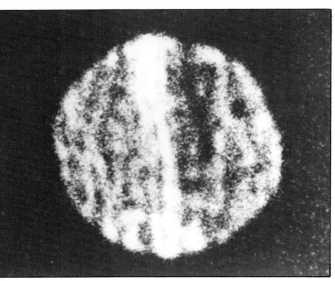

Sightings like those reported by Lord Clancarty, witnessed by people with unimpeachable credentials, and which cannot be explained in terms of known phenomena, are the mainstay of the UFO believers' case. Among other convincing accounts of sightings is the famous New Zealand sighting of 30/31 December 1978. In this instance the UFO was not only spotted by eyewitnesses and tracked by radar, but was also filmed.

The story, briefly stated, is this. On 30 December 1978, a film crew led by an Australian television reporter, Quentin Fogarty, took off from Blenheim Airport in South Island, New Zealand, on a flight to Wellington. They were aboard the flight—a newspaper delivery run—because Fogarty had been asked by his office in Melbourne to investigate a UFO which had, apparently, tracked another plane down the coast for some 12 miles (19 km) a few nights earlier. At around midnight, they encountered some bright lights above the town of Kaikoura, on the northeast coast, and Wellington radar confirmed that they too had been picking up unidentified targets in the area. While the amazed reporter taped a commentary, the cameraman managed fleetingly to capture some of the lights on film. On the return journey something even more remarkable happened: a bright object, which the cameraman described as having a brightly lit base with a sort of transparent dome, appeared on the starboard side of the aircraft. When the pilot headed for the object, it kept its relative distance from the plane, and then, when the pilot returned to his previous course, it sped in front of the aircraft, to the left, and then disappeared beneath it. Once again, ground radar confirmed unidentified targets in the area.

As soon as the film was shown on television throughout the world, astronomers were offering explanations. Some suggested that the film crew had seen meteors, others a planet—Jupiter and Venus were the favourites—and yet others maintained that atmospheric conditions had caused the

Nancy Hawes

lights of a Japanese fishing fleet in the area to be reflected in the sky. At the time, they seemed quite plausible explanations, but an impressively detailed examination of the film and of the eyewitnesses leaves the case still wide open. It was conducted by a US Navy optical physicist, Dr Bruce Maccabee. In his lengthy report, he considers all the explanations advanced but none of them provides a convincing answer. For example, he was able to dispose of the planetary explanation by showing that Venus was not yet visible when the sightings were made, and that other planets were not bright enough and in the wrong direction. Similarly, the Japanese fishing fleet was, among other things, too far away for its lights to have been seen by Fogarty and his colleagues.

In an attempt to bring some order to the thousands of UFO reports that come in every year, an American astronomer, Dr J Allen Hynek, has invented categories of sighting: close encounters of the first, second and third kind. Thanks to the feature film of the same title, close encounters of the third kind—actual meetings with humanoids or aliens—are the best known but are very rarely reported, and are hotly disputed when they are. The New Zealand UFO falls into the first category, since it was what Hynek calls 'a close-at-hand experience without tangible physical effects' on the

observer. These are undoubtedly the commonest occurrences, but UFO advocates can point to many examples of the second category, which, according to Hynek, entails 'measurable physical effects on the land and on animate and inanimate objects'. One such, from the Moses Lake area of Washington State, has received little publicity, despite its extraordinary nature.

One night in August 1965, Mrs Nancy Hawes and her sons Philip and Cliff were asleep in their house a few miles from the township of Moses Lake. Mrs Hawes' husband was away on business in Canada, and she was therefore terrified when, at half past two in the morning, she heard a sound like a bell ringing somewhere above her head, and a loud commotion from outside, made by her dog and the horses, which were in the neighbouring field. The whole house was filled with a strange bright light. For some reason, which she is unable to explain, Nancy Hawes did not look out of the window, but, instead, checked that her children were still asleep before returning to bed. The next morning, a neighbour's child came to play with the Hawes children: their favourite pastime being to go into the paddock where the horses were and dig for arrowheads dropped there in the past by Indians. When the boy, Philip Evans, reached the field, however, ahead of the Hawes boys, all thoughts of searching for arrowheads were abandoned, for there, on the ground, were giant footprints leading for 150 ft (46 m) from a bowl-shaped depression in the ground, before turning back again. There were also marks which looked as though they had been made by a tripod.

Although the ground was hard, the footprints had sunk several inches into the soil. When the boys measured them, they found they were all 22 in (56 cm) long, and what Mrs Hawes calls the 'leg positions' were all 18 in (46 cm) in diameter. The strides were 6 ft (1.8 m) long on the 'outward journey', and 10 ft (3 m) long on the 'return'. Mystified, Mrs Hawes called the local police who could offer no plausible explanation for the marks on the ground, or for the ringing sound (Mrs Hawes had already established it had not been made by her alarm clock), the wild behaviour of the horses in the middle of the night, or the strange light that had filled the house. A team from the nearby Larsen Air Force Base was also called in, but they too were baffled according to Mrs Hawes.

Even more disconcerting was the rough treatment experienced by a forester working for the Livingston Development Corporation in Scotland on Friday 9 November 1979. At ten o'clock that morning, Bob Taylor was making a routine check of woodland outside the town, when he turned a corner in the forest and was transfixed by the sight of a large metallic cone sitting in a clearing. Bob Taylor says:

'I just came round this corner and I was amazed to see this vehicle sitting there. I was just rooted to the spot. It was like a huge spinning top, 20 ft or so wide and the same in height with a huge flange right round about it. There was a rod sticking out of this flange with what I took to be blades on top and portholes behind those blades going right round the dome.'

Suddenly, two balls with long, spiked supports raced towards him from the UFO. He blacked out, and when he came round— he cannot tell how much later—his trousers were ripped and he had a bad headache. He felt 'drained of energy', but was eventually able to struggle home after abandoning his van at the roadside. His trousers had been ripped in a strange fashion—with long upward tears in the strong fabric, his thighs were scratched and there was an unpleasant taste in his mouth, similar to the smell he remembered just before blacking out.

Once again the police were called and they photographed a 15 ft (4.5 m) diameter ring of 'spiked holes'. The holes themselves were 4 in (100 mm) deep and 3½ in (8.8 mm) in diameter. But neither the police nor Bob Taylor, who had worked at Livingston for sixteen years, could solve the mystery.

Since the number of UFO reports is increasing all the time, as Lord Clancarty pointed out, the case advanced by the people who believe that UFOs are extraterrestrial craft discreetly spying on earth seems to be a strong one, and it has certainly inspired many costly investigations. In the early days, soon after Kenneth Arnold's original sighting, the US Air Force began the first of several enquiries into the possible existence of the phenomenon. This was 'Project Sign', which, in turn, led to 'Project Blue Book' in 1949, and, finally, to the Condon Committee, which reported in 1969. While all these committees were unable to explain certain cases, they were also unable to establish the existence of UFOs as alien spacecraft. Today, the French government has based a small team of investigators known as *Gepan* in Toulouse, and at least one private organization, Project Starlight International of Austin, Texas, is monitoring UFO reports with sophisticated equipment. In California, a teacher operates special classes for hopeful people on what to do if they meet an alien, and in France an airfield was specially laid out to welcome extraterrestrial visitors before closing after several years due to lack of business.

UFOs: mistaken identity

However, many people still remain unconvinced, despite the weight of 'evidence' from the sightings. Certainly, among the speakers in the House of Lords debate, there were many sceptics. Lord Trefgarne, for example, declared that he had flown for many hours as an aircraft pilot across the Atlantic, and yet he had never seen a UFO; Lord Kings Norton was of the opinion that many were of terrestrial origin, like aircraft, satellites and rockets, and that those of extraterrestrial origin were phenomena like meteorites or the Northern Lights; while Lord Hewlett had consulted the noted astronomer Sir Bernard Lovell, who had told him that, not only had his telescope at Jodrell Bank never picked up a UFO in thirty years, but that the skies were littered with pieces of broken rocket as well as natural debris. While the UFO believers feel they have a strong case, the sceptics also feel there is much to justify their stance. Their main platform, as the subject matter of many of the speeches referred to above makes clear, is that the vast majority of people who report seeing UFOs are not lying but are merely mistaken.

The sceptics point to many cases of this type. Among the more comic stories of mistaken identity was that of the two Englishmen who were reported in the newspapers as having seen 'a large illuminated dome' near their home in Nottinghamshire. But, when local UFO investigators looked closely, they decided that the mysterious object was no more than 'a brown and white cow in the moonlight!'

Mistakes can be made by the most reliable people. Consider this account culled from a UFO sighting questionnaire completed by a man from Atlanta, Georgia in 1973. He said that, at about 7.15 pm Eastern Standard Time one evening in October 1969, he had seen a UFO appear from the west, 'about thirty degrees up'. It was brighter than the background of the sky, and, at one time, was 'as bright as the moon'. Its size varied 'from brighter/larger than planet to apparent size of moon'. It 'came close, moved away—came close then moved away.' It was 'maybe 300–1,000 yards [274 m–914 m] away'. But when an energetic UFO sceptic, Robert Sheaffer, re-examined the evidence, the mystery was quickly exploded, for Sheaffer established that since the eyewitness had been with members of the Leary, Georgia, Lions Club on the day in question, the date of the sighting must have been 6 January 1969. When he examined star charts for that night, taking into account the witness's statement of the bearing and elevation of the object he had seen, Sheaffer was able to conclude, beyond all reasonable doubt, that what the man had seen was the planet Venus. It might seem odd that anyone should have taken the trouble to establish the true identity of a 'UFO' seen many years before,

Venus: 'Queen of UFOs'

but this one had become an important pillar of the UFO lobbyists' case, because the eyewitness happened to be Jimmy Carter, later President of the United States.

Venus is so often mistaken for some sort of spacecraft, that she has been called the 'Queen of the UFOs'. A well-earned title if the following passage from a characteristically wry article by the eminent British intelligence expert and physicist R V Jones is anything to go by. He wrote:

'My own contact with the subject goes back to about 1925, when I was told at Oxted in Surrey of a bright light that slowly made its way across the sky every night. In fact, I knew of one married couple who sat up all night to watch it. It was Venus, which had attracted them by its brilliance; they never before noticed that all the planets and stars seem to move across the sky. Venus, indeed, has caused much trouble through the years. In 1940 or 1941 there was an alarm that the

Germans had a new high-flying aircraft, because this was what was reported by the predictor crew of an anti-aircraft battery somewhere, I think, in the Borders. The aircraft, they said, was showing a light and they had determined its height with their rangefinder. The answer was, as far as I can remember, 26,000 ft and we wondered how they had managed to get such a precise measurement. Investigations showed that this was the last gradation on their range scale and that what they had tried to range upon was, once again, Venus. The same explanation has been true of several flying saucers that have come to my attention in the north of Scotland; it has sometimes been possible to predict the nights on which reports would come in, depending on whether or not Venus was bright and visible.'

In fact, almost anything that flies in the sky has been mistaken, at one time or another, for UFOs. One sceptic, Donald H Menzel, even went so far as to make a list of 'selected examples', which range from material objects in the upper atmosphere like rocket firings and ionosphere experiments, through clouds, blimps, migrating birds and aircraft landing lights in the lower atmosphere, to paper kites, spiders' webs, feathers and parachutes in the very low atmosphere, and lighthouses, weathervanes, reflections from windows, and icebergs on or near ground or sea level. Menzel also listed meteorological phenomena like noctilucent clouds, sun- and moondogs, and ball lightning; astronomical manifestations like planets, meteors and comets; physiological effects like after-images from street lights or even matches; eye defects like astigmatism or myopia; or the results of psychological problems like hallucinations.

Individual researchers have been able to make out convincing cases for explaining some UFO reports in terms of hitherto-unsuspected natural phenomena. For example, Philip S Callahan and R W Mankin, two employees of the US Department of Agriculture, Agricultural Research Service at Gainesville, Florida, showed in laboratory experiments that swarms of insects can be lit up by the phenomenon known as St Elmo's fire while flying into high electric fields brought about by thundery weather conditions. They then went on to demonstrate a correlation between a wave of UFO sightings and insect infestation in the Uinta Basin, Utah between 1965 and 1968. They showed that the UFOs had appeared at a time when an insect called the spruce budworm was infesting trees in nearby forests, and, since individual spruce budworms had emitted St Elmo's fire in the laboratory tests, Callahan and Mankin suggested that swarms could have appeared as shining UFOs in stormy conditions.

Sceptics also point to a large body of explained sightings which are the result, not of mistaken identification, but of hoaxes, misreporting or fraud. One of the best sustained UFO hoaxes of all time was perpetrated by two schoolboys in Sheffield, England, in 1962. They claimed to have taken what the newspapers hailed as 'the world's best UFO snap' of five craft in the sky over the Sheffield suburb of Mosborough. For the next decade, it was a prize exhibit in the UFO supporters' case, until one of the boys, David Brownlow, confessed in October 1972 that they had merely photographed a piece of glass on which they had painted five saucer shapes. Interestingly, not only was the original publication of the boys' picture followed by a spate of UFO sightings in the area, but the hoaxers were quoted as saying that they had found it difficult to persuade people to believe them when they admitted the joke. Similarly, much play is made of reports that NASA astronauts have sighted UFOs on space missions. The stories received such wide circulation that James Oberg of the Johnson Space Center in Houston, a diligent and sceptical investigator, examined all the quoted cases, and found none of them to have any real substance. Many of the

Right: Lenticular or 'flying saucer' cloud

stories had been simply made up, while others had become distorted in the reporting. For example, Jim Lovell and Edwin Aldrin were said to have seen four UFOs linked in a row during their Gemini 12 flight on 11 November 1966. In fact, Oberg discovered, they knew what they were seeing: they had been talking about four bags of trash which they had thrown overboard an hour earlier. That same year, on 12 September, astronauts Richard Gordon and Charles Conrad were said to have reported a 'yellow-orange UFO' several miles away, which turned out, on investigation, to be a Russian satellite, Proton 3, and not an alien spacecraft.

The case of the UFO spotted at Runcorn in Cheshire, England, on New Year's Eve 1978 is, however, rather different. That day, Dominic Valdez had spent the afternoon arranging chairs for a party that was due to be held that night at the school where he is caretaker. At about seven that evening,

The drawing of the flying saucer seen by Stephen Darbyshire over Coniston, Lancashire, 4 February 1954, made before his photo was developed

his sister, Mrs Veronica Scantlebury and her husband arrived to go to the party. Mr Valdez and his children had gone out to greet them, when Mrs Scantlebury, who had just got out of the car, said 'My God! What's that?' There, about 1,500 ft (460 m) up in the sky above the terraced houses on the other side of the street, was a brightly lit craft which looked like no aircraft any of them had ever seen. It was a cold, clear night. Both Mr and Mrs Scantlebury and Dominic Valdez watched the craft for at least a minute and a half and were able to remember it clearly. The craft had shining portholes, was cigar-shaped, and flames seemed to be coming from its tail. A different kind of light shone from its nose. It moved silently on what seemed to be a straight course, and appeared to be so low that it looked as if it might crash onto the rooftops. It was an eerie experience, but mystifying though it was, it was not an alien spacecraft. It was, experts were later able to explain, the remains of a Russian rocket which had launched a space satellite, COSMOS 1068 on 26 December. Its descent to

Stephen Darbyshire's photograph developed *after* he had made the drawing for his father who had at first been sceptical

earth was reported by many people (including Lord Gainford in the House of Lords debate) before it crashed near Hanover in West Germany.

It is very reminiscent of a celebrated instance in 1968, when on 3 March UFOs were reported from at least nine of the United States. The Air Force was besieged with calls, and some eyewitnesses maintained that the craft they had seen had had lit-up windows, others that it looked like a 'long jet airplane'. The Air Force, however, was unruffled, as a few inquiries established the nature of the strange, fiery object. It, too, was a Russian spacecraft, this time a satellite called ZOND IV, which, instead of reaching its planned orbit, plummeted to earth in burning fragments. An interesting facet of this case was that the reporting, though graphic, tended to be inaccurate, with eyewitnesses maintaining, for example, that the craft flew low or skimmed the trees, when ZOND IV was, in fact, 75 miles (120 km) up in the sky.

Sceptical arguments of this kind were put forward by the British government spokesman Lord Strabolgi when he rose to wind up the House of Lords UFO debate after three hours of discussion. He bluntly stated the position, as he and his colleagues saw it: 'There is nothing to convince the Government that there has ever been a single visit by an alien spacecraft, let alone the numbers of visits which the noble Earl, Lord Clancarty, claims are increasing all the time.' To advance his argument, Lord Strabolgi posed a series of questions which, in one form or another, are put by all UFO sceptics. Assuming, for the sake of argument, that there were an advanced civilization elsewhere in the universe, with the technology to enable travel over the vast distances of space, 'What', he asked to begin with, 'is the point of this alleged huge number of visits to our planet, over three decades or more, to no apparent purpose?'

'There seem to be internal inconsistencies

in the idea. To put it simply, if these alleged aliens prefer to keep out of the way, the number of reported sightings would surely be only a tiny proportion of the actual UFO movements, which would run into many millions. If they do not prefer to pass unnoticed, we could surely expect unmistakable appearances.

'Why have they never tried to communicate with us? Why has there been no evidence on radio of attempts at communication? And would not such a large number of movements be picked up by our defence radar system? Why has not a single artifact been found? Assuming that each visit does not represent a journey from a distant star, where are these alien spacecraft supposed to be hiding?'

Lord Strabolgi did not rest his case there, however. He went on to describe all kinds of natural aerial phenomena that have been mistaken for UFOs, concluding that:

'There really are tens of thousands of strange things to be seen. It is the custom to call such phenomena "UFOs", and to transpose this easily into "alien spacecraft". The appearance is too fleeting and the description too imprecise for a particular cause to be attributed. All we can say is that there is a great variety of plain explanations. There is no need, I suggest, for the far-fetched hypothesis of alien spacecraft.'

And so saying, Lord Strabolgi, on behalf of the British government, rejected Lord Clancarty's plea for an investigation into UFOs, and was also at pains to explain that there was no 'cover up' of the truth. While UFO reports were analysed to see if they contained anything of defence interest, he explained they were only kept confidential because of the identities of the people who had reported them.

At the end of this debate, nothing more concrete had been achieved than the setting up of a House of Lords UFO Study Group and an airing of views. However, the speeches had highlighted the crucial problem confronting each side. The believers, for all their accumulation of sightings and analyses of eyewitness reports, and for all their conviction that UFOs must exist, have yet to produce indisputable evidence of a sighting after more than thirty years of intensive study. Still, as one of their favourite slogans goes, absence of evidence is not evidence of absence, and the sceptics are, for their part, faced with the impossible task of proving for certain that something does *not* exist. Whatever their views, it would be surprising if, as they left the Houses of Parliament on that January night, believers and sceptics alike did not glance up into the sky for a moment and wonder.

Arthur C Clarke comments:

Every few years I find myself writing an article: 'Last Words on UFOs'. (For the previous last words, see *The View from Serendip*.) Well, here we go again.

I have now observed so many UFOs that the subject bores me to tears, and I wouldn't cross the street to see another. Having said that, I hasten to add that in every single case my UFO eventually turned into an *Identified* Flying Object. Almost every one would have fooled most laymen: a couple fooled me for a while, and I consider that I have some expertise on the subject.

The last specimen I saw is one of the best: It was late afternoon and I was standing in the shadow of my Colombo house, pointing out the planet Venus to one of my friends. (The fact that Venus is easily visible in broad daylight is a great surprise to most people, and is itself responsible for a large number of UFO reports.)

I pointed to the tiny, dazzling star high in the western sky, about forty degrees above the hidden sun. 'There she is!' I said.

My friend pointed almost a right angle round to the north and said: 'No—there!' The argument lasted for some time: finally, to my utter astonishment, I realized that Venus had an identical twin. At about the same elevation in the northwest was a brilliant, motionless star.

For a few fleeting instants I had visions of astronomical fame as the discoverer of Supernova Clarke, and I wondered what bribe would be sufficient to secure my friend's silence. Then I ran for my telescope, and the mystery was resolved.

It was the local meteorological balloon, released every afternoon to measure conditions in the upper atmosphere. Hanging becalmed perhaps 10 km above the earth, it was catching the last rays of the setting sun. There was *no* way in which the naked eye could have distinguished it from Venus.

I could give a dozen more examples from my own experience. They all add up to this: even expert, honest witnesses can be completely fooled by unusual objects (or phenomena) in the sky. And the evidence of the *in*expert (even when it is not distorted by excitement or prejudice) is utterly worthless. When anyone tries to tell me about the bright moving object he once saw in the sky, I beg to be excused. This is not stubborn obscurantism, or even laziness. He *may* have seen the Mother Ship from Proxima Centauri going into its parking orbit. But as there's simply no way of either proving or disproving this, I refuse to waste my time listing the scores of possible explanations.

So—what to do? UFOs are a serious and fascinating problem. Some of the hundreds of varieties may even (though I doubt it) lead to important scientific discoveries. The only thing I'm reasonably sure about UFOs is that they're *not* spaceships. *That* explanation is too naïve and geocentric.

In my opinion, what UFOs need is a decade or so of benign neglect. Let's ignore all the things in the sky and concentrate on the only reports that matter—the 'Close Encounters of the Third Kind'—which, as everyone knows, are unmistakable face-to-face confrontations with alien vehicles or creatures. Either they occur, or they do not, and there's a lot of high-powered lying and hysterical self-delusion going on. In any event, only time will tell . . . perhaps.

UFOs may simply go away, like the witches of the Middle Ages, when no one believes in them any more. That would be a pretty convincing proof that they are a purely psychological phenomenon.

Or they may turn out to be caused by some hitherto unknown phenomenon, perhaps like ball lightning, which is still totally unexplained (and even denied by some sceptical scientists, see Chapter 12).

Or—

—I think I will stop here, merely reminding you of J B S Haldane's famous aphorism: 'The universe is not only queerer than we imagine—it is queerer than we *can* imagine.'

11
Strange Skies

The Chronicle of Gervase, written in flowing medieval script, picked out with illuminated capitals, is preserved in the magnificent library of Trinity College, Cambridge. Its author was a monk of the monastery attached to Canterbury Cathedral. Little is known of Gervase's life, except that he became a monk in 1163, at the height of the tragic conflict between King Henry II and Thomas à Becket. Some of the most striking passages in the manuscript, however, deal not with the affairs of church and state, but with astronomical events including an eclipse of the sun and a spectacular display of the *aurora borealis*. Most intriguing of all is a report of an extraordinary occurrence on 18 June 1178 (Julian calendar):

'In this year, on the Sunday before the feast of St John the Baptist, after sunset when the moon had first become visible, a marvellous phenomenon was witnessed by some five or more men who were sitting there facing the moon. Now there was a bright new moon, and as usual in that phase, its horns were tilted toward the east and suddenly the upper horn split in two. From the midpoint of this division a flaming torch sprang up, spewing out, over a considerable distance, fire, hot coals and sparks. Meanwhile the body of the moon, which was below, writhed, as it were, in anxiety, and, to put it in the words of those who reported it to me and saw it with their own eyes, the moon throbbed like a wounded snake. Afterwards it resumed its proper state. This phenomenon was repeated a dozen times or more, the flame assuming various twisting shapes at random and then returning to normal. Then after these transforma-

tions the moon from horn to horn, that is along its whole length, took on a blackish appearance.'

The five men of Canterbury must be numbered among an unlikely group of people who occupy a special place in the history of astronomy. It includes an American tycoon, a French country doctor, some Chinese civil servants and the Three Wise Men. For they share a common experience, they have witnessed a phenomenon in the sky so fleeting that the rest of the world has been mystified by its nature or doubted its very existence.

The story of the Canterbury sighting remained a fascinating, but baffling, curiosity to those few scholars who came across it. Only Gervase's affirmation that 'the present writer was given this report by men who saw it with their own eyes, and are prepared to stake their honour on oath that they have made no addition or falsification in the above narrative' has prevented it from being dismissed as pure fiction. In fact, the episode is a rarity in more ways than one, for not only is there no description of an astronomical event like it in ancient literature, but it is a mystery which, after eight hundred years, may finally have been explained.

One day in the mid-1970s, Dr Jack B Hartung, of the State University of New York at Stony Brook, was browsing through a book when he came across a brief reference to Gervase's report of the extraordinary event witnessed by the five men of Kent. Intrigued, Hartung sought out the full text of *The*

Right: The sun in eclipse. During the eclipse of 1878, the astronomer, James Watson, 'had a view of a celestial object . . . which to my mind, without any doubt is the long-sought Vulcan'

'Giordano Bruno', the moon crater, which perhaps the five men of Kent saw created in 1178

Chronicle, and when he read the details of the moon's appearance, he at once realized what they might mean.

He first discounted any possibility that the witnesses had seen something which had occurred not on the Moon but in the earth's atmosphere, perhaps as a result of cloud layers or turbulence, or of the entry of a meteoroid on the men's line of sight. For the report mentions only the moon itself, not clouds or bad weather. Thus Hartung could explain the phenomena in Gervase's report in terms of an enormous impact on the surface of the moon. It was a suggestion he was supremely qualified to make, since much of Hartung's work at New York State University consisted of the study of craters made by meteorites which have struck the earth. Phrase by phrase, Gervase's account reinforced his conviction: 'the upper horn split in two' indicated that dust or cloud was produced by the impact, obscuring part of the moon's crescent from the watchers on

earth: the 'flaming torch . . . spewing out fire, hot coals, and sparks' suggested that gases or liquids were released when the surface was struck, and gases forming a temporary 'atmosphere' around the region of the impact could have made the moon seem to writhe or throb 'like a wounded snake' Although some of the phenomena reported by the witnesses were not easily explained, Hartung believed that the men in 1178 might have been the only people to have witnessed the formation of a large crater on the moon. The question now was: where exactly had the impact been, and was there a crater there?

Hartung knew what phase the moon was in on 18 June 1178: it was very new—only a thin crescent in the sky—which narrowed down the possible impact area. Gervase's report provided plenty of additional clues. The Kentish men had noticed that the strange events had occurred at the 'midpoint' of the 'upper horn' of a 'new moon', which, Hartung calculated, meant somewhere near latitude 45°N and longitude 90°E. The fact that so much had been seen on earth with the naked eye suggested that the cloud thrown up by the impact would have been more than 60 miles (100 km) across and that the crater itself would have been at least 6 miles (10 km) in diameter, surrounded by long 'rays' of light-coloured debris.

With the latest photographs taken by lunar orbiter and Apollo missions, Hartung searched for a crater which fitted his theoretical calculations: it had to be somewhere in an area between latitude 30° to 60°N and longitude 75° to 105°E with a diameter greater than 6 miles (10 km) and surrounded by bright rays. At 36°N and 103°E, he found it: a crater about 12 miles (20 km) in diameter named Giordano Bruno, after the sixteenth-century philosopher. For hundreds of miles around it, there were the tell-tale signs of a vast impact, bright rays caused by the reflection of light on dust particles one of which ran for at least 750 miles (1,200 km), and showed up clearly in NASA's photographs. Astonishingly, the five men from Kent saw with their own eyes signs of the actual gouging of a vast crater from the surface of the moon on 18 June 1178 and recorded it for posterity. Hartung noted that

'. . . In any given three thousand-year period (a rough estimate for all of recorded history), the chances are about one in a thousand that such an event would occur anywhere on the moon. The chance that a record of such an event would be preserved for us is still lower because only half of the moon can be seen, observations have not been made continuously, observations made may not have been recorded and records may not have been preserved. In short, the probability of our having a recorded observation of a 20-mile impact event is extremely small.'

The Planet of Romance

While most of Jack Hartung's fellow astronomers agree that his interpretation of Gervase's 'marvellous phenomenon' is likely to be correct, no such consensus exists over an observation made by a French country doctor called Lescarbault on the afternoon of 26 March 1859.

Lescarbault, who practised in the small village of Orgères about 100 km from Paris, was a keen amateur astronomer, and had built a small observatory onto his house. On that March afternoon in 1859, he had snatched a few minutes from his work to observe the sun. As he watched it through his telescope, he saw a dot appear near the upper left-hand edge of the sun's disc and move gradually downwards. He watched fascinated, since, as he was an experienced astronomer, he knew that the object was certainly not a sunspot. Soon afterwards, he was called away to see a patient, but when he returned, the object was still there, moving steadily down the sun. Lescarbault watched it for several hours, until it disappeared.

It was not until the following December that the country doctor realized that his observation might be an astronomical discovery of sensational importance. For

Lescarbault's observatory at Orgères

France's leading astronomer, Urbain Jean Joseph Leverrier, had just announced a theory which could explain the problem of the planet Mercury, which was not behaving in the manner predicted by Sir Isaac Newton; something seemed to be disturbing it as it revolved in the sky. Leverrier claimed that Mercury was being perturbed by an unknown object between it and the sun, and his theory was not to be discounted, since he had predicted the position of the planet Neptune thirteen years earlier by studying irregularities in the orbit of Uranus and his calculations had led to its discovery.

When Dr Lescarbault heard of Leverrier's theory, he realized that the black disc which he had seen travelling across the sun in the previous March might be the object in question and, in his innocence, he sent details of his observation to the great astronomer. He explained that he had not liked to mention it earlier because he had not yet been able to make another sighting to confirm the first.

At once, Leverrier set off from Paris to question the doctor. By the time he had reached Dr Lescarbault's house, after a 19 km walk from the nearest railway station, Leverrier, once described as 'one of the rudest men in history', was in a towering rage. The meeting that followed was graphically summarized in a nineteenth-century astronomical handbook:

particulars regarding his discovery. On speaking of the rough method adopted to ascertain the period of the first contact, the astronomer inquired what chronometer he had been guided by, and was naturally enough somewhat surprised when the physician pulled out a huge old watch with only minute hands. It had been his faithful companion in his professional journeys, he said; but that would hardly be considered a satisfactory qualification for performing so delicate an experiment. The consequence was, that Leverrier, evidently now beginning to conclude that the whole affair was an imposition or a delusion, exclaimed, with some warmth, "What, with that old watch, showing only minutes, dare you talk of estimating seconds? My suspicions are already too well founded." To this Lescarbault replied that he had a pendulum by which he counted seconds. This was produced, and found to consist of an ivory ball attached to a silken thread, which, being hung on a nail, is made to oscillate, and is shown by the watch to beat very nearly seconds. Leverrier is now puzzled to know how the number of seconds is ascertained, as there is nothing to mark them; but Lescarbault states that with him there is no difficulty whatever in this, as he is accustomed "to feel pulses and count their pulsations", and can with ease carry out the same principle with the pendulum.'

Urbain Leverrier (left) (1811–1877). The French astronomer being received by Louis Philippe after his discovery of the planet Neptune

'On calling at the residence of the modest and unobtrusive medical practitioner, he refused to say who he was, but in the most abrupt manner, and in the most authoritative tone, began, "It is then you, Sir, who pretend to have observed the intra-Mercurial planet, and who have committed the grave offence of keeping your observation secret for nine months. I warn you that I have come here with the intention of doing justice to your pretensions, and of demonstrating either that you have been dishonest or deceived. Tell me then, unequivocally, what you have seen." The doctor then explained what he had witnessed, and entered into all the

And so the interrogation went on, with the doctor's telescope being produced for inspection, along with the original memorandum noting the find now 'covered with grease and laudanum'. Even Dr Lescarbault's calculations of the distance of the planet from the sun were written on a plank: 'Lescarbault's method, he being short of paper, was to make his calculations on a plank, and make way for fresh ones by planing them off'. Finally, Leverrier was satisfied, and returned to Paris to announce the discovery.

Predictably, it caused a sensation through-out the world, and astronomers waited eagerly for an opportunity to see for them-selves the new planet, which Leverrier had named Vulcan. Thus, between 29 March and 7 April 1860, almost exactly a year after Lescarbault's sighting, the telescopes of the world were constantly manned in the vain hope that Vulcan would appear as it made the transit of the sun predicted by astronomi-cal calculation. There was no sign of a planet whatever.

Professional astronomers became un-easy; some of them publicly doubted the very existence of Vulcan. Despite this, Leverrier continued to make detailed calculations about a planet which he himself had never seen. A few reports did crop up occasionally from amateurs, such as Richard Covington, whose observation appeared in *Scientific American* in the United States:

'I was residing then in Washington Territory, and was superintending some work on a prairie, a few miles from Fort Vancouver, on the Columbia River. A range of mountains was in the distance

from behind which the sun had reached an altitude of about 30° above the horizon, when a small boy asked me what was the matter with the sun. On looking at it I saw a planet, a perfectly rounded, well-defined dark spot . . . I watched its progress till its completion with a telescope, merely glancing with partially closed eyes at very short intervals.'

But such reports were scarce and failed to convince the astronomers, and in 1877, Leverrier died with his ambition to estab-lish Vulcan's existence unfulfilled and his advocacy of it discredited. Yet in 1878 specu-lation revived when two professional as-tronomers reported seeing Vulcan during the eclipse of the sun in July of that year.

The first was James C Watson of Ann Arbor University in Michigan, who had already discovered many asteroids and who, being passionately interested in Vulcan, decided to search for it during the eclipse. An eclipse is traditionally the best oppor-tunity for seeing objects close to the sun, for even the smallest and dimmest have a chance of showing up at the side of the blackened disc. And so it was that James C Watson journeyed in the summer of 1878 to the Bad-lands of Wyoming Territory, a place from

James Watson and Thomas Edison were among those who watched the 1878 eclipse near Rawlins, Wyoming

which he calculated he might be able to get the best view of the eclipse. He reached a halt on the Union Pacific Railroad called Separation, 13 miles (21 km) miles west of the small township of Rawlins. The place does not exist now, and only a pair of stone telescope piers remain in the undergrowth. In July 1878 however, Separation was busy and important, because not only had Watson come there to observe the eclipse, but it was the site chosen for the camp of the US Naval Eclipse Expedition, led by one of the leading astronomers of the day, Simon Newcomb.

Watson set up his telescope in a small hollow by the railroad track, next to the other astronomers. The weather was blustery, and windsheets had to be put up to protect the telescopes from dust, but, when the time came for the eclipse, conditions for observation were good. When the sun disappeared for the few brief minutes of totality, the astronomers worked feverishly to make the observations they had planned. About halfway through, Watson suddenly noticed that there were two objects in the constellation of Cancer which did not appear on his astronomical charts. Leaving his telescope, he rushed across to Professor Newcomb, asking him to verify that he could see them too. But time was running out, and Newcomb, who was no believer in Vulcan, summarily dismissed Watson and carried on with his work. It was only much later that Watson discovered that he had not been alone in his sighting, for letters had begun to appear in the scientific journals from Dr Lewis Swift of Rochester, N.Y. One of them began: 'During the total phase of the late solar eclipse, as observed at Denver, Colorado, I had a view of a celestial object not down in Argelander's charts, which to my mind, without any doubt, is the long-sought Vulcan.'

Watson himself became famous and was acclaimed by the popular press. The scientific journals, too, were keen to congratulate both him and Swift: *The Observatory*, for example, had no doubts in its report on the eclipse that 'the great achievement was the discovery by Professor Watson and Mr Swift of what appears to be the long-sought inter-Mercurial planet'. But the critical reaction was not long in coming, and by 1880 when Watson died of pneumonia while building a telescope to continue his search for Vulcan, most astronomers were satisfied that he had mistaken the star Theta Cancri for Vulcan in his desire to prove the existence of the unknown planet.

Although a few professional astronomers after Watson still scanned the sky for Vulcan, none of them saw the elusive planet. When Albert Einstein published his General Theory of Relativity in 1915, the strange perturbations of Mercury which had inspired Leverrier's original theory were explained: the eccentricity of the planet's orbit was caused by the gravitational field of the sun. Leverrier's dream of finding a planet between Mercury and the sun seemed to be dead. Richard Baum, a British amateur astronomer who has made a detailed study of the Vulcan story, sees it like this:

'Some astronomers at the end of the nineteenth century called it the Planet of Romance. I think they put their finger right on the pulse to begin with. It *was* the Planet of Romance—a splendid romance . . . like an astronomer's search for the Holy Grail, we might say. But beyond that, there was nothing. It was as though the Heavens were laughing at us all the time. We can look forever for the footprints of Vulcan in the sky, but those footprints are ghosts, footprints of ghosts, and no more than that.'

Yet even if Einstein had shown that Leverrier's theory that Mercury was being perturbed by another planet was wrong, what had Dr Lescarbault seen? Possibly, one of the minor planets which exist between Mars and Jupiter had moved into his line of sight on an eccentric orbit, so that the country doctor mistook its place in the solar system and assumed it to be between Mercury and the sun. On the other hand, it may after all have been a new planet. Eclipse-watching is now a sophisticated business. Astronomers no longer stare at the darkened sun, frantically hoping to notice something unusual: they use cameras, and study the photographs taken by them at their leisure. It was while he was studying photographs shot during the eclipses in Brazil in 1966, and in Mexico and North Carolina in 1970, that an American scientist, Dr Henry C Courten of Dowling College on Long Island, noticed a number of mysterious pinpoints of light-traces which he thinks could only have been left by tiny objects in the vicinity of the sun. The tracks are very faint, but Courten has discounted the possibility of their being what astronomers have dubbed 'Kodak Stars'—flaws on the plates themselves. The search for Vulcan has claimed many reputations, so Courten's approach is cautious, but

The enormous canyon, Valles Marineris, stretching nearly a third of the way round the planet Mars: perhaps one of Lowell's 'canals'

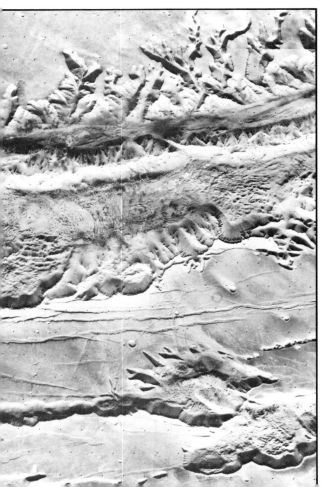

he will admit that he may have photographed the remains of a small planet which has fragmented recently. This would not have been the planet the great Leverrier was seeking to confirm his theories of the strange behaviour of Mercury, but perhaps it *was* the small black disc noticed by the humble country doctor in France on that spring afternoon in 1859 which gave birth to one of the most elusive searches in the history of astronomy: the quest for the planet Vulcan.

The Canals of Mars

While the controversy over Vulcan was confined mainly to the pages of scientific journals, the saga of the canals of Mars made headlines in the world's press for decades. In 1877, an Italian astronomer, Giovanni Schiaparelli, reported a phenomenon he had noticed while studying Mars, which was then in favourable opposition to the Earth. He noticed a latticework of lines covering the surface of the planet. Others before Schiaparelli had noticed them, but the Italian had seen them more clearly, and his account of the '*canali*', as he called them, caused no more than a mild sensation. It was not until 1894 that, through Percival Lowell, they became headline news.

In 1892, Lowell, a keen astronomer who had inherited a substantial fortune, heard that Schiaparelli's eyesight was failing and that the Italian would therefore not be able to continue his study of Mars. Lowell decided not merely to continue the hunt for the '*canali*' himself, but actually to build an observatory specially for the purpose. Time was short, for Mars was due to be in a particularly favourable position for observations in October 1894. Undaunted, Lowell sent his assistant to test the atmosphere all around Arizona and find a site, where the night sky was free of the extraneous light of cities, and high above sea level where the air was as clear as possible. As a result, Lowell decided to erect his telescope in the 'great pine oasis of Flagstaff in the midst of the Arizona desert'. Here, above the small

The American astronomer, Percival Lowell

township, he built the Lowell observatory.

In October 1894, the Red Planet came into focus through the new telescope high on Mars Hill, and at once Lowell could make out the lines which Schiaparelli had described fifteen years before. He counted himself lucky that he had exceptional eyesight for, as he wrote later:

'Not everybody can see these delicate features at first sight, even when pointed out to them; and to perceive their more minute details takes a trained as well as an acute eye, observing under best conditions. When so viewed however, the disc of the planet takes on a most singular appearance. It looks as if it had been cobwebbed all over. Suggestive of a spider's web seen against the grass of a spring morning, a mesh of fine reticulated lines overspreads it, which with attention proves to compass the globe from one pole to the other. The chief difference between it and a spider's work is one of size, supplemented by greater complexity, but both are joys of geometric beauty. For the lines are of individually uniform width, of exceeding beauty, and of great length. These are the Martian canals.'

Lowell's technique was to draw what he saw while he looked through his telescope, and his notes, still preserved at Flagstaff, are full of tiny and delicate drawings of the surface of Mars. These were to form the basis of the elaborate maps of the Martian canal system which the Lowell Observatory produced during his lifetime. But mere observation was not enough, and after a few weeks of studying the planet, Lowell formulated an extraordinary theory to explain the existence of the canals, and he clung to it for the rest of his life. Schiaparelli, in using the word 'canali', had meant merely that the lines he had noticed on Mars might be channels—a better English translation. But Lowell's was a great age of canal building—the Suez Canal, built in 1869, was still one of the modern wonders of the world— and Lowell insisted that what Schiaparelli had discovered were also canals, built by a Martian civilization.

Lowell first satisfied himself that Mars was habitable: the changing appearance of what he took to be the polar ice-caps convinced him that the planet had an atmosphere; a blue band which showed up from time to time near the poles, he took to be water, and the dark, blue-green areas which grew and then faded at different times of the year, were undoubtedly vegetation. Lowell's suggestion that Mars could be habitable was revolutionary enough. However, it was not this which captured the public imagination, but his theory that the canals of Mars were the last cry of a doomed Martian civilization, struggling to survive as desert overwhelmed the planet.

Lowell believed that all planets followed roughly the same course of evolution, from the early stages when the land was fresh and green enough to support life, through a period when encroaching desert laid waste vast areas, to a time when a dead, bare planet turned lifelessly in space. In the solar system there were three planets which exemplified what he meant: the moon was the dead planet, the earth the verdant one, teeming with life, and Mars was dying. The canals had appeared on Mars because its inhabitants had realized that the only way to survive was to irrigate their planet with water from their last remaining source, the polar ice-caps. The Martians had therefore constructed an elaborate network of canals, circling the entire planet and running for thousands of miles, linking the oases which were the last refuge of life. Lowell was careful, however, not to let speculation go too far and refused to describe the characteristics of the Martians themselves.

In expounding his theory, Lowell became a prophet of the Earth's future. There, deserts like the Sahara were growing, and it was only a matter of time before humanity would suffer what the Martians had already undergone: 'Not only are the desert belts in existence', he wrote of Mars, 'but the whole surface, except for the sea bottoms, has gone the same way. Five eighths of it all is now an arid waste, unrelieved from sterility by surface moisture or covering of cloud. Bare itself, it is pitilessly held up to a brazen sun, unprotected by any shield of shade'. The fate of Mars was sealed: 'The drying up of the planet is certain to proceed until its surface can support no life at all. Slowly but surely time will snuff it out. When the last ember is thus extinguished, the planet will roll a dead world through space, its evolutionary career forever ended.' Earth's future was already clear: 'Study of Mars proves that planet to occupy earthwise in some sort the post of prophet. For, in addition to the side-lights it throws upon our past, it is by way of foretelling our future.'

The public was soon won over by Lowell's ripe prose and every time the planet came into favourable opposition, Marsmania gripped the world. Lowell's lectures were packed out with people eager to hear the latest developments in the tragic struggle of their planetary neighbours, and newspaper editors and their readers pounced upon every new

Part of Lowell's map of Mars

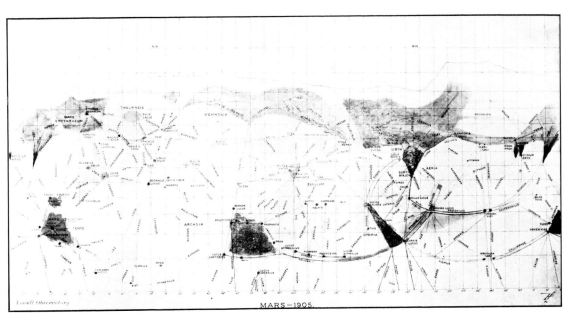

drawing and canal map issued from the observatory on Mars Hill. As the years passed, the details of the canal system were revealed to be more complex: now new canals, double canals and canal distribution points were constantly appearing. As the maps grew more elaborate, so did the theory: the construction of the network, Lowell contended, must have demanded the efforts of the whole population, thus demonstrating that Mars was a Utopia of peace and industry.

Astronomers, however, were less easily convinced, for the simple reason that few of them could see the canals at all, and certainly not in the profusion that Lowell claimed for them. Even Andrew Douglass, Lowell's assistant, who had shared in the initial sightings, and had made drawings of the developing system as he watched through the observatory telescope, began to wonder whether the whole thing was not a psychological phenomenon after all. He tried studying discs set up a mile away from the telescope for markings similar to those found on the planet. These and other investigations increased his doubts, and finally he left Flagstaff. Other astronomers were sure that the Martian canals were in the eye of their beholder, and were outspoken in their criticism. Some believed that there were defects in the telescope, while one of them, the Englishman E W Maunder, mounted an elaborate experiment at the Royal Hospital School in Greenwich, London, to test whether the canals were an optical illusion. He chose a room with good natural light, and asked schoolboys sitting at different distances to copy a drawing on the other side of the room which, unknown to the pupils, contained features depicted on maps of Mars. Many of the boys reproduced the drawings reasonably faithfully, but others joined up surface features with straight lines, as Maunder's published results show, he was satisfied that

'the canals of Mars may in some cases be ... the boundaries of tones or shadings, but that in the majority of cases they are

A E Douglass seated in the dome of the 24 in Clark refractor at Flagstaff

simply the integration by the eye of minute details too small to be separately and distinctly defined. It would not therefore be in the least correct to say that the numerous observers who have drawn canals on *Mars* during the last twenty-five years have drawn what they did not see. On the contrary they have drawn, and drawn truthfully, that which they saw; yet, for all that, the canals which they have drawn have no more objective existence than those which our Greenwich boys imagined they saw on the drawings submitted to them.'

Lowell, however, contemptuously dismissed Maunder's interpretation of what he had seen as the 'Small Boy Theory' and new data on the canals and the progress of the struggling Martians continued to flow from Flagstaff into the scientific journals and the newspapers. Lowell grew more confident about the existence of the canals with every passing year, although the problems of photographing them clearly enough for reproduction frustrated him. There was time, too, for the occasional stunt, like the balloon trip over Regent's Park in London during his honeymoon, when he took photographs of the pathways to help him estimate the size of the Martian canals.

By the time Lowell died in 1916, the canals of Mars were more than a theory, they were an article of faith. Even after the gaudy scenario of the dying civilization had faded from the popular mind, nagging doubts about the existence of the canals lasted until the 1960s when the Mariner fly-by missions first obtained close-up pictures of the planet. In 1971, a great duststorm cleared, and allowed Mariner 9 to take more than 7,000 photographs of the planet's surface. These finally killed the theory of the canals of Mars since there was absolutely no trace of them on the planet's surface—unless of course, as some wags suggested, the Martians, with their superior intelligence, had seen the space-probes coming and had hidden every vestige of their activities.

What, then, had Lowell seen through the great telescope at Flagstaff? How had he and his assistants been able to make thousands of drawings of the 'spider's web' of canals for at least twenty years? Lowell was a serious astronomer: it was he who laid down criteria for siting observatories which are still followed today. He passionately espoused the now accepted view that life must exist on other planets and it was his work which led, many years after his death, to the discovery of Pluto, the planet whose name begins with his initials. It is therefore not likely that he was the knowing perpetrator of a hoax. After the Mariner 9 mission, two noted American scientists, Carl Sagan and Paul Fox, reviewed Lowell's canal system in the light of the new photographs. They found that, although a few of the canals corresponded to the valleys, ridges and chains of craters on the surface of Mars, most of them had nothing to do with the actual topography of the planet. 'The vast majority of the canals,' say Sagan and Fox, 'appear to be largely self-generated by the visual observers of the canal school, and stand as monuments to the imprecision of the human eye-brain-hand system under difficult observing conditions.'

But that does not pretend fully to explain the affair, for in 1971, the year Mariner 9 mapped Mars, two American astronomers, Peter Boyce and Jim Westfall, had a curious and unnerving experience as they watched the sky through one of the most sophisticated telescopes in the world at Cerrotollollo in Chile. For three hours, as they studied the planet, they saw the canals of Mars. That night, Boyce remembers, conditions for observation were among the best he has ever known. Suddenly, as he scanned Syrtis Major—one of the dark triangular markings usually to be seen on the planet's surface—Boyce saw a classic Lowellian canal stretching from its pointed tip. As he watched in amazement, other markings appeared, including more lines and even 'oases'. Boyce's colleague Jim Westfall, working at a different telescope, also saw them: 'Things are popping up all over the place.' he said. Boyce is absolutely certain about what he saw, although he also is well aware from the Mariner photographs that there are no canals on Mars. He speculates that the lines may be caused by the passage of dust across the planet's surface. This, however, is no more than a guess, yet another attempt to explain what Percival Lowell actually saw. Sadly, it is all far less romantic than the saga that 'unfolded' before the eyes of the astronomers at Flagstaff and seemed to them to point to the future of our earth.

The Star of Bethlehem

Among the papers preserved in the Lowell Observatory Archives is a letter to Lowell about the greatest of all mysterious short-lived astronomical phenomena, the Star of Bethlehem. 'May I know please', wrote one Ellen S Hunter of Leesburg, Florida, 'where, and at what time, to look for the "Star of Bethlehem", and what is the astronomical

The star that guided the wise men. It has been
suggested that Giotto had seen Halley's comet.
(Adoration of the Magi, Scrovegni Chapel, Padua)

his star in the east, and are come to worship
him . . . Then Herod, when he had privily
called the wise men, inquired of them
diligently what time the star appeared.
And he sent them to Bethlehem, and said,
Go and search diligently for the young
child; and when ye have found him, bring
me word again, that I may come and worship him also. When they had heard the
king, they departed; and, lo, the star,
which they saw in the east, went before
them, till it came and stood over where the
young child was. When they saw the star,
they rejoiced with exceeding great joy.'

These few clues supplied by St Matthew
were enough to encourage the great German
astronomer Johannes Kepler (1571–1630)
to formulate a theory which is still widely
held today. Kepler suggested that the Star
of Bethlehem was really an astrological
event: a triple conjunction of two planets,
Saturn and Jupiter, in the constellation of
Pisces. Kepler himself witnessed such an
event in 1603 and 1604; first on 17 December
1603, when Saturn and Jupiter moved close
together in the sky. Within six months,
the planets came together twice more in a
similar fashion, once with Mars also nearby,
a phenomenon known as 'the massing of the
planets'. Kepler calculated that a triple
conjunction such as this took place only
once every 805 years, and had therefore
occurred previously in AD 799 and in 7 BC.

If this were right, then Christ must have
been born earlier than the calendar con-
ventions AD and BC suggest, and there is
some justification for this. The present
calendar was drawn up by a Roman monk
called Dionysius Exiguus, who unfortunately left out of his calculations the four-
year reign of the Emperor Augustus, when
he ruled under his own name of Octavian.
Moreover, Matthew specifically says that
Christ was born 'in the days of Herod the
King,' and his death can be precisely dated
by another astronomical event: the ancient
historian Flavius Josephus says that Herod
died within days of an eclipse of the moon

name and magnitude of the star?' Since she
clearly regarded Lowell as the fount of all
astronomical knowledge, Ellen Hunter was
no doubt rather disappointed with the
reply from Lowell's assistant, Vesto Melvin
Slipher, who said that 'no satisfactory
explanation has yet been offered'. That
reply came in 1910, and it is still true today.

The Star of Bethlehem may not have been
an astronomical phenomenon at all of
course, but rather a myth or a miracle. Even
if it is susceptible to an astronomical explanation there is very little information
to work with. The Star is, in fact, mentioned
only in St Matthew's Gospel. The second
chapter begins:

'Now when Jesus was born in Bethlehem
of Judaea in the days of Herod the king,
behold, there came wise men from the east
to Jerusalem, saying, where is he that is
born King of the Jews? For we have seen

which has been dated as occurring on the night of 12 and 13 March in 4 BC. Christ, therefore, must have been born before then, and according to the Bible was in Egypt when Herod died. It is, therefore, quite possible that Christ was born in 6 or 7 BC.

No one knows exactly who the wise men were, or even whether they existed, but if they did, we can safely assume, as most commentators have done, that they were skilled not only in astronomical observation but also in astrology. Thus, a triple conjunction of Saturn and Jupiter in the constellation of Pisces could have had a special significance for them and caused them to make the journey, for it has been suggested that Jupiter signified royalty, Saturn protected Israel, and the background to the conjunction, Pisces, also signified Israel. Interestingly, there is a tablet in a Berlin museum inscribed with calculations predicting the very triple conjunction Kepler believed might have been the Christmas star, which shows that it was an event of recognized significance to the astronomers and astrologers of the ancient world. Certainly, the triple conjunction hypothesis helps to

Johannes Kepler (1511–1630)

explain some of the more puzzling aspects of the biblical account, such as why the wise men were prompted to set out for Jerusalem or why Herod himself had not seen 'the star', it may also explain why the star 'went before them'. It is even possible to piece together the sequence of events, as David W Hughes, the British authority on the Star, has done. He suggests that the Magi could have been inspired to make the journey to Israel by the conjunction of 27 May in 7 BC. Allowing time for the Magi to make preparations, they could have set out in June, with the second of the conjunctions on 6 October, serving to confirm that they were heading in the right direction. By this reasoning, the third conjunction, on 1 December, would have taken place after the meeting with Herod, and would have pointed the way south to Bethlehem.

However, although the triple conjunction would have had considerable astrological significance, it was an unspectacular event, since the planets, always the width of two moons apart, never merged into something which looked like one star. One nineteenth-century reviewer of the evidence evaded this problem by suggesting that the Magi must have been so shortsighted that the planets (which were about one degree apart) merged into one star!

To many astronomers the triple conjunction theory seems too complicated to account for the Star of Bethlehem, and they have directed their energies towards trying to identify a single star in the sky at the time of the birth of Christ. This is not an impossible task, because there are at least two sets of detailed records of astronomical events in the ancient world. The best were kept by the Chinese who, in the days before telescopes, employed civil servants who lay on their backs scanning the heavens in the hope of seeing new events. Their observations were eventually included, in a special astronomical chapter, in the Annals of every Chinese dynasty, and similar records were also kept by the Koreans. These documents still survive, and are much studied by astronomers in the hope of identifying the origins of radio stars, the pattern of eclipses and the return of comets. Predictably, they have also been studied for evidence of any star which might be identified with the Star of Bethlehem.

One such historical astronomer is an Englishman, Dr Richard Stephenson of Liverpool University, and his knowledge of Chinese enables him to make a direct study of the ancient texts. With two colleagues, he decided to make a thorough search for a single especially bright star in the astronomical records covering the period from 10 BC to AD 10. He struck lucky in the *Chien-Han-Shu*—the astronomical treatise of the former Han Dynasty—which says 'Second year of the Ch'en-ping high period, second month, a "Hui-Hsing" appeared at Ch'ien-niu for over seventy days.'

Dr Stephenson and his colleagues knew that the term *Hui-Hsing* is usually applied to a broom-star—a comet with an obvious tail, but since the Chinese usually mentioned the motion of such bodies, they concluded that the object was more likely to be a nova, a star which has exploded into prominence. What struck Stephenson was that the dates of the star mentioned by the Chinese correspond well to the estimated date of Christ's birth: it appeared between 10 March and 7 April in 5 BC. The nova fits the bill in other ways too: it was in the right part of the sky to be seen before dawn, and was reasonably bright, though not so bright that it would have caught the eye of people like Herod who were unused to studying the sky. It was in the sky for seventy days, which could have been long enough to help the Magi on their way.

Stephenson recognizes there are problems in marrying up the Chinese record with the star mentioned in St Matthew, notably that the star 'went before' the Magi. But he points out that any star high in the sky seems to go along with a traveller. Of the 5 BC nova, he says:

'I think it fits in as well as might be expected. The account in St Matthew is quite detailed in some ways. He, it must be remembered, was not an astronomer, and he never wrote as an astronomer or for a scientific audience. But the dating is about right. It was in vision for quite an extended period, and visible in the right part of the sky, and perhaps that's as good as we can hope for.'

The Chinese records do, however, throw up one alternative possibility. One of them mentions yet another nova which flared up on 23 February in 4 BC, and an American mathematician, A J Morehouse, believes that this was the third in a sequence of events which may explain the Star of Bethlehem. The first was the series of conjunctions of Saturn and Jupiter, which took eleven months, the second was the nova of 5 BC which appeared about eleven months later, and the third was the nova of 4 BC which, according to the records, occurred exactly eleven months after the first nova. While the eleven-month sequence might have had an astrological significance in the ancient world, Morehouse, in his discussion of the 4 BC nova, points to an even more intriguing possibility: *the Star of Bethlehem may still be in the sky.*

Morehouse believes this to be possible, because the Chinese records actually say where the nova was: it turns out to have been in a group of stars which we know as α, β and γ Aquilae. Now if the nova was unusually

Planetary nebula in Aquila where the star of Bethlehem may still be shining

bright—the records describe it as 'scintillating', it may have been a supernova star about 10,000 times brighter than a nova. Morehouse knew that when supernovae decline, they turn into pulsars, burnt-out stars which send radio pulses out into space. As it happens, there are many pulsars in the region of α, β, γ Aquilae, but Morehouse believes that only one really fits the bill, a binary pulsar with the unbiblical name of PSR 1913 + 16b, and Morehouse's conviction grew when his calculations showed that, to anyone standing at the South Gate of Jerusalem, this star would have appeared over Bethlehem. Morehouse's theory has not gained universal acceptance, partly because 4 BC seems to be too late a date for the birth of Christ: but it is, at least, a new contribution to an argument which has gone on since the days of the early church. Since no one can now know the true identity of that most mysterious herald of the greatest mystery of all, the Star of Bethlehem will keep its secret long after Saturn and Jupiter have swung once again into conjunction in Pisces in the year 2409, and the pulses of PSR 1913 + 16b have faded from the skies.

Arthur C Clarke comments:

The Tunguska Explosion (Chapter 9) reminds us that large meteors must hit the Moon, as well as the Earth: so there is nothing at all impossible about the observation recorded in *The Chronicle of Gervase*.

Indeed, we know just what such an event would look like, because the Voyager 1 spacecraft photographed great explosions (probably volcanic) on Jupiter's satellite Io—which is almost exactly the same size as the Moon, and equally airless.

It is hard to decide whether the Rise and Fall of the Martian Canals is a comedy or a

A volcanic explosion on Jupiter's satellite Io throwing debris a hundred miles into space (Photographed by Voyager 1)

tragedy. On the one hand, there is the sad spectacle of a brilliant man, Percival Lowell, obsessed by an illusion. Yet that very obsession focused interest upon the planets, led to worthwhile discoveries—and, not least, inspired a vast body of fiction which has given pleasure for generations. Lowell's real and abiding legacy is to be found in the writings of Edgar Rice Burroughs and Ray Bradbury.

And, as for the Star of Bethlehem, many years ago I made it the basis of what is perhaps my best-known short story. If you want my interpretation, please see 'The Star' (in the collection of my stories called *The Other Side of the Sky*).

12

Giants in the Earth

The Cardiff Giant

When a mystery turns up, a scientist is often quickly on the scene, hoping to analyse and evaluate the evidence. Sometimes whole platoons of scientists take up the case—like the Russian commissions to investigate Neanderthal Man or the expeditions to investigate the cause of the Tunguska explosion—sometimes lone investigators like Professor Derek de Solla Price, who investigated the Antikythera Mechanism, tackle the mystery. Scientists were certainly not slow to come forward in the autumn of 1869, when the body of a giant was unearthed in a field in an obscure village called Cardiff in New York State.

On the day of that remarkable discovery, 16 October 1869, a gang of workmen had been digging a well in a field owned by a farmer called William C Newell. Suddenly, just below the surface of the soil, one of the men's spades struck something hard. As he dug deeper, a huge petrified foot appeared, and the astonished workmen carried on digging until they had uncovered the mummified body of a huge man which seemed to have been turned to stone. He was 10 ft 4½ in (3.16 m) tall, and was later found to weigh 2,999 lb (1,360 kg). In the circumstances, the reaction of one of the workmen could be said to be rather restrained: 'Jerusalem, it's a big Injun!'

The Cardiff Giant, as it was named, really did become an overnight sensation. By the next day, word had got round and the local people flocked to see it. The following morning, farmer Newell had erected a tent over the Giant's grave and, for fifty cents, the

Left: The Cardiff Giant, after being exposed as a hoax, was reverently reburied

public was treated to a fifteen-minute viewing and a lecture on what the barkers called the latest and perhaps the most remarkable, of all the wonders of the Americas. Cardiff became a boom town, with its shops doing record business; Newell became rich by selling his find to a group of businessmen, and there was not a hotel room to be found in nearby Syracuse where the Giant was soon put on show.

Among the crowds there were scientists, newly versed in the works of Charles Darwin, and burning to find, or at least see, the 'missing link' in man's evolution. While the public debated the mystery over oysters in the nearby 'Giant Saloon', the scientists began to examine the Giant in detail. Many of them had studied fossils and compared him to fossilized creatures in their collections. One investigator announced that any man who declared the Giant to be a hoax 'simply declared himself a fool'; and at least four doctors insisted the Giant had once been a living creature. One investigator drilled a hole in his enormous skull and claimed that he was able to make out fascinating aspects of the Giant's anatomy. This was very odd indeed because there was nothing there. The Cardiff Giant was indeed a fake, much to the chagrin of the scientists who had endorsed him as the preserved corpse of a member of a lost race (and to the delight of the few who had maintained that the whole thing was humbug). He had been planted at the farm by one of Newell's relatives, a cigar manufacturer called George Hull. Hull had been provoked into perpetrating the hoax by a revivalist preacher, of whom there were many in that part of New York State in the mid-nineteenth century. The preacher was the Reverend

Turk, and he and Hull had had a furious argument over the line from Genesis, 'There were giants in the earth in those days'. Turk believed it to be literally true, while Hull, an agnostic, refused to have any truck with such dogmatic assertions.

He decided to teach Turk and his kind a lesson, and made elaborate preparations. At Fort Dodge in Iowa, he found a huge block of gypsum, which he had carved in the utmost secrecy into the form of a giant by two sculptors in Chicago. When the figure was completed, it was said to look remarkably like Hull himself. Hull now set about giving the statue's body the appearance of petrified flesh and bone: one of the methods he devised to achieve this was to insert hundreds of large darning needles into a block of wood before hammering it all over the 'body' to simulate the pores of the skin. Finally, after dowsing the Giant with sulphuric acid to make it look suitably old, Hull had it transported hugger-mugger to Newell's farm, where it was buried by night to await the great moment of discovery.

Everything went better than Hull had dared to hope: the revivalist ministers were completely taken in and he also made a great deal of money. By the end of the year, however, the fraud had been well and truly exposed, but few people seemed to mind: in fact, the public continued to pay to see the Cardiff Giant, and he was, indeed, so popular that the great showman P T Barnum, having failed to buy the original, exhibited his own version on Broadway. The only real casualties of the affair were the experts who had enthusiastically declared that the Giant was a petrified body. Their reputations were now in tatters.

The Moving Stones

There have been many hoaxes like the Cardiff Giant in the past, so it is hardly surprising that scientists are wary of many of the 'mysteries' presented to them. So many hard-won reputations have been ruined by the rash espousal of theories subsequently proved wrong, with the result that many experts refuse publicly to investigate strange occurrences. Which is unfortunate, for in many cases, scientists have been able to shed considerable light on phenomena that seem to offer few clues to the public. One such mystery is the stones that move by themselves in the lonely wastes of California's Death Valley.

All over Racetrack Playa, a dried-up lake on the edge of Death Valley, there are tracks gouged out of the surface of what was once the lake floor, which is made of sand, silt and clay. Some of the tracks are more than 100 yd (90 m) long, many of them curve and loop like squiggles in a child's drawing book, and at the end of them sits a stone. Everyone who has taken more than a cursory look at the tracks is convinced that they have been made by the movement of the stones, some of them weighing up to 600 lb (270 kg). But the curious thing is that, although there are dozens of tracks, no one has ever reported seeing a stone move: one day it is in one place, the next day in another.

When the phenomenon was first brought to the attention of scientists in the 1940s, the whole thing sounded like a joke, but the more they thought about it, the more in-

Death Valley, California

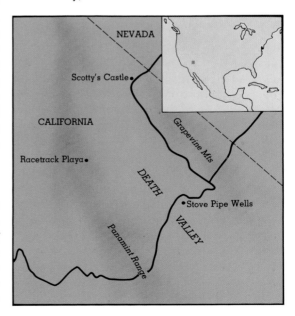

triguing the problem became. The obvious explanation was that the stones were being moved by people. There were, however, many considerations which ruled this out; not least the fact that to move hundreds of stones many times and on many occasions would be an uncommonly fruitless exercise, especially as many of the larger ones were extremely cumbersome.

There were other theories, too: for example, that the stones had moved as a result of some kind of magnetic effect or even of mysterious vibrations, or that they had been swept along the Playa by floods.

In 1968, two Californian geologists, Robert P Sharp and Dwight L Carey decided to begin a long-term study of the moving stones. Their first move was to label twenty-five of the stones with a name and a letter. Thus Mary Ann, Sue, Sally, Milly, Jane, Carmen, Margie and the others were chosen, and their positions marked with a steel stake.

Over a period of seven years Sharp and Carey, while not considering the mystery of the moving stones as a matter of great scientific importance, gathered an impressive array of facts. They found, for example, that stones were not the only things which moved by themselves on Racetrack Playa: there were tracks left by twigs, brush, burro droppings and possibly sheets of ice. The tracks were often complex: one stone, I (Kristy), moved north for 165 ft (50 m), and travelled back in a south-southwest direction, while eight of the twenty-three stones that moved in the winter of 1973–74 went north-northeast for 100 ft (30 m). Sometimes, whole groups of stones would move, sometimes only a single one would take off, leaving the others behind. Over the seven-year period, the champion traveller was H (Nancy), which notched up a track of 860 ft (262 m) in a series of movements—although, at other times, stones may have moved more than $1\frac{3}{4}$ miles (3 km).

More important, the scientists felt they could discount one theory which had been advanced to account for the phenomenon:

The intriguing mystery of the stones that move in California's Death Valley

that the stones moved when they were caught up in blocks of ice. There was ample evidence against this, including the fact that when stones were in groups some moved and others did not and when more than one did move, the distances they travelled were different. Furthermore, the tracks of two neighbouring stones often did not remain parallel, and sometimes crossed each other. One ingenious monitoring device was to make a 'corral' of stakes to surround some of the stones. The idea was that, if ice blocks did cause the movement, they would now be unable to get to the stones or to escape with them if they formed within the corral. In fact a stone soon moved out of a corral, which was another blow to advocates of the ice-block theory.

While all these factors were inconsistent with their being caught up in a block of ice, what, then, did account for their movement? Seven years of observation had provided a clue: the greatest number of movements had occurred during the winters of 1968–69, 1972–73 and 1973–74, and always in the wake of a storm. However, the investigators also established that the stones did not move every time the Playa was wet. The conditions, therefore, had to be just right, and in their report, Sharp and Carey summed them up:

> 'Wetting of the Playa surface is required to the extent that a thin, slimy, water-saturated mud layer overlies a still firm base. This condition is attained within an hour or two after water gathers on the surface. Stained areas forward of some moved stones suggest that only a thin film of water lay on the Playa surface at the time these stones moved.'

Once the Playa was slippery enough, the stones almost certainly began to move after being rocked by abnormally strong gusts of wind, and, 'once underway, the stones, judging from their tracks, literally sail across the Playa surface', at a pace which the scientists describe as 'something more than a slow creep'.

Of course, no one has yet seen one of the stones actually move, and it is possible that Sharp and Carey's hypothesis might still be discounted. Their conclusion is, however, a reasonable and justifiable one to draw after seven years of thought and observation, and few people can believe that an impenetrable mystery now remains on Racetrack Playa or, indeed, on any of the other half dozen playas in California or Nevada where stones have been known to move.

The Dark Day

In shedding light on this mystery, the investigators were working well within the capabilities of tried and tested scientific method. They were able to observe the phenomenon carefully, over a considerable period of time, and were then able to make their deductions. This is, of course, even easier to do if a scientist is actually present during a strange occurrence.

This does not happen often, but it did in America on 19 May 1780 when, between ten and eleven o'clock in the morning, the famous 'Dark Day' began, and New England was plunged into darkness which lasted until the following night. One contemporary account records some of the uncanny events that followed:

> '. . . the birds having sung their evening songs, disappeared, and became silent: the fowls retired to roost; the cocks were crowing all around, as at break of day; objects could not be distinguished but at a very little distance; and everything bore the appearance and gloom of night.'

As the darkness covered the land, the bewildered settlers of early America began to panic. There were extraordinary scenes in the Connecticut legislature, which was in full session at the time. When the darkness fell, many members thought that the end of the world had come and some proposed

Mysterious mid-afternoon darkness on 24 September 1950 in Main Street, Buffalo, NY

that the house should adjourn. Whereupon, a Mr Davenport arose and said 'Mr Speaker, —it is either the day of judgment, or it is not. If it is not, there is no need of adjourning. If it is, I desire to be found doing my duty. I move that candles be brought, and that we proceed to business.'

However, the politicians and people did not have to contemplate the end of the world for long, for the darkness soon lifted, and everyone was able to go about their business as before. And an explanation for the strange dark day was soon forthcoming from a Professor Samuel Williams of Massachusetts, who had been able to study the phenomenon while it was happening. He wrote:

> 'It is well known that in this part of America it is customary to make large fires in the woods, for the purpose of clearing the lands in the new settlements. This was the case this spring, in a much greater degree than is common. In the county of York, in the western parts of this state, and in Vermont, uncommonly large and extensive fires had been kept up.'

Williams, by studying the weather conditions, and analysing scum that fell during the darkness—it turned out to be the ashes of burnt leaves—had correctly concluded that enormous forest fires can cause Dark Days. Something similar happened in September 1950, when the sun turned blue in the Scottish capital of Edinburgh, a few days after many American cities had been plunged into such darkness that baseball match floodlights had had to be turned on in the early afternoon. The cause, once again, was forest fires, this time in Alberta.

Frogs in the rock

No scientist, as far as we know, has had direct experience of another type of mystery: the extraordinary tales of frogs and toads that can apparently survive for very long periods entombed in rocks. Over the years, there have been persistent reports of coalminers or quarry-

A mummified toad in a flint nodule

men breaking open a rock or a lump of coal, only to see a frog or a toad hop out. One graphic example of a 'toad in the hole' was found by a British geologist, Dr Jack Treagus, of Manchester University, and described in an 1811 report by the noted Derbyshire geologist, White Watson. He said that 'in Bolsover Field in 1795 on breaking open a block of limestone a ton and a half in weight, a toad was discovered alive in the centre, which died immediately.' Another report concerns a toad called 'Old Rip' who apparently survived being entombed in the cornerstone of a courthouse in Schenectady for more than thirty years.

Intrigued by such reports, the famous English naturalist, Dr William Buckland, embarked on a series of rather grotesque experiments to test the validity of the claims contained therein. On 26 November 1825, he buried twenty-four toads in sealed cells, some in solid and some in porous limestone. When he dug them up, just over a year later, on 10 December 1826, all the toads entombed in the solid limestone were dead and had obviously been dead for many months. Some of those in the porous limestone, however, were still alive, although they finally starved to death when they had to undergo another year's imprisonment in the name of science. Death had also overtaken some more toads which were sealed up in the trunk of an apple tree. Having established that toads cannot live for a year enclosed in stone, entirely without air, and that they certainly cannot live for two years entirely without food, Dr Buckland declared:

'... we may, I think find a solution of such phenomena in the habits of these reptiles, and of the insects which form their food. The first effort of the young toad, as soon as it has left its tadpole state and emerged from the water, is to seek shelter in holes and crevices of rocks and trees. An individual, which, when young, may have thus entered a cavity by some very narrow aperture, would find abundance of food by catching insects, which like itself seek shelter in such cavities, and may soon have increased so much in bulk as to render it impossible to get out again through the narrow aperture at which it entered. A small hole of this kind is very likely to be overlooked by common workmen, who are the only people whose operations on stone and wood disclose cavities in the interior of such substances.'

Such an explanation could almost certainly account for the mummified toad now preserved in the Brighton Museum, with the flint nodule in which it was found. It turned up when two workmen found an unnaturally light stone in Lewes, and excited a great deal of interest at the time. It is probably the only known example of a 'toad in the hole' now in captivity, and certainly proves that there is a basis for the reports of the phenomenon. In fact, soon after its discovery, investigators found a tiny hole at one end of the stone, which no one had noticed before, since it had become filled up with silted chalk.

Ball lightning

If good observation were enough, however, scientists would have sorted out the problem of ball lightning long ago, because there are countless eyewitness reports of the phenomenon, dating back many centuries. According to those who have seen it, ball lightning is a terrifying sight. Often a luminous ball suddenly appears, advancing noisily towards the witness, occasionally burning people and objects, often disappearing after a violent explosion. For example, the unfortunate Diane de Poitiers (the mistress of Henry II of France) was said to have been burned by a flame which ran round her bedroom on her wedding night in 1557. In 1596, according to one account, an alarming thing happened while a Dr Rogers was preaching his first sermon in Wells Cathedral:

'In his sermon, according to a text which he had chosen, and having made no prayer, he began to discourse of spirits and their properties; and within a while after there entered in at the west window of the church a dark and unproportionable thing of the bigness of a football, and went along the wall on the pulpit side; and suddenly it seemed to break but with no less sound and terror than if an hundred cannons had been discharged at once; and therewithal came a most violent storm and tempest of lightning and thunder as if the church had been full of fire.'

All very dramatic, but, despite such stories, to later scientists this type of event presented a puzzle: no one could decide whether ball lightning really existed or not. There was no real problem before the 'scientific age' brought new discoveries about the nature of electricity: people were content to accept that ball lightning, like thunder or torrential rain, was just another manifestation of an unpredictable and often hostile universe. In the nineteenth century, however, scientists who studied electricity were unable to reconcile their knowledge with the idea that something like lightning could exist in a self-contained round ball. In the laboratories of the world, reports like this one from 1892 were often treated with disdain:

'... a family were in a house with doors and windows open, and a luminous ball seemed to leap from the wire, pass through the open door and a window, and pursue its course some rods through the open space

Roy Jennings took this photograph of the path and point of explosion of ball lightning at 2 am during a storm at Castleford, Yorkshire

behind the house. A boy in the room grasped his thumb and cried out, "I'm struck", and Mr Hewett felt a sensation in his left arm for some time. A girl seized her shawl and rushed out of the house to chase the ball. She reported that she pursued it some distance, while it bounded lightly along, until it seemed to be dissipated in the air without an explosion. . . .'

In more recent times, however, many scientists have come to recognize that ball lightning may, after all, exist. This is partly because their increased understanding not only of meteorology but of plasma physics has begun to provide a framework within which they can examine and begin to understand the problem, and partly because the flow of eyewitness reports has not abated.

There was, for example, an extraordinary manifestation of the phenomenon at the small Scottish seaside resort of Crail in August 1966. On the afternoon in question, Mrs Elizabeth Radcliffe was returning home from a walk along a concrete path near the seashore.

'I looked up and saw what I thought was a sort of light, and almost instantaneously it turned itself into a ball, between the size of a tennis ball and a football. It crossed the path and changed colour slightly into the colour of the path. Then it passed over the grass and turned greenish, and, very quickly disappeared towards a café and went bang.'

Inside the café, Mrs Evelyn Murdoch was in the kitchen, cooking for the customers.

'The café was busy, everything was normal. Then, all of a sudden there was an awful disturbance: terrible cracking sounds, and they increased all the time. I looked through the kitchen window, and people were running from the beach screaming and shouting, and the noise got louder. Then, all of a sudden, there was one vicious crack. It seemed to go all through the hut, and the whole kitchen lit up with a luminous glare. I never saw anything like it in the whole of my life. . . .

'The customers all ran out of the café, and a man with a wooden leg who usually sat at a table just next to the counter was gone with all the rest. You never saw anybody move so quickly in your whole life.'

Later, Mrs Murdoch found that the thick cast-iron top of the café's big stove had been split from end to end. Mrs Murdoch's daughter, Mrs Jean Meldrum, was visiting the beach café when the fireball struck. She had left her baby son outside in his pram, and, as the strange noise grew louder and louder, she rushed to rescue him. It was then that she saw the ball of fire.

'It was a luminous orange in the middle, and pure white all round the side, and it rolled right along the wall of the café. It came to the window, and, when I stood up to see what it was, the thing came out of the window and battered across the front of my chest, and then just vanished.

At a nearby caravan site, Mrs Kitty Cox was out walking her two dogs.

'Suddenly, there was a tremendous clap of thunder, and then from the land right across in front of us I heard screaming, and children ran away, and this hissing ball came in front of me trailing what looked like a copper ribbon two or three inches wide at the back of it. My dogs

The clear round hole in the window at Edinburgh University's Department of Meteorology attributed to ball lightning and shown here actual size

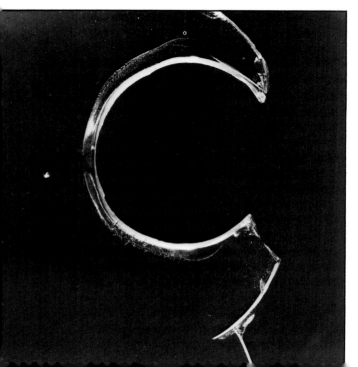

panicked, and I watched as it went past very quickly, hissing and whirring, and went right across into the sea.'

From America comes the extraordinary story of Clara Greenlee and her husband who witnessed a reddish-orange ball of lightning shoot through the screen of the concrete patio in their home at Crystal River, Florida. The ball, the size of a basketball, rolled along the floor, whereupon Mrs Greenlee batted it with a fly swat which she happened to be holding in her hand. The ball exploded with the sound of a shotgun blast. 'That ought to have got the fly,' said Clara Greenlee's neighbour, Mrs Riggs.

In the African state of Cameroon in 1960, Mrs Joyce Casey was going to the kitchen one night, when 'a thing like a car headlamp' rushed towards her down the passage. As it came near her, it turned aside into the bathroom and disappeared down the washbasin.

Now, an increasing number of scientists have themselves seen ball lightning or at least experienced its effects. At Edinburgh University's Department of Meteorology a hole was found in a window of the building after a storm, and, since the glass was fused on the inside, the event has been attributed to ball lightning.

One of the most detailed sightings by a scientist was made in March 1963 by Professor R C Jennison of the Electronics Laboratories at the University of Kent in unusual and alarming circumstances. He reported in *Nature* that he had been sitting near the front of the passenger cabin of an Eastern Airlines night flight from New York to Washington, when the aircraft was caught up in a violent electrical storm. Not only was it then 'enveloped in a sudden bright and loud electrical discharge', but, Professor Jennison wrote, 'some seconds after this a glowing sphere a little more than twenty centimetres in diameter emerged from the pilot's cabin and passed down the aisle of the aircraft approximately fifty centimetres from me, maintaining the same height and course over which it could be observed.'

One aspect of this sighting casts doubt on one widely held theory about ball lightning: that it was no more than an optical illusion, the 'after-image' on the retina of the eye of a conventional lightning flash. For Professor Jennison also reported that the ball was witnessed by another person, 'a terrified air hostess who was strapped in her seat on the opposite side and farther to the rear of the aircraft. She saw the ball continue to travel down the aisle and finally disappear towards the lavatory at the end.'

Ball lightning has also been photographed, although some scientists are wary of such evidence, believing that it is easy to confuse some other light phenomenon for the real thing. One man, however, has obtained not just still photographs but 16 mm film of what may be a ball lightning event. He is Professor James Tuck, who was born in England but is now an American citizen. In a distinguished scientific career, he worked as Chief Scientific Adviser to Winston Churchill's colleague Lord Cherwell, and then went on to join the Manhattan Project, which made the atomic bomb, at Los Alamos. Today, Professor Tuck still lives in Los Alamos, and it was here that he began an experiment to study ball lightning in the laboratory: something that many researchers had attempted in vain.

Professor Tuck had heard that ball lightning occurred from time to time in submarines, as a result of an incorrect manipulation of switch gear taking power from the battery. If an error was made, fireballs, it was said, would come out of the rear of the switch gear and sometimes burn the clumsy submariners' legs. Tuck's attempts to investigate the phenomenon actually on board a submarine were frustrated, but he discovered that, at Los Alamos itself, there was a two-million-dollar submarine battery that had been installed for another research programme, but was now lying idle. He was given permission to work with it, and a series of 'bootleg' experiments thus began, with Tuck and his colleagues working on the project during their lunch hour or outside of their normal working periods.

Although they produced some extremely large power discharges from the battery, James Tuck and his colleagues were unable to produce anything like ball lightning. As the months went on, they found themselves under pressure to finish their experiments, so that the building that housed the battery could be cleared to make room for another research programme. Suddenly there was no time left. Outside, the bulldozers were ready to begin work. The scientists had tried almost everything they could think of, but had produced no ball lightning. As a final desperate attempt to achieve their aim, they decided to add something to the atmosphere around the switch. Thus, they built a small cellophane box around the switch and blew a low concentration of methane into it. They had thought that the amount of gas was small enough to be non-inflammable—nevertheless, they were, fortunately, crouching behind sandbags, when the switch was turned on. There was a sheet of flame and a thundering roar, and all any of them later remembered seeing was the roof of the building lifting off.

It was the end of their experiment, but it was not until film of the event, taken from different angles by two cameras, came back from processing, that they discovered what else had happened. On about a hundred frames, there was a ball of light about 10 cm in diameter. Professor Tuck is certain that it is not something produced by a defect in the film or by the processing. That said, he is not certain what it is, except that it may be some phenomenon related to ball lightning.

James Tuck is now attempting to classify the characteristics of ball lightning, and has isolated several potentially important factors. Among them, that the phenomenon usually occurs after a stroke of conventional lightning, the ball is, on average 15 cm in radius, usually coloured yellow to red, is not markedly hot, and often gives off a hissing sound.

From picking through these characteristics, a theory acceptable to most scientists may emerge. Tuck favours a chemical re-action as the origin of ball lightning, but the scientific literature is full of other theories, from 'anti-matter meteorites' to variations on the optical illusion theme. Today, despite a growing list of character-istics formulated from reliable eyewitness reports, almost nothing is certain about ball lightning, but many scientists now feel increasingly confident that they will, one day, be able to explain it.

The story of the gradual acceptance of ball lightning as a real phenomenon has been repeated many times when science has en-countered mysteries. Today, it is astonishing to recall that the existence of meteorites was once totally denied and hotly debated in the French Royal Academy of Sciences. The scientists simply could not believe that stones could fall out of the sky, and although they were familiar with meteors in the sky and with strange 'thunderstones' that had fallen on France, they failed to connect the two because there was not only no body of

observation to connect them, but also there was no scientific theory to account for them. It was only when the respected German physicist, Ernst Chladni, postulated the existence of meteorites that scientists took them seriously enough to make observa-tions. Once they had embraced this new attitude, confirmation that meteorites did fall from the heavens soon followed.

Many of the mysteries in this book may undergo the same process. At the moment, 'official' science considers the existence of phenomena such as UFOs, yetis and lake monsters to be highly unlikely. Yet, as we have seen, scientists once took a similar view of meteorites and, more recently, of ball lightning. Many of the mysteries in this book are certainly susceptible to investiga-tion; as techniques of detection improve, convincing explanations for sightings of mysterious creatures or UFOs may emerge.

Mysterious mounds

Paradoxically, it may ultimately prove that the most difficult mysteries to solve may be those that we have definite physical evidence for. No amount of scientific method and apparatus can now tell us the thoughts

Silbury Hill drawn by the eighteenth-century antiquarian William Stukely. This strange artificial mound was built 4,500 years ago

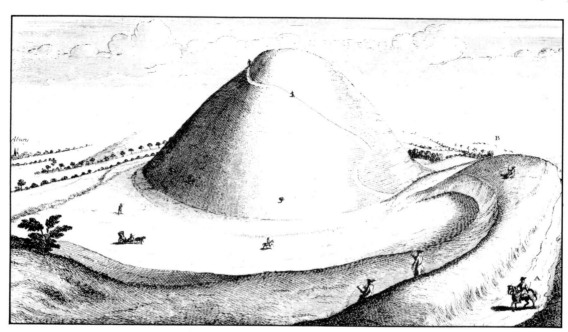

The Great Serpent Mound of Adams County, Ohio, investigated by the archaeologist F W Putnam

and intentions of people who, many many centuries ago, left behind them strange relics of their civilizations. In Britain, Silbury Hill, an artificial mound built 4,500 years ago, is arguably the most puzzling of all. It is huge—its base alone covers 5 acres (2 ha)—and to build it would have taken, say, five hundred people ten years of continuous labour, since it is made of the equivalent of thirty-six million basketfuls of chalk. It stands like an upturned pudding basin in a hollow beside the old London to Bath road: nearby is the vast stone circle of Avebury.

Many early visitors assumed that it was some sort of burial mound, others suggested that it contained treasure. In 1776, a shaft was dug from the top right into the middle of the hill; in 1849 a tunnel was dug, also into the centre, and in 1968, archaeologists once again penetrated the heart of Silbury Hill, thanks to another tunnel skilfully engineered, and dug with the aid of modern min-

ing techniques. These and other smaller-scale excavations have established that the hill was built in great steps, with enormous care taken to ensure that the structure did not collapse, and that one of the first things the builders did was to erect a fence on the site. But no treasure, no burial and no memorial has been found and excavation has revealed no clues as to why Silbury was built.

The New World also has an old world that only grudgingly yields up its secrets. All over the United States, remains of civilizations that flourished long before Columbus, mark the landscape of the open country and loom up in the shadow of the freeway. Many relics are earthen mounds, built on a scale so vast that early settlers believed them to have been beyond the capabilities of the Indians they found there, preferring to hark back instead to a nobler race of 'mound-builders'. These, some thought, were itinerant Danes or Welshmen or even refugees from Atlantis. We know now that the mounds were, after all, built by ancient Indian tribes: some as tombs for the dead, and others as platforms for great temples.

In September 1883, however, F W Putnam, one of the 'fathers' of American archaeology, turned his attention to the puzzle of another type of ancient construction, known as the Effigy Mounds. There are still some of them in existence: pictures of birds and animals made by shaping piles of earth. It was to the greatest of these that Putnam came that autumn: the Great Serpent Mound of Adams County, Ohio. Today, as then, the Serpent winds sinuously for more than 400 yd (365 m) along the top of a cliff above a creek. Its tail is in a tight spiral, and the main part of its body is pleated as though it is about to strike. But the strangest aspect of all is its head: its jaws gape, and it seems to be in the act of swallowing an egg. Like many visitors since —and the Serpent Mound is now the focal point of a National Park—Putnam was overwhelmed by his first sight of the creature as he scrambled up the steep hillside from the wagon he had travelled in. He wrote later:

'The most singular sensation of awe and admiration overwhelmed me at this sudden realization of my long-cherished desire, for here before me was the mysterious work of an unknown people, whose seemingly most sacred place we had invaded.'

Thanks partly to Putnam, American archaeologists had made great advances during the nineteenth century in the understanding of their country's past, but the true purpose of the Effigy Mounds still eluded them. Putnam, however, was determined that this state of affairs should not last.

'Reclining on one of the huge folds of this gigantic serpent, as the last rays of the sun glancing from their distant hilltops, cast their long shadows over the valley, I mused on the probabilities of the past: and there seemed to come to me a picture as of a distant time, of a people with strange customs, and with it came the demand for an interpretation of this

mystery. The unknown must become known!'

Accordingly, Putnam decided to return to Ohio later, to solve the mystery of the Great Serpent Mound once and for all through the standard archaeological method of excavation. He therefore cut sections through the Serpent itself and dug into the mounds surrounding it. His finds were disappointingly meagre: practically nothing in the Serpent and the stone tools, flint knives and skeletons that were unearthed nearby could tell him no more than that there had been considerable Indian activity on the spot. But there was nothing at all to help him achieve the aim he had set himself during that sunset reverie on his first visit to the mound: to solve the mystery of why a great serpent had been constructed in this remote stretch of country so long ago. This did not, however, prevent him from speculating about its purpose, and peopling the landscape in his mind with tribes who came to worship at this sinuous shrine. After all, when conventional methods of investigation have been thoroughly tried and found wanting, then speculation, that most pleasurable aspect of the study of mysteries, can finally come into play. For while science has its limits, the imagination has none.

Arthur C Clarke comments:
This final chapter—let's frankly admit it—is a patchwork made from some of the unclassifiable fragments left over from our researches. We could have used many others, for the catalogue of mysterious events, strange phenomena and archaeological enigmas is endless. . . . Indeed, we must ourselves be creating many for our remote descendants to puzzle over. Why did the Americans and Russians dig those mysterious holes in the ground, capped with heavy metal lids like the lairs of giant trapdoor spiders? What is *really* going on in those ancient films of 'rock concerts'—could they be some kind of religious ceremony? Did Charlie Chaplin, James Bond, David Frost,

Tarzan, Stalin really exist, or are they purely mythical? And so on. . . .

This might be a good place at which to make some final observations about mysteries. In the Introduction, I classified them according to our degree of understanding, which could range from total ignorance to complete comprehension—at which point, of course, the 'mystery' vanishes.

But another way of classifying them would be by their importance. Some—like the moving stones—are quite trivial; though interesting, they are not likely to improve human welfare or advance our knowledge of the universe. Others may have the potential to change our world.

UFOs could fall into this category, though personally I doubt it. So could paranormal phenomena; indeed, I have devoted one novel (*Childhood's End*) to this theme. But the mystery on which I'd put most of my money is ball lightning.

We live on a solid earth, sailing its seas, breathing its air. But most of the matter in the universe is *not* in the three familiar states of solid, liquid, gas. It is a 'plasma' —an enormously hot, electrically charged fluid—the stuff of stars and atomic fireballs.

Ball lightning may be a bit of plasma brought down to earth by some trick of Nature.* If we can discover the laws that control it, we may have found the secret of eternal power—because it is in a controlled plasma that scientists hope to release the energy of hydrogen fusion.

But whether they are important or not, easily seen through or impossible of solution —mysteries are *fun*. Even if they are only Nature's practical jokes, they add to our enjoyment of the marvellous universe around us; and my colleagues and I hope that we have conveyed some of that enjoyment to you.

And, perhaps, we may have helped to unravel some of these mysteries by the very act of presenting them to a wide public. If we can find the answers to as many as ten per cent, I should be very pleased—and surprised.

And even if we got the answers to one hundred per cent, there are plenty more where they came from. . . .

---

*Ball lightning seems to have a preference for high altitudes. I once said to J B S Haldane: 'I understand that your father did some work on ball lightning at the top of Pike's Peak.' (The 4,300-m high mountain in Colorado.) 'No,' replied JBS 'Ball lightning did some work on my father.' That was all I could get out of him.

Acknowledgments

The mysteries in this book would be even more mysterious if it were not for the dedicated work of a disparate but single-minded collection of individuals in many corners of the globe. They have devoted, if not their lives, then certainly their imaginations to the task of, like Theo Brown, tracking the Footprints of the Devil across the English countryside, or, like Jim Woodman, taking to the air in the most Heath Robinson of machines to photograph the Nazca Lines in Peru.

In the top security atom bomb headquarters of Los Alamos in New Mexico, Professor James Tuck did not blanch at blowing the top off a building in his search for the secret of ball lightning. Tim Dinsdale saw the Loch Ness monster and promptly gave up his job and twenty years of his life to trying to find it again. There is the man in Canada who relentlessly rides the Greyhound buses in pursuit of fish-falls and mysterious explosions; Dr Krinov who lost a toe to frostbite in the quest for the Great Siberian Explosion; and Chicago Professor, Roy Mackal, who trekked into the darkest Congo jungle in search of a living dinosaur.

If the spaceships really do want to contact us poor earthlings, then at least Ray Stanford and hundreds of thousands of dollars' worth of hardware are ready and waiting, day and night, in Austin, Texas.

If Bigfoot should ever step out of the Cascade Mountains, then Dr Grover Krantz is also prepared. He never travels without a loaded .44 calibre rifle.

From Professor Michael O'Kelly, waiting alone in the dark of an Irish night to prove his theories about the oldest building in the world, to Aubrey Burl dreaming by moonlight of death and human sacrifice beside the ancient Scottish circle of Castle Fraser, it is the insight and imagination of inspired individuals which has sustained and enlightened us in our researches.

As Nobel Prizewinner Richard Feynman said, 'It does no harm to the mystery to know a little about it.' If we know a little more, it is thanks to such men and women who have risked not only their reputations, but often life and limb, to illuminate the darker corners of Nature and human nature.   Simon Welfare and John Fairley

The authors and publishers thank Victor Gollancz Ltd for permission to reproduce an extract from Arthur C Clarke's *The View from Serendip* and *Rendezvous with Rama* which is published in the US by Harcourt Brace Jovanovich, Inc; Ernest Benn Bros Ltd, London and St Martin's Press Inc, NY for the extract from the *Complete Short Stories* of H G Wells; and Paul Elek Ltd for the extract from F A Mitchell-Hedges' *Danger My Ally*. The authors also thank their colleagues at Yorkshire TV, in particular John Fanshawe and Michael Deakin.

The illustrations on the pages indicated below are reproduced by permission of:

Aerofilms 87; Frederick Aldrich 72; K. M. Andrew 60; American Anthropological Research Foundation 25 *bottom*; Associated Press 174, 204; BBC Hulton Picture Library 52, 142, 197; Bettmann Archive 200; Chris Bonington/Bruce Coleman Ltd 18; Janet and Colin Bord 59; Borough of Brighton 205; Paul and Lena Bottriell 136; British Museum/Aldus Books 32; British Tourist Authority 84; Cambridge University Collection 119; Camera Press *Rear endpaper*; Bruce Coleman Ltd 16 *bottom*, 31, 86; Robin Constable 6, 34, 35, 91; Eric Crichton/Bruce Coleman Ltd 122; Crown copyright reserved 89; Crown copyright. Science Museum 67; Lester Davies 17; Devon and Exeter Institution 47; Tim Dinsdale 111, 112; Francisco Erize/Bruce Coleman Ltd 144; Robert Estall 90, 97, 118, 125; Express Newspapers 109 *bottom*; Fortean Picture Library 23, 25 *top*, 27, 33, 38, 45, 79, 113, 114, 172, 181; Arlene Gaal 105; Gamma/Hermann 152; Dr Georg Gerster/John Hillelson Agency 128, 129, 130, 211; Richard Griffiths 43; Jack B. Hartung/N.A.S.A. 186; from Hughes 'Scouring of the White Horse' 1859 121; Lord Hunt 13; The Illustrated London News 55, 56, 57, 125, 203; Roy Jennings/Frank W. Lane 207; Kyodo News Enterprise Co. 107; Lowell Observatory, Flagstaff 192, 194; M.E.P.L. 69, 76, 210; Macmillan (Australia) 147; Mansell Collection 73, 78; John Massey-Stewart 150, 166; Edwin Mickleburgh/Ardea 95; W. G. Miller 126; Pat Morris/Ardea 137; Tony Morrison 131; Musée de l'Homme, Paris 54; Museum of Mankind 50; National Museum of Ireland 44; Naval Ocean Systems Center 70 *top*; Novosti 149; Veronica Papworth 37; Patterson/Gimlin © 1968 Dahinden 24; Pelizaeus-Museum, Hildesheim 63; Photri 185, 198; Bernard Pickard 123; Popperfoto 15 *bottom*, 19, 109 *top*, 162, 170, 180; Rainbird Picture Library 41, 64 *left*, 64 *right*, 80, 141, 143, 154, 158, 159, 160, 163, 171 *right*, 175, 187; Slavomir Rawicz/William Tschernezky 28; Bernard Regent/Alan Hutchinson Library 68; G. R. Roberts 120; Roger-Viollet 188; Ann Ronan Picture Library 71, 77, 85; Royal Commission on the Ancient and Historical Monuments of Scotland 62; Royal Geographical Society 16 *top*; Royal Scottish Museum 81; Scala, Florence 196; Philippa Scott/N.H.P.A. 148; Scottish Tourist Board 93; Myra Shackley 30; Ian Shepherd 58; Derek de Solla Price 65, 66, 67; Sovfoto 165; Space Frontiers/N.A.S.A. 157, 168, 177, 191, 199; Spectrum 15 *top*; St Augustine Historical Society 75; Sunday Times 96; Syndication International 101, 108; Kojo Tanaka/Animals Animals/O.S.F. 138; Ron and Valerie Taylor/Ardea 70 *bottom*; R. Thompson/Frank W. Lane 179; The Times 140; Topix 103; Torquay Natural History Society 46; Universal Pictorial Press 171 *left*; University of Edinburgh 208; U.S. Department of The Interior 189; Wolfgang Volz 133; Ralph Wetzel 139; Don Whillans *Front endpaper*, 12; J. S. Whyte 21; Jim Woodman 116, 132; Yorkshire Television 92, 98, 110.

Index

Page numbers in *italics* refer to illustrations.

Abominable Snowman, *see* Yeti
Adam, A R, 106
Aldrin, Edwin, 180
Allison, Susan, 103
Allsop, Christopher, 118
Alma, 27, 30, 31
Alpine chough, 17
Amesbury, 85
Andrews, John, 80
Antikythera Mechanism, 64, *65, 66,* 67
Arnold, Kenneth, 170, 171, *171,* 172, 173, 176
Atacama Giant, *116,* 132
Atkinson, Prof. Richard, 87, 89, 94
Atluri, C R, 164
Aubrey, John, 86, 120
Avebury, 86, 87, *87,* 89, 97, 211

Baghdad battery, 62, *63,* 64
Ball lightning, 183, 206, 207, 208, 209, 210, 213
Barnum, P T, 106, 202
Barringer, Daniel, 158
Baskerville, Thomas, 120
Battell, Joan, 37
Baum, Richard, 190
Bayanov, Dr, 24, 29
Beck, Fred, 22
Behme, Mrs Robert L, 23
Bellamy, Robert, 23
Belcher, Sir Edward, 68
Bermuda Triangle, 10
Berry, Clive, 145
Bigfoot, 13, 14, 21–27, 30, 31
Black beast of Ponenegamook, 105
Blakiston, Captain, 41
Blythe Giants, 117, 127
Bonacase, Serge, 141, 143
Bordet, Abbé, 17, 21
Bottriell, Paul & Lena, 136
Bourne, Dr Geoffrey, 145
Bowen, Patrick, 136
Boyce, Peter, 195
Branner, Johnny, 40
Braunholtz, H J, 53
Brontosaurus, 149, 150
Brown, John, 164, 165
Brown, Theo, 47, 48
Buckland, Dr William, 205, 206
Bullen, F T, 72
Bunyip, 101

Burchak Abramovich, Prof., 13
Burke, Father Matthew, 102
Burl, Dr Aubrey, 97, *98,* 99
Burney, Sidney, 53, 54
Burton, Dr Maurice, 110, 114, 115
Burtsev, Dr Igor, 24, *27*

Cadborosaurus (Caddy), 79, 80, 105
Caesar, Julius, 60, 85
Callahan, Philip S., 178
Campbell, Alex, 102, 110, *110,* 111
Campbell, Sherri, 105
Cardiff Giant, 201, *201,* 202
Carey, Dwight L., 203, 204
Carrdus, Kenneth, 126, 127
Carter, Jimmy, 177
Casey, Joyce, 208
Castle Fraser, 97, 98
Castlerigg, Cumbria, 89, *90*
Cerne Giant, 121, 122, *122,* 123, 124, 125, 126
Chacoan peccary (*Catagonus wagneri*), 139, *139,* 140
Champ, 101, 106
Champlain, Samuel, 106
Chapman, Jan, 45
Cherhill White Horse, 118, *118*
Childe, Gordon, 61, 62, *62*
Chinese seals, 43, *44,* 45, 49
Chladni, Ernst, 210
Chumbi, Khunjo, *19,* 20
Circle of Stenness, 92
Clancarty, Earl of, 169, 170, *171,* 173, 174, 176, 181, 182
Clark, Anthony, 126
Clark, Burton, 76
Clava Cairns, 89
Cochran, Jack, 22
Coffeyville Hailstone, 41, 42
Conrad, Charles, 180
Covington, Richard, 189
Cowan, Clyde, 164
Cox, Kitty, 208
Cox, Lt R E Grimani, 71
Cronin, 15
Cromwell, Debbie, 41
Crystal skull, 51, *51,* 54, 55
Cullers, Wilbert, 40, *41*

Dall, Prof. W H, 74
Däniken, Erich von, 133
Darbyshire, Stephen, 180, 181
Darwin, Charles, 14, 201
'Dark Day', 204, 205
Davenport, Mr, 205

Davies, Sqn Ldr Lester, 17
Davies, Peter, 113
Davidson, Lt R N, 71
de Solla Price, Prof. Derek, 65, 66, 67, 201
'Devil's footprints', 45–58, *45*
Dinsdale, Tim, 111, *111*
Doig, Desmond, 19, 20, 21, 31
Domani, Lakhpa, 15
Donskoy, Dr, 24
Doroshenko, N, 83
Douglass, Andrew, E, 194, *194*
Doveton, Mr, 46
Dun Lagaidh, 59 (fort)
Dunnideer, 59

Eastnor, Lord, 39
Edwards, Sqn Ldr John, 14
Effigy Mounds, 212
Einstein, Albert, 190
'Elder Brother', 127
Eggebrecht, Dr Arne, 63, *64*
Egorov, 28
Ellacombe, Reverend H T, 46, *47*
Encke, 165
Evans, Philip, 175
Exiguus, Dionysius, 196
Ezekiel, 170

Fawcett, Captain, 142
Fedorovich, Professor B A, 29
Fish, Mr, 47
Flanagan, Dennis, 67
Fletcher: Diane, 104; Ed, 103, 104
Folden, Art, 104
Fogarty, Quentin, 174, 175
Forstner, Georg von, 80
Fort, Charles, 33, *33,* 36, 37, 43, 45, 49; Forteana, 33, 48
Fox, Paul, 195
Franssen, Lt, 136, 137
Fraser, Janet, 109
Fraser, Constable John, 102
Frazer, Dr, 44, 45
Frogs in the rock, 205, 206
Fursdon, Henrietta, 46

Gaal, Arlene B, 104
Gale, Mr and Mrs, 34, 35
Gallon, M, 148
Gamache, Sgt Larry, 22
Gardner, George, 142
Gavin, James, 78
Geddes, Tex, 78
Gennaro, Joseph, 75

Gervase, 184, 186, 187
Getty, Edmund, 44
Giant Balls, 51, 55–58, *55*
Gigantopithecus, 17, 20
Gimlin, Bob, 23
Gomez, Dr Luis Diego, 58
Gordon, Richard, 180
Grant, Arthur, 113
Gravett, K W E, 125
Gray, Hugh, 108
Great Serpent Mound, 21
Greenall, John, 39
Greenland whale, 83
Greenlee, Clara, 208
Grieve, Dr D W, 24
Griffiths, Dr Richard, 42
Grønningsæter, Arne, 74
Guiller, Dr Eric, 146

Ha'ak, 127
Hackpen horse, 119
Hagenbeck, Carl, 150
Haldane, J B S, 183, 213
Halley's comet, 164, 196
Hansen, Frank, 27
Harkness, Mrs William, 138, 139
Harry, Muchalat, 22
Hartung, Dr Jack B, 184, 186, 187
Hawes, Nancy, 175, *175*, 176
Hawkins, Gerald S, 128
Heel Stone, 85
Heinz, Father Victor, 142
Helith, Helis, Helethkin, 124
Helm, Thomas, 78, 79
Hercules, 124, 126
Herod, 196, 197, 198
Heuvelmans, Dr B, 26, 27, 78, 141
Hewett, Mr, 207
Hewlett, Lord, 176
Hichens, Capt. William
Hillary, Sir Edmund, 19, *19*, 20, 30
Hobbes, Reverend W E, 109
Hod Hill, 123
Hook, Mr, 47
Hopwas, 37
Hottinger, Sgt Carl 'Butch', 40, *41*
Hoyle, Sir Frederick, 49
Hughes, David W, 164, 165, 197
Huband Smith, Joseph, 43
Hull, George, 201
Hunt, Lord, 13, 15, 21
Hunter, Ellen S, 195, 196
Hutchins, Reverend John, 123
Hutchinson, Derek, 83
Hynek, Dr J Allen, 175

Io, *199*
Irvine, Malcolm, 111
Issie, 101, 107, *107*

Jackson, A A, 164
Java Man, 24
Jennings, Roy, 207
Jesus Christ, 196, 197, 198, 199
Johanson, J C, 150

Jennison, Prof. R C, 208, 209
Jones, L R, 106
Jones, R V, 177
Josephus, Flavius, 196
Juszczyk, Wiktor, 28, 29

Kangchenjunga, 17, 18, 31
Kawaji, Yutaka, 107
Kazantsev, 166
Keel Cross, 86
Keith, Sir Arthur, 144, 145
Kent, five men of, 184, 186
Kepler, Johannes, 196, 197, *197*
Khalkov, Prof., 31
Kilburn Horse, 118
Kimberley, Earl of, 170
Kings Norton, Lord, 170, 176
Kintraw, 93, 94
Koffmann, Marie Jeanne, 29
Kolchak, Admiral, 153
Kolpachnikov, G N, 29
Komodo dragon, 139, 147, *148*
König, Wilhelm, 62, 63
Kosok, Paul, 127, 128
Kraken, 71, *71*, 72, 74
Krantz, Dr Grover S, 13, 25, *25*
Krinov, 160
Kulik, Leonid, 153, 154, 155, 156, 157, 158, 159, 160, 161

Lágarfljótsormur, 101, 102, 103
Lagoeira, Senhor, 142
Lapova, Koso, 156
Leblond, Paul H, 80
Lehman, Dr Robert, 40
Lescarbault, 187, 188
Leverrier, Urbain Jean Joseph, 187, 188, *188*, 189, 190, 191
Libby, W, 162, 164
Loanhead of Daviot, 98
Loch Ness Monster, 101, *101*, 102, *103*, 108, *108*, *109*, 110, 111, *112*, 113, 114, 115, 169
Locke, Tom, 106
Lockyer, Sir Norman, 91
Long Man of Wilmington, 125, *125*, 126
Long Meg and Her Daughters, 89, 93
Lothrop, Dr Samuel, 55, 56, *56*, 57
Love, Bob, 112
Lovell, Sir Bernard, 176
Lovell, Jim, 180
Lowell, Percival, 173, 191, 192, *192*, 193, 194, 195, 199
Loys, Francis de, 134, 143, 144, 145
Loys' ape, *134*, 143, 144
Lucia, Morris, 102
Ludlum, David, 36
Lyttelton, Dr, 122

Maccabee, Dr Bruce, 175
Machrie Moor, 89
Mackal, Prof. Roy, 150
Mackie, Dr Euan, 94

Maclean, R P, 105
McLeod, Dr James A, 103
Macleod, Torquil, 113
Macnab, Mr & Mrs, *110*
McNeely, J, 15
M'Quhae, Capt. Peter, 77
Maes Howe, 92, 93, *93*, 98
Manipogo, 101, 103, 105, 106
Mankin, R W, 178
Marlborough White Horse, 118
Marples, George, 118, 119
Mars, 192, 193, 196; Canals of, 191, 192, 194, 195, 198, 199
Martin, J C, 76
Martin, Rilla, 146
Matsubara, Sumiaki, 101, 107
Maunder, E A, 194
Megamouth shark, 70, *70*
Meldrum, Jean, 208
Menzel, Donald H, 178
Miller, Graham, 126, 127
Minnesota Ice Man, 26, *26*
Mitchell-Hedges: Anna, 51, 52, 53, 55; F A ('Mike'), 51, 52, *52*, 53
Moffat, Mr, 42
Moir, George, 145
Monmouth, Geoffrey of, 96
Monnard, Dr A, 150
Montandon, Dr Georges, 144, 145
Moody, Roland, 34, *34*, 35
Morant, Dr G M, 54
Morehouse, A J, 198, 199
Morgawr, *79*
Morrison, Tony, 129, 130
Mortlake Studd, General E, 46
Mowday, Sylvia, 36, 37
Murdoch, Evelyn, 207, 208
Musgrave, Reverend George, 47

Na-ha-ha-itkh *see* Ogopogo
Nazca lines, 117, 127, 128, *128*, 129, *129*, 130, 131, 133
Neanderthal Man, 13, 21, 26, 27, 30, 31, 201
Neely, Erin, 101, 104
Neptune, 187, 188
Nessie, *Nessiteras rhombopteryx*, *see* Loch Ness monster
Newcomb, Prof. Simon, 190
Newell, William C, 201, 202
Newgrange, 91, *91*, 92, 93, 95, 96, 98
New Guinea dragon, 147
New Pewsey Horse, 118, 119
Nisbet, Helen, 61
Nodens, 123, *123*, 124, 126
Nott, Julian, 131
Nunda, 134

Oberg, James, 178, 180
Ogopogo, 101, 103, 104, 105, *105*
Okhchen, Vasiley, 155, 157
Okapi, *137*, 138
O'Kelly, Prof. Michael, 91, 92, 95, *96*
Oliveira, Miguel Gastão de, 142

Omagari, M, 107
Osborne, Mr & Mrs, 34, 35, *35*, 36
Osborne, Fermin, 22
Osmington White Horse, 119
Other Side of the Sky, The ('The Star'), 199
Owen, Sir Richard, 48, 146

Palmer, A H, 109
Palmer, George, 117
Papworth, Veronica, 37, *37*
Patey, Ian, 39
Patterson, Roger, 23, *24*, *25*
Phillips, Joseph, 39
Pickard, Bernard, 123, 124
Piggott, S, 97, 120, 121, 124, 126
'Piltdown Man', 145
Pithecanthropus erectus, see Java Man
Pittman, John W, 37
Plenderleath, Reverend, 118
Poitiers, Diane de, 206
Porchnev, Dr Boris, 28, 29
Potapovich, Il'ya, 154, 155, 156, 157
Putnam, F W, 211, 212
Przhevalski, N M, 28
Pygmy elephants, 136, 137

Queensland tiger, 134, 145, 146

Radcliffe, Elizabeth, 207
Rankin, Charles, 81, 82
Rawicz, Slavomir, 28
Rayner, Dick, *110*
Red Horse of Tysoe, 126, *126*, 127
Rehaluk, Steve & Ann, 106
Reiche, Maria, 127, 128, 129, *129*
Rendezvous With Rama, 167
Rennie, James Alan, 48
Rentsch, L G, 145
Revelstoke, 165
Riggs, Mrs, 208
Rines, R H, 101, 113, *113*, 114, 115
Ring of Brodgar, 92, 94, *95*
Rintchen, Prof., 28
Robertson, Mrs, *110*, 111
Robinson, Don, 110
Rockley Down Horse, 119, *119*
Rogers, Dr, 206
Rolandson, Lt, R N, 71
Rollright Stones, 96, *96*
Rourke, J C, 22
Rusticus, Philalethes, 121
Ryan, M P, 164

Sagan, Carl, 195
St Elmo's fire, 178
Sasquatch, *see* Bigfoot
Scantlebury, Veronica, 180
Schiaparelli, Giovanni, 191, 192
Scott, Sir Peter, 103, 114
Sea serpent, 9, 68–83, *77*

Setzler, Frank M, 127
Shackleton, Ernest, 162, 165
Shackley, Dr Myra, 30
Shanafelt, Fred, 102
Sharp, George, 145
Sharp, Robert P, 203, 204
Sheaffer, Robert, 177
Shipton, Eric, 15, 16, *16*, 17, 21
Siberian mammoth, 146, 147, 148, 149, *149*, *150*
Sibert, John, 80
Slaughter, Gary, 104
Slipher, Vesto Melvin, 196
Smith, Gwen & Peter, *110*, 112
Smythe, F S, 15
Snell, John Blashford, 147
Snow leopard, 16, *16*
Sowerby, Captain Paul, 79, *80*
Spence, Magnus, 93
Spencer, Ron, 38
Staines, Harry, 104
Stais, Spyridon, 65
Staniukovich, K V, 29
Star of Bethlehem, 195, 196, *196*, 197, 198, 199
Starkey, J D, 74
Steller's sea cow, 83
Stephenson, Dr Richard, 198
Stevens, Capt. Leicester, 149
Stockley, Mrs & Patrick, 34, 35
Stonehenge, 85, *85*, 86, 87, 89, 91, 94, 96, *99*, 120, 128
Storsjön monster, 101
Strabolgi, Lord, 181, 182
Strehle, Dietrich and Patricia, 146
Stronin, A, 29
Stronsa beast, 81, *81*
Strukov, 159
Stuart, Lachlan, 109, 110
Stubbs, Philip, 122
Stukeley, William, 86, 91, 124, 210
Swift, Dr Lewis, 190

Tap O'Noth, 58, *58*, 59
Tasmanian tiger, 134, 146, *147*
Tatsl, Igor, 29
Taylor, Bob, 176
Taylor, Dan, 112
Taylor, G E, 111
Taylor, Thomas, 118
Tenzing, Sherpa, 20
Terhaar, Father Anthony, 22
Thom: Dr Archie, 89, 94;
   Prof. Alexander, 89, 93, 94
Thomas, Glenn, 23, *23*
Thorneycroft, Wallace, 61
Tibetan blue bear, 20, 134
Timofeyevich, Ermak, 148
Tomaszczuk, Janusz, 19
Treagus, Dr Jack, 205
Trefgarne, Lord, 176
Tschernezky, Dr W, 17, 28

Tuck, Prof. James, 209, 210
Tucker, Dr Denys, 102
Tunguska, 153, 156, 157, 160, 161, 162, *163*, 164, 165, 166, 199, 201
Turtle Lake monster, 105
Tyler, Janet, 106

Uffington: 'Pastime', 120, *121*; White Horse, 119, 120, *120*, 121
UFO, 7, 8, 11, 33, 96, 169–83, 210
Uranus, 187

Valdez, Dominic, 180
Vasilieyev, Dr, 162, 163
Venus, 97, 174, 175, 177, *177*, 178, 182
Veo, Lt Verdell, 27
Vereshchagin, Prof. N K, 147, 149
Verne, Jules, 68, 74
Victorian panther, *see* Queensland tiger
View from Serendip, The, 182
Vitrified forts of Scotland, 58–62
Vogelgesang, Lillian, 101, 102, 104
Vulcan, 184, 189, 190, 191

Wallis, Wing Cdr Ken, 112
Walter of Coventry, 124
Ward, Michael, 16
Watson, James, 184, 189, 190
Watson, White, 205
Webb, David, 80
Webb, Dr De Witt, 74, 75
Weber, William, 15
Westfall, Jim, 195
Wetzel, Dr Ralph, 139, 140, 146
Whillans, Don, 6, 13, 18, *18*
Whipple, F, 164
Whitley, Gilbert, 38
Whyte, Constance, 113
Wick, Captain Emil, 17
Wickramasinghe, Prof. N C, 49
Wilkins, Mr, *110*
Williams, Prof. Samuel, 205
Wilson, Colonel Robert, 109
Wood, F G, 75, 76
Wood, Dr John Edwin, 89
Woodman, Jim, 117, 130, 131, 132, 133
Woodward, Arthur, 117
Woolborough Horse, 119
Wright, Bruce, 76

Yano, Michihiko, 82
Yasuda, Dr Fujio, 82, 83
Yeti, 6, 13, *13*, 14, *14*, 15, *15*, 16, 17, *17*, 20, 28, 30, 31, 169, 210
Young, Robert, 150

Zaire, 137
Zarzynski, Joe, 106
Zima, Reymondo, 142
Zolotov, Academician, 163

Endpaper: The Loch Ness monster (Macnab 1955)